Increase Your Web Traffic

In a Weekend®

Revised Edition

Send Us Your Comments:

To comment on this book or any other PRIMA TECH title, visit Prima's reader response page on the Web at **www.primapublishing.com/comments.**

How to Order:

For information on quantity discounts, contact the publisher: Prima Publishing, P.O. Box 1260BK, Rocklin, CA 95677-1260; (916) 632-4400. On your letterhead, include information concerning the intended use of the books and the number of books you wish to purchase. For individual orders, visit PRIMA TECH's Web site at **www.prima-tech.com.**

Increase Your Web Traffic

In a Weekend

Revised Edition

WILLIAM R. STANEK

PRIMA TECH

A Division of Prima Publishing

A Division of Prima Publishing

In a Weekend, Prima Publishing, and colophon are registered trademarks of Prima Communications, Inc., Rocklin, California 95677.

Publisher: Matthew H. Carleson
Managing Editor: Dan J. Foster
Senior Acquisitions Editor: Deborah F. Abshier
Project Editor: Kevin W. Ferns
Assistant Project Editor: Kim V. Benbow
Technical Reviewer: Emily B. Kim
Copy Editor: Robert Campbell
Interior Layout: Phil Quinn
Cover Design: Prima Design Team
Indexer: Katherine Stimson

Prima Publishing and the author have attempted throughout this book to distinguish proprietary trademarks from descriptive terms by following the capitalization style used by the manufacturer.

Information contained in this book has been obtained by Prima Publishing from sources believed to be reliable. However, because of the possibility of human or mechanical error by our sources, Prima Publishing, or others, the Publisher does not guarantee the accuracy, adequacy, or completeness of any information and is not responsible for any errors or omissions or the results obtained from the use of such information. Readers should be particularly aware of the fact that the Internet is an ever-changing entity. Some facts may have changed since this book went to press.

ISBN: 0-7615-1398-1
Library of Congress Catalog Card Number: 98-67612
Printed in the United States of America
99 00 01 02 DD 10 9 8 7 6 5 4 3 2

To my children, Sapphire, William Jr., and Jennifer.

Thanks for the joy, the laughter, and the light.

Always chase your dreams…

CONTENTS AT A GLANCE

CONTENTS

Acknowledgments

Wow! What a wild year for the Internet! Dozens of IPOs. Thousands of new Web sites. Millions of new Web users. And I want to thank the people behind the scenes that make this happen.

I'd also like to thank bookstores, booksellers, book buyers, book distributors, and book reviewers. Your awards and recognition are truly appreciated. Your efforts helped this book receive honors as a Top 5 Internet business book (October 1997, Amazon.com), a Top 50 bestseller (January and February 1998, Ingram Book Group), and the topic of conversation at CNN-FN (June 1998, CNN-FN Online).

Last but not least, special thanks to the employees at 3Com, Adobe, Apple Computer, America Online, AT&T, Cabletron Systems, Cisco Systems, Compaq Computer, iCat, Intel, Macromedia, Microsoft, Net Objects, Netscape, Oracle, PC Magazine, Prima Publishing, Real Networks, Sun Microsystems, W3O, and Yahoo!.

About the Author

William Stanek (webpromotion@tvpress.com) has a Master of Science in Information Systems and more than a decade of hands-on experience with advanced programming and development. He is a leading Internet technology expert, an award-winning author, and an expert Web site designer. Over the years, his practical advice has helped Web publishers, programmers, and developers all over the world. William is also a columnist and features writer for *PC Magazine.*

William served in the Persian Gulf War as a combat crew member on an Electronic Warfare aircraft. During the war, he flew on numerous combat missions into Iraq and was awarded nine medals for his wartime service, including one of the United States' highest flying honors, the Air Force Distinguished Flying Cross.

INTRODUCTION

These days, everyone seems to have a home page or a Web site. However, just because you create and publish a Web page doesn't mean that anyone will visit it. The reality is that of the millions of Web pages, only a handful actually attract a steady readership; and these same Web pages are the ones that attract advertisers.

What can you do when you build a home page that no one visits? What can you do to earn money on your Web site? Is there an easy way to attract readers and advertisers without spending a fortune? Fortunately, there are low-cost ways to attract readers and advertisers to your home page or Web site, and *Increase Your Web Traffic In a Weekend, Revised Edition* shows you how.

What's This Book About?

With 100 million Web users from dozens of countries around the world, the Web has an extremely diverse audience. Trying to tap into the tremendous potential of the Web can be a daunting task. Enter *Increase Your Web Traffic In a Weekend, Revised Edition.* The goal of this book is to lay out a cost-effective, comprehensive plan that both Web beginners and experts can use to build an audience for a home page or a Web site.

I gathered the low-cost Web-promotion and advertising techniques in this book from years of practical experience. I haven't shared these secrets with anyone. Secrets that have helped me attract millions of readers to my Web sites and the Web sites of my customers. Secrets that could save you thousands of dollars. Now, that's something to think about!

The plan that I lay out isn't for the faint of heart. You will need to roll back your sleeves and really dive into the project at hand, which is to promote the heck out of your Web site using the techniques revealed here. Although this will require some effort on your part, the plan *is* designed to be implemented in a weekend. Do you already see the light at the end of the tunnel? You should.

How Is This Book Organized?

Making this book easy to follow and understand was my number one goal! I really want anyone, skill level or work schedule aside, to be able to learn the secrets of successful Web promotion and advertising.

To make the book easy to use, I've divided it into five sessions. The book begins with a Friday evening preview of what is ahead for the weekend. Saturday is broken down into morning and afternoon sessions. These sessions are designed to help you understand the following:

✿ Who is currently visiting your home page

✿ How to track and analyze visitor statistics

✿ How to put those statistics to work

✿ How to direct visitors to popular areas of your Web site

✿ How to gain readers who otherwise would be lost because they used the wrong URL

Sunday is also divided into morning and afternoon sessions. These sessions are designed to help you understand:

✿ Where to publicize your home pages for free

✿ How to register with search engines

✿ How to get your home page listed as the Cool Site of the Day

✿ Techniques that you can use to attract the masses

✿ The right way to sell your site through e-mail

✿ How to create, track, and manage banner advertising

✿ How to place ads on other sites without spending a dime

Who Should Read This Book?

Anyone who wants to learn how to attract visitors to a home page or a Web site should read this book.

✪ Are you disappointed with the results that you've achieved through Web publishing?

✪ Have you created wonderful Web pages, yet receive only a few visitors?

✪ Do you think that the lack of visitors means that your ideas, interests, or products aren't interesting?

✪ Do you want to reach a larger audience?

✪ Do you want to learn how to attract a steady readership to your Web site?

✪ Do you want to learn the secrets of Web promotion and marketing?

✪ Do you want to attract advertisers to your Web site?

✪ Do you want to learn how to tap into the tremendous potential of the Web?

✪ Do you want to learn the secrets of marketing without spending a dime?

If you answer yes to any of these questions, this book is for you.

What Do You Need to Use This Book?

The most important ingredients for using this book are a connection to the Internet and a home page or Web site that you want to promote. For some of the concepts discussed, you will need access to the server log files for your Web site. On Saturday, I present ways that you can obtain statistics without server logs. Depending on the alternative that you decide to use, you may need to install a CGI script. If you have no idea what server logs or scripts are used for, don't worry—all these elements are explained in the book. All you need to do before you get started, though, is to ask your Internet service provider where log files and CGI scripts are stored on the server.

What Do You Need to Know to Use This Book?

Increase Your Web Traffic In a Weekend, Revised Edition guides you through everything you need to successfully promote your Web site or home page. To get the most useful information into your hands without the clutter of a ton of background material, I assume several things. I hope that you already have a home page or Web site and, although you certainly don't need to be an HTML wizard, you should know at least the basics of HTML. Finally, you should also know the basics of Web browsing. If this is all true, you're on the right track.

Conventions Used in This Book

I've used a variety of elements to help keep the text clear and easy to follow. You'll find code terms and listings in monospace type, except when I tell you to actually type a command. In that case, the command appears in **bold** type. When I introduce and define a new term, I put it in *italics*.

Other conventions include these:

Notes enhance a discussion in the text by drawing your attention to a particular point that needs emphasis.

Tips offer helpful hints or additional information.

I truly hope you find that *Increase Your Web Traffic In a Weekend, Revised Edition* provides everything you need to attract the masses to your home page or Web site.

Promoting Your Web Site to the World

- ✿ You Built It, But Will They Come?
- ✿ Can You Really Promote Your Web Site without Spending a Fortune?
- ✿ Getting Your Web Site Noticed
- ✿ Making the Web Work for You
- ✿ Promoting Your Web Site to Joe Web Surfer
- ✿ Using The Web Promoter's Log Book

Thousands of Web publishers have created home pages to sell products and services, or simply to share ideas. Often they are disappointed with the results they achieve through Web publishing. They create wonderful pages and yet receive only a few visitors. These publishers may think that their ideas, interests, and products aren't interesting, but nothing could be further from the truth. Capitalizing on available resources and knowing how to promote your site are the keys to increasing your Web traffic. By the end of this weekend, you'll know a great deal more about how to do that.

So go ahead—get started. It's Friday evening (at least if you're following the schedule). This evening's session provides an overview of what you need to get started and gets you acquainted with crucial issues and resources on which you'll focus to get your Web site noticed by the masses.

Increase Your Web Traffic In a Weekend, Revised Edition is designed as a guide to everything that you need to successfully promote your Web site or home page. In this book, promotion encompasses publicizing, marketing, advertising, and all the other techniques that help build traffic to a Web site. Although promotion is 35 percent inspiration and 65 percent perspiration, promoting your Web site can be an awful lot of fun.

You Built It, But Will They Come?

As incredible as it may seem, cyberspace contains more than 350 million Web pages. As if the virtually limitless possibilities that these millions of pages provide weren't bad enough, there are no Web maps and relatively few signposts to guide readers anywhere. So how can anyone find your Web site? Unfortunately, no easy answer to this question exists.

After you've spent hours of your time and possibly hundreds or thousands of dollars creating a home page, it is certainly disheartening when no one visits your site, or the traffic is so minimal that it might as well be nonexistent. Take a look at Figure 1.1. Early in 1994, this was one of the first Web sites I created. When I created the Writer's Gallery, I added a counter that told me every time the page was accessed. I really thought the counter was quite wonderful. Not only could I see how many times my pages were accessed, but I could show the world these numbers as well. Though I dreamed of a great flood of visitors, the numbers told me otherwise.

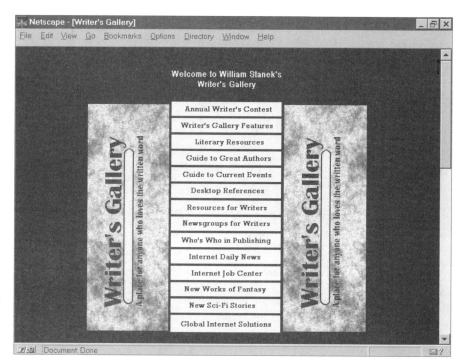

Figure 1.1

A cool Web site can't be found unless it is promoted properly.

All right, I thought, perhaps not that many people are interested in literature. What else do I know about that might interest people? At the time, I was using the Web daily to search for a new career. I had a ton of information covering online job hunting and job resources on the Internet, so I put together the site shown in Figure 1.2. I waited, but again, the great flood of visitors didn't come.

Usually, the next step for many Web publishers is to try to launch their own promotion campaign. They register with all the search engines they can find, blanket the newsgroups and mailing lists with information about their home page, tell everyone they know to visit their home page—in other words, they explore all the promotion avenues that they've heard and read about. Unfortunately, unless you truly understand Web marketing and promotion, these types of blanket efforts are like throwing good money after bad.

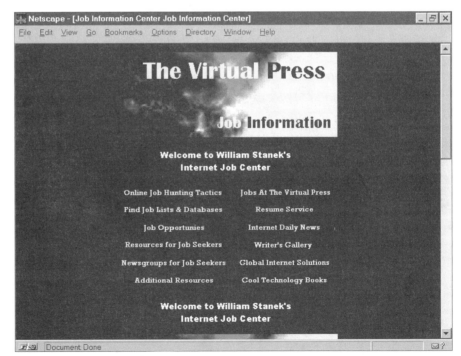

Figure 1.2

Another snazzy home page, but how come no one visited?

You could register with search engines till your fingers won't type any more. But unless you truly understand how search engines work and how to use their indexing features, you are wasting your time.

You could send out tons of e-mail through mailing lists and news-groups. But unless you know what you are doing, you will get so much hate mail that you will truly wish you had never published a home page in the first place.

In the end, when the euphoria over getting a new Web page noticed wears off, many Web publishers wake up to the cruel reality that creating a Web page doesn't automatically create visitors to it. Now you may be thinking, "All right, if none of this works, why not sit back and hope that people stumble into my home page?" In truth, you have better odds of winning the New York State lottery than having someone wander into your unannounced, unregistered home page.

Fortunately, there are reliable and low-cost or free ways to get your Web site noticed as well as to substantially increase traffic to your Web site, and in this book I show you every single one. By the end of this book, you will have everything you need to successfully attract a following to your Web site, gain an audience for your ideas, and promote your Web site to the world. As a case in point, millions of people now visit my Web sites every year, and the Internet Job Center and the Writer's Gallery are two of my most popular attractions. But it is a long way from zero to hero.

Can You Really Promote Your Web Site without Spending a Fortune?

Invariably, the first question people ask when I tell them about my proven Web promotion and marketing techniques is, "How much will it cost?" If you've been publishing on the Web for a while or have done some considerable browsing, you have probably come across sales pitches like the following:

✿ Get 325 e-mail addresses for the top magazines, newspapers, and e-zines—only $325!

✿ We'll submit your site everywhere for $275!

✿ Send e-mail promotions to millions for pennies apiece!

Unfortunately, whether these types of pitches sell you on a pennies-apiece concept or a flat-fee-per-use concept, they are usually nothing more than cleverly designed ways to get you to open your pocketbook. For example, out of the list of 325 top magazines, newspapers, and e-zines, usually only a handful are really interested in the topic that your site covers, and you could get these e-mail addresses simply by visiting the related Web sites yourself. So why pay $325 for a few e-mail addresses that you could get yourself in less than an hour? I certainly don't have that kind of money to throw away, and you probably don't either, which is why I sought out every possible avenue for effective and low-cost promotion.

When I say low-cost promotion, I mean it. In fact, most of the techniques or concepts I explore in this book are cost-free. That said, the Web is constantly changing and what may be free or low-cost today may not be tomorrow. For this reason, I try to present more than one alternative for each specific technique or concept that I explore.

Getting Your Web Site Noticed

Increasing your Web site traffic starts with taking a closer look at your Web site to understand the big picture—who is visiting your Web site and why. Trying to promote your Web site without understanding the big picture is like trying to play baseball without a ball—you just can't do it.

I would like to tell you that there is a magic button to press to give you the big picture for your Web site. Unfortunately, there is no such button. The only way to get from A to Z is to roll back your sleeves and dive in. Diving in involves slogging through the server log files, examining your Web site with an honest eye, and taking a look at problem areas at your Web site.

By examining the server log files, you will see firsthand the pages at your Web site that get the most visitors, and the pages at your Web site that don't get any visitors. When you dig through the server log files, you are gathering statistics—stats that will tell you many things about your Web site's current traffic.

When you examine your site's traffic, you will move beyond tracking file accesses and zero in on the things that matter, such as page views and the actual number of visitors. When you look at page views and visitor counts, some of the questions that you can answer about your Web site include these:

- ✪ What are the busiest days of the week?
- ✪ What are the busiest hours of the day?
- ✪ What are the most requested pages?
- ✪ Where do visitors live and work?
- ✪ What is the average number of page views per day?
- ✪ What is the average number of visitors per day?
- ✪ What is the average number of page views per visitor?
- ✪ What is the length of the average visit?
- ✪ What is the total number of visitors?

You will use stats not only to understand who is visiting your Web site right now and why, but also to put together a promotion campaign for your Web site. By digging deeper through the server logs, you can find out whether people like what they see or are just racing through. You also can discover problem areas at your Web site that may cause you to lose visitors who otherwise might come back to your Web site repeatedly. You'll find more information on working with server logs and finding trouble spots at your Web site on Saturday morning.

TIP If you find that you can't access your server log files for whatever reason, don't worry. Later, on Saturday morning, you'll discover ways that you can gather stats without server log files.

To make tracking stats easier, I put together the Web Promoter's Log Book, which you will find on this book's Web site at **www.tvpress.com/promote/log/**. You can use this log book to help track your Web site's stats. The log book also has pages for keeping records on the key information that you need to maintain your Web site, such as a record for where files are kept and a page revision history.

After I help you develop a clear understanding of your Web site, I take you through the steps necessary to put your Web site's stats to work. The first step is to summarize the stats and transform them into meaningful data. Then you will use the stats to make your Web site a better place to visit by taking care of the following:

- ✪ Cleaning up unused pages
- ✪ Clearing out dead ends
- ✪ Fixing errors

You can also use the stats to build cross-traffic and to attract users to popular areas of your Web site. Learning how to put the stats to work is the subject of the section within Saturday afternoon's coverage called "Transforming the Numbers into Meaningful Data."

Making the Web Work for You

Making the Web work for you means conducting your Web promotion campaign. As with any campaign, your promotion efforts start with careful planning and a firm understanding of the subjects that you plan to tackle—such as Web site promotion through search engines. Although everyone has used search engines to find Web resources, few people truly understand how search engines do what they do. Now it is time to make those search engines work for you. Rather than visit InfoSeek's Web site (**www.infoseek.com/**), shown in Figure 1.3, to find other Web sites, you will use InfoSeek to bring visitors to your Web site.

You start by learning to take advantage of the way search engines find and retrieve information. Although the inner workings of search engines aren't exactly state secrets, each individual search engine does things differently, which is why you will use many different techniques to make your Web pages more friendly to search engines. Web pages that are optimized for search engines using the techniques covered in the Saturday Afternoon session under "Capitalizing on Search Engine Fundamentals" will help put your Web site on the map. These techniques make obtaining references to your Web pages easier.

After you gain a firm understanding of how search engines work, you should register your Web site with the search engines used by the majority of Web users. Although your promotion efforts begin with search

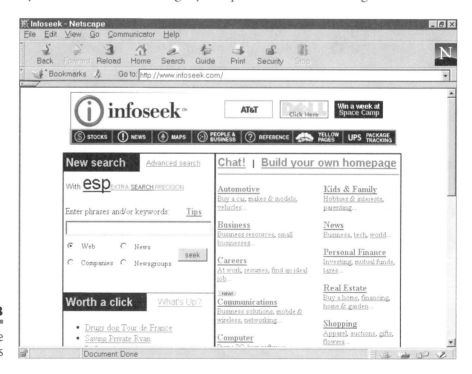

Figure 1.3

InfoSeek: One of the top search engines

engines, you don't stop there. Afterward, you move on to Web guides, lists, and directories, such as Yahoo! (**www.yahoo.com**), shown in Figure 1.4.

Just as few people understand how search engines work, few people take the time to plot out how to get the most out of Web guides, lists, and directories. You will create your own personal plan of attack in the Saturday Afternoon session, in the section called "Submitting Your Site to the Top Guides, Lists, and Directories." The reason for targeting the best directories is to encourage you to use your time and resources wisely. Why waste your time registering with every single search engine and directory on the planet when 90 percent of Web users find what they are looking for through the top 10 percent of the Web search and directory sites?

In the best search sites, you will find many other search sites and directories that focus on specific types of information. These include Yellow Pages directories, category-specific directories, and specialty directories. Although these search and directory sites generally have narrow focuses,

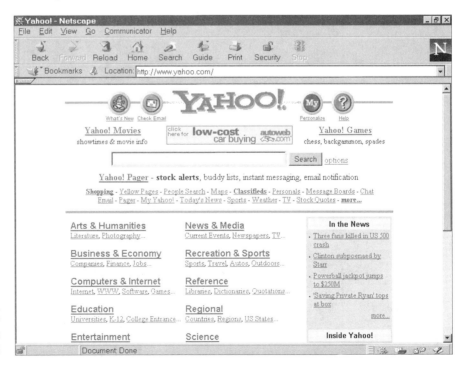

Figure 1.4

Yahoo!—one of the top Web directories

they are popular and frequently used to find information. For example, anyone looking for a business listing can use a Yellow Pages directory, such as ComFind (**www.comfind.com/**), as shown in Figure 1.5.

Promoting Your Web Site to Joe Web Surfer

Joe Web surfer is your average person browsing the Web. He's been there and done that. Now he's out looking for a bit of excitement or trying to find something—gasp!—useful. He's looking for a site like yours. He just doesn't know it yet. Well, to help Joe on his way, you have to give him a bit of prodding and grab his attention.

In the real world, you could grab Joe's attention by putting up a flashing neon sign that says, "Hey, Joe, over here!" In cyberspace, you grab Joe's attention using the tools of the Web promotion trade.

Figure 1.5

ComFind: A Yellow Page directory

If Joe is looking for something cool, you grab his attention by getting your site listed as the Cool Site of the Day. Although Cool Site of the Day is one of the key awards that will get your Web site noticed, many other awards exist that will get him to notice your site as well. He may be looking for sites like those featured as the Craziest Site of the Week (**www.verycrazy.com/crazysites/**) by Very Crazy Productions (see Figure 1.6).

NOTE You'll find more information on these and other awards in the Sunday Morning session, under "Getting Your Site Listed as the Cool Site of the Day."

If Joe is looking to get something for nothing, you grab his attention with freebies, such as a giveaway. Then again, Joe may be interested in some other type of freebie, such as a contest, sweepstakes, or treasure hunt. Catching his eye when he's looking for freebies is covered on Sunday after-

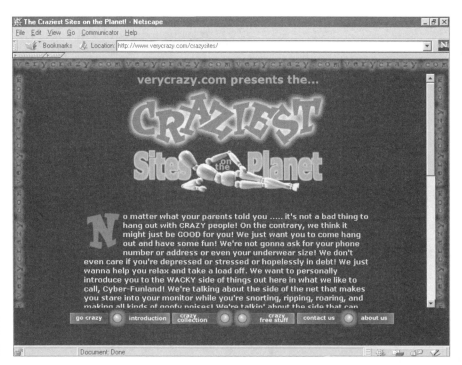

Figure 1.6

The Craziest Site of the Week

noon under "Attracting the Masses with Giveaways, Contests, Sweepstakes, and More."

Other ways to grab Joe's attention include using straightforward Web advertising. Most Web users have a newsgroup or mailing list they like to follow, and Joe is no exception. So to get Joe where he lives, you have to visit the discussion groups and forums where he hangs out. If Joe is interested in topics similar to those covered at your Web site, chances are good that you will find him hanging out in a like-minded newsgroup or mailing list. Web site promotion through newsgroups and mailing lists is featured on Sunday afternoon under "Selling Your Web Site through E-mail."

Sometimes, the best way to get Joe's attention is to use good old-fashioned advertising. On the Web, this means using a banner advertisement. You have to admit that sometimes you do click on them, and so does Joe. If something grabs his eye, he's going to click on it, and when he does, you want it to be your site that he visits. To help Joe on his way, you can use the cost-free advertising techniques that you'll explore on Sunday afternoon under "Cost-Free Banner Advertising: No Joke."

Using The Web Promoter's Log Book

You will find the Web Promoter's Log Book at the companion Web site (**www.tvpress.com/promote/log/**). You can use the Web Promoter's Log Book to keep track of just about everything you do in this book. The purpose of the log book is to make maintaining and promoting your Web site easier, as well as to help you develop a record that you can use to gauge the long-term performance of your Web site. The log book is divided into three sections: Stat Tracking Logs, Web Site Maintenance Logs, and Site Registration Logs.

I designed the stat tracking logs to help you keep track of statistics for individual pages and areas at your Web site. You should use the stat tracking logs whenever you examine the stats for your Web site. Individual logs that you can find in this section of the log book include:

- ✿ **Weekly Hit Summary:** Used as a weekly record of hits for an entire Web site or area of a Web site by date and hit total.

- ✿ **Monthly Hit Summary:** Used to record monthly hit summaries for an entire Web site or area of a Web site by month and hit total.

- ✿ **Page Views:** Used to record page views for specific pages at your Web site; also includes a column for tracking average page views per day.

- ✿ **Area Summaries:** Used to summarize all the hits and page views for a specific area within your Web site. An *area* is a collection of Web pages with a similar theme.

You can use the Web site maintenance logs to help you track Web site maintenance, schedule updates, and find your files. You should use the Web site maintenance logs whenever you work with Web pages, images, or banners. Logs that you can find in this section of the log book include:

- ✿ **Directories for Web Files:** Helps you track your Web-related files on your hard disk and the corresponding directory for the files on your Web server.

- ✿ **Web Page Change Log:** Helps you track the revision history of your Web pages and whether you need to update the directory listings for these Web pages.

- ✿ **Image Change Log:** Helps you track the revision history of your Web-related images.

- ✿ **Banner Change Log:** Helps you track banner advertisements and banner exchange advertising.

You can use the site registration logs to help you track when and where you've registered your Web site, and to record essential information that will make updating such facts as your account name and password easy at a later date. The site registration logs come in handy to track the details of your promotion campaign. The logs that you can find in this section of the log book include:

- ✿ **Search Engine Registration Log:** Helps you track the Web sites that you've registered in search engines.

⚙ **Directory Registration Log:** Helps you track the pages that you've registered in Web directories.

⚙ **Yellow Pages Registration Log:** Helps you track the pages that you've registered in Yellow Pages directories as well as related account information.

⚙ **White Pages Registration Log:** Helps you track the pages and e-mail addresses that you've registered in White Pages directories, as well as related account information.

⚙ **Web Guide and Awards Registration Log:** Helps you track the pages that you've submitted for awards and recognition, as well as when you may want to submit your site again.

⚙ **Specialty Directory Registration Log:** Helps you track the pages that you've registered in specialty directories.

⚙ **Freebies and Contest Registration Log:** Helps you track freebies and contests.

⚙ **Banner Exchange Registration Log:** Helps you track your accounts with banner exchanges.

As you explore the promotional techniques that I outline in this book, be sure to record your efforts in the log book. Although some of the information you will be asked to record may not make sense right now, I want you to know about the log book before you start using any of the promotion techniques that I outline. In this way, you will be able to see your progress and record all the information that will make maintaining and promoting your Web site easier over the long term.

Wrapping Up and Looking Ahead

It makes sense to promote for a few hours a Web site that you spent days creating and weeks perfecting. Promoting your Web site to the world starts with taking a closer look at your Web site and carefully planning a promotion campaign. Now that the preview of what's ahead is over, it is time to roll back your sleeves and get ready to dive in. In the next section, I will show you how you can use Web statistics to understand who is visiting your Web site and why.

Working with Statistics and Logs

- ⚙ Using Web Stats to Understand Your Site's Visitors
- ⚙ Unlocking the Secrets of the Access Logs
- ⚙ Understanding Visits and Page Views
- ⚙ Introducing Counters

Before you launch a promotion campaign that'll bring the masses to your Web site, you really need to understand what is happening at your Web site right now. The way to do this is to examine your current traffic. Your site's stats are the single most important means for discovering what people really think about your Web site, and you will probably be surprised when you discover which of your resources are bringing in readers, and which resources aren't.

If you're tempted to pay only cursory attention to this section, ask yourself this: What do I really know about the flow of traffic to my site? How do I know which pages are drawing visitors and which ones are being skipped? If you make assumptions about your readers that the stats don't support, then your lack of awareness could cost you dearly.

So settle in with a good cup of coffee or some juice to get you alert—it's Saturday morning and time to roll. By the end of the morning, you'll know how to find out who is visiting your site, and why. You'll also know how to make use of the stats to begin increasing your Web traffic right away.

Using Web Stats to Understand Your Site's Visitors

Web site stats tell you much more than which Web pages at your site interest readers. By tracking stats, you also learn many things about those

who visit your Web site, such as how long they visit, whether they really read the pages that you present or just skip on by, what days of the week are the most popular, what time of day is the best time to make updates, and a whole lot of other things.

You need to know what kind of people are drawn to your site so that you can keep them coming back for more and attract others like them. You need to know about errors and other circumstances that could make your site an obstacle course that prevents visitors from coming or staying. You need to know how to use logs effectively so that you can interpret the data and make informed decisions. This effort will remove your site from the ranks of hit-or-miss Web sites and give it the stamp of professionalism.

Web Site Stats Are a Necessary Evil

Yes, Web site stats truly are a necessary evil. We all hate the thought of statistics, which is why I present this topic early in the book. If you don't track the stats at your Web site, however, you never truly understand who is visiting your Web site and, more importantly, why.

Before you start having flashbacks of high school algebra class, you should know that tracking and analyzing Web site stats isn't rocket science. As a matter of fact, tracking and analyzing stats is fairly easy as long as you follow the practical advice I give you in the next couple of days. In this section, I show you how to obtain stats for your Web site using server logs. Next, I show you how to use those stats to get the big picture for your Web site.

NOTE Although my server log files are located in the directory /www/logs/, the location of server log files is defined when a server is installed, which means that the server log files you need are probably located somewhere else. The best way to find the server log files is to ask your service provider or the Web master for your server where these files are located.

Keep in mind that if you have your own domain, such as www.yourname.com, you should have separate log files regardless of whether you actually have your own server or you use someone else's. If multiple domains are served by the same server, the logs probably have a prefix that indicates the domain. Otherwise, you, like anyone using a service provider, will share server logs with everyone else using the server.

Here are a few reasons that you may have to track stats:

- ✿ To discover popular resources
- ✿ To learn more about the people who visit your site
- ✿ To find out when people visit

Discover Popular Resources

By tracking and analyzing stats, you can discover which of the pages at your Web site are the most visited. Although you may think that your top-level home page is the most popular, this isn't always the case. In fact, your analysis may reveal that most people visit some other page at your Web site. The reason for this is that the Web allows anyone to visit any page at your Web site, and visitors don't have to start at your home page.

An example of tracking page accesses is shown in Figure 2.1. You can see how Web site stats can be analyzed using a software application. When I

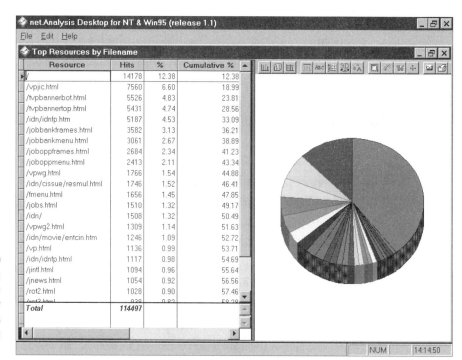

Figure 2.1

Tracking page accesses can help you learn many things about who's visiting your site and why.

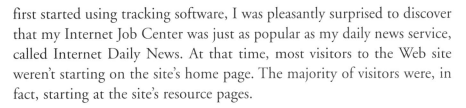

first started using tracking software, I was pleasantly surprised to discover that my Internet Job Center was just as popular as my daily news service, called Internet Daily News. At that time, most visitors to the Web site weren't starting on the site's home page. The majority of visitors were, in fact, starting at the site's resource pages.

Using the techniques detailed in this book, I drew those same visitors to the site's home page, and now the home page is the most popular resource at the site. I wanted to give visitors the chance to learn about everything the site had to offer. It worked wonderfully.

Learn More about the People Who Visit Your Site

By tracking your site's stats, you also can learn more about the people who visit, such as where they live, where they work, and how they access your Web site. One of the best ways to learn more about your site's visitors is to examine the domain that the visitor uses.

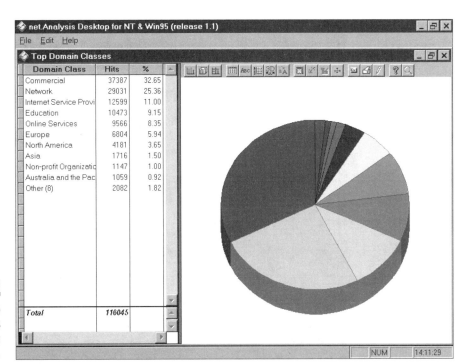

Figure 2.2

Get an idea of who the reader is by tracking domain classes.

Figure 2.2 shows an example of how you can track domain classes. Each domain class can tell you something about the person who uses it. For example, users from the education domain—addresses ending in .edu— are usually college students or faculty members. For more information on domain classes, see "The Host Field" in this morning's session.

Find Out When People Visit

Finding out when people visit your Web site is extremely useful, especially if you use this information to plan updates for your Web pages. As Figure 2.3 shows, you can use stats to determine the activity level at your Web site throughout the week. In this example, Monday is the busiest day of the week, and the weekend is the slowest time of the week.

My discovery that most people visited this site on a Monday and that weekends were the slowest time of the week opened a whole new world of possibilities. Before this discovery, I made weekly updates to this Web site

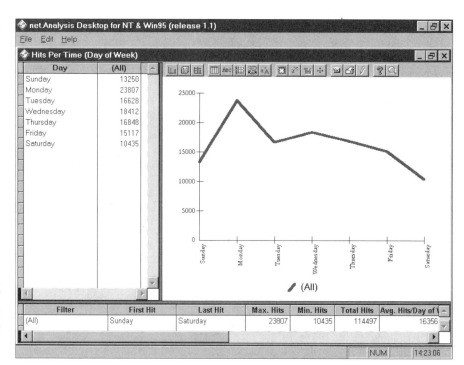

Figure 2.3

The busiest days of the week may reveal important trends.

on Wednesdays because I assumed that the busiest times were Fridays and weekends.

As it turned out, the news tidbits that I posted on Wednesday weren't read by the vast majority of visitors until five days later. By moving the updates to Sunday evenings, I gave the Monday crowd truly fresh information. As a result, the site as a whole gained more readers over time.

Tracking Stats: The Basics

When you analyze your site's stats, you may be in for a big surprise. Often, people track Web site stats by counting file accesses rather than actual visitors. Unfortunately, the number of file accesses alone isn't an accurate way to measure the popularity of a Web site.

Understanding Hits

File accesses are also referred to as *hits*. When you browse a Web page, every file that is accessed to display the page in your browser is considered a hit. If you access a Web page with five graphics, up to six hits could be generated. One of these hits would be for the page itself. The other five hits would be for each of the images displayed with the page.

To put this in perspective, take a look at Figure 2.4, which shows the original home page for Internet Daily News. When you access the home page, these files are loaded into your browser:

- index.html—The HTML source for the page
- glnet.gif—The first image
- glmail.gif—The second image
- site2.gif—The third image
- site1.gif—The fourth image
- cal.gif—The fifth image
- wpupr.gif—The sixth image
- fpu97.gif—The seventh image

Thus, every time that the home page for Internet Daily News is accessed in a graphics-capable browser, eight hits are generated. If you follow a link to an article in the newspaper, up to six more hits are generated. When you put both page accesses together, you get a total of 14 hits. As you can see, 14 hits definitely does not equal 14 visitors, and it is rather unfortunate that the hit is sometimes used to advertise the popularity of a Web site.

Recording Hits

Hits are logged in a special file on the server called an *access log*. When a browser requests a resource at a Web site, the server retrieves the file and then writes an entry in the access log for the request. Entries in the server access log indicate many things about the file transfer, including the success or failure of the transfer. You'll learn more about the access log in the upcoming part of this morning's session, titled "Unlocking the Secrets of the Access Logs."

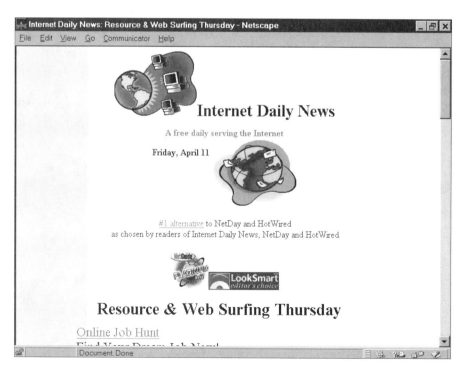

Figure 2.4

Loading this page generates eight hits.

The access log is not the only server log file. If the server can't find the file or if an error occurs, the server usually makes an entry in the access log and in an *error log*. The error log provides more detail about each specific error. Although the error log is useful, many service providers save space on the file system by configuring the Web server so that error logs aren't used at all.

TIP

Errors can tell you many things about your Web site. By examining errors, you can find links or references that are broken in your Web site. Fixing these errors can help you build a steady readership at your Web site.

You'll learn more about errors later this morning in "Gaining Lost Readers from the Error Logs." If your service provider doesn't use error logs, don't worry. Errors are still recorded in the access logs.

The wonderful thing about server log files is that they are ordinary text files, which means that they contain no special formatting characters or codes other than those used for standard ASCII text. Generally, entries in the server logs are entered chronologically, with new entries appended to the end of the log.

Unlocking the Secrets of the Access Logs

The access log is the key to discovering who is visiting your Web site and why. Every time someone requests a file from your Web site, an entry goes into the access log, making the access log a running history of every successful and unsuccessful attempt to retrieve information from your Web site. Because each entry has its own line, entries in the access log can be extracted easily when you want to compile stats for your Web site. Compiling stats from access log entries is covered later this morning under "Understanding Visits and Page Views."

The most basic format for server access logs is the *common log file format*. In the common log file format, entries in the log file have seven fields. These fields are as follows:

- Host
- Identification
- User Authentication
- Time Stamp
- HTTP Request Type
- Status Code
- Transfer Volume

As you'll see, the common log file format is fairly easy to understand, which makes it great as a stepping stone to more advanced log file formats. Listing 2.1 shows entries in a sample access log. As you can see from the sample, log fields are separated with spaces. In the sections that follow, I examine each of these fields and explain what they mean.

Listing 2.1 Sample Entries from a Server Access Log

```
pc4.att.net - - [02/Mar/1998:12:37:20 -0800] "GET / HTTP/1.0" 304 -
pc4.att.net - - [02/Mar/1998:12:37:22 -0800] "GET /lightn.jpg
   HTTP/1.0" 304 -
pc4.att.net - - [02/Mar/1998:12:37:23 -0800] "GET /ns.gif HTTP/1.0"
   304 -
pc4.att.net - - [02/Mar/1998:12:37:28 -0800] "GET /writ.htm HTTP/1.0"
   304 -
pc4.att.net - - [02/Mar/1998:12:37:28 -0800] "GET /wpupr.gif
   HTTP/1.0" 304 -
pc4.att.net - - [02/Mar/1998:12:37:28 -0800] "GET /wpd.gif HTTP/1.0"
   304 -
pc4.att.net - - [02/Mar/1998:12:37:28 -0800] "GET /fp97.gif HTTP/1.0"
   304 -
pc4.att.net - - [02/Mar/1998:12:37:28 -0800] "GET /dice.gif HTTP/1.0"
   304 -
```

```
pc4.att.net - - [02/Mar/1998:12:37:29 -0800] "GET /ticket.gif
   HTTP/1.0" 304 -

pc4.att.net - - [02/Mar/1998:12:37:29 -0800] "GET /keyb.gif HTTP/1.0"
   304 -

pc4.att.net - - [02/Mar/1998:12:37:42 -0800] "GET /wdream.htm
   HTTP/1.0" 304 -

195.173.163.34 - - [02/Mar/1998:13:22:04 -0800] "GET / HTTP/1.0" 200
   1970

ds.ucla.edu - - [02/Mar/1998:13:37:57 -0800] "GET / HTTP/1.0" 200
   1970

ds.ucla.edu - - [02/Mar/1998:13:38:06 -0800] "GET /ns.gif HTTP/1.0"
   200 1052

ds.ucla.edu - - [02/Mar/1998:13:38:28 -0800] "GET /writ.htm HTTP/1.0"
   200 5835

ds.ucla.edu - - [02/Mar/1998:13:38:31 -0800] "GET /dice.gif HTTP/1.0"
   200 1714

ds.ucla.edu - - [02/Mar/1998:13:38:31 -0800] "GET /wpupr.gif
   HTTP/1.0" 200 6376

ds.ucla.edu - - [02/Mar/1998:13:38:31 -0800] "GET /wpd.gif
   HTTP/1.0" 200 10423

ds.ucla.edu - - [02/Mar/1998:13:38:31 -0800] "GET /fp97.gif
   HTTP/1.0" 200 5306

ds.ucla.edu - - [02/Mar/1998:13:38:38 -0800] "GET /keyb.gif HTTP/1.0"
   200 1934

ds.ucla.edu - - [02/Mar/1998:13:38:41 -0800] "GET /ticket.gif
   HTTP/1.0" 200 2015

195.173.163.34 - - [02/Mar/1998:13:22:04 -0800] "GET /ns.gif
   HTTP/1.0" 200 1970
```

The Host Field

The first field in the common log file format identifies the host computer requesting a file from your Web server. The value in this field is either the fully qualified domain name of the remote host, such as:

```
pc4.att.net - - [02/Mar/1998:12:37:20 -0800] "GET / HTTP/1.0"
   304 -
```

or the value is the IP address of the remote host, such as:

```
195.173.163.34 - - [02/Mar/1998:13:22:04 -0800] "GET /
   HTTP/1.0" 200 1970
```

Examining Domain Names

When an entry has the fully qualified domain name of the remote host, you can examine that domain name to learn a great deal about the user accessing your server. Divisions within the domain are separated by periods, such as:

```
pc4.att.net - - [02/Mar/1998:12:37:20 -0800] "GET /
  HTTP/1.0" 304 -
```

In this example, the domain name is broken down into three divisions:

> `pc4`—Identifies the remote host as a terminal
>
> `att`—The organization associated with the remote host, AT&T
>
> `net`—The domain class for the host

The first piece of the puzzle, the identity of the remote host, isn't as important as the organization and the domain class with which the host is associated. With most service providers, remote host names are allocated dynamically when you dial up and connect, which is why you may see identifiers in the first field such as PC4, AT1, or CLIENT99.

The second piece of the puzzle tells you about the organization with which the remote host is associated. Often, several fields may be here, which identify divisions within the organization, such as the human resources department at IBM. Here, you might see an entry of `pc3.hr.ibm.net` where the hr identifies the department.

The final piece of the puzzle is the domain class, which can tell you where the user lives and works. Table 2.1 describes the basic domain classes.

Domain classes are also organized geographically. These domain classes end in a two- or three-letter designator that tells you the state or country the user lives in, such as `wheel.dcn.davis.ca.us`. Because there are hundreds of state and country designators, I won't outline them here and I don't recommend memorizing them, either. Just make a note that if you see a domain class you don't recognize, it is probably a designator for a specific state or country.

Domain Name	Description
ARTS	Organizations emphasizing cultural and entertainment activities
COM	Commercial; users from commercial Internet services and Web sites
EDU	Education; users from colleges and universities
FIRM	For businesses or firms
GOV	All U.S. government agencies, except military
INFO	Information; for organizations providing information services
MIL	U.S. Military; users who work at a military installation
NET	Network sites, includes service providers and true network developers
NOM	Nomenclature; for those wanting individual or personal nomenclature
ORG	Nonprofit organizations; users who work for nonprofit organizations
REC	Recreation; for organizations emphasizing recreation activities
SHOP	Online shop; businesses offering goods to purchase
WEB	Web-related organization; for organizations emphasizing activities related to the World Wide Web

TABLE 2.1   BASIC DOMAIN CLASSES

Examining IP Addresses

IP addresses are the numeric equivalent of fully qualified domain names. Here's an example:

```
195.173.163.34 - - [02/Mar/1998:13:22:04 -0800] "GET /
  HTTP/1.0" 200 1970
```

Although the bunch of numbers that you see in the host field doesn't tell you much, there are ways to equate the IP address with a specific host name, and your server can even be configured to do this job for you. Keep in mind, though, that resolving an IP address to a host name requires server resources and usually isn't worth the effort in the end. Suffice it to say that if you see an IP address in the host field, moving on to the next entry or simply working with the remaining fields in the current entry is easier.

The Identification Field

The second field in the common log format is the identification field. Although this field is meant to identify users by their usernames, this field is rarely used. Because of this, you will generally see a hyphen (-) in this field, as appears here:

```
ds.ucla.edu - - [02/Mar/1998:13:37:57 -0800] "GET /
  HTTP/1.0" 200 1970
```

The problem with the identification field is that even if only by chance you do see something in this field, the username cannot be trusted. The username is not validated, so it could be made up.

The User Authentication Field

The third field in the common log format comes into play whenever you have protected areas at your Web site. Unless you have a password-protected area at your Web site, you will usually see a hyphen (-) in this field, such as:

```
ds.ucla.edu - - [02/Mar/1998:13:37:57 -0800] "GET /
  HTTP/1.0" 200 1970
```

If you have a password-protected area at your Web site, users must authenticate themselves with a username and password that is registered for this area. After users validate themselves with their username and password, their username is entered in the user authentication field. Keep in mind that the entry in this field is not the actual username but rather the username for your Web site.

The Time Stamp Field

Beyond what generally equates to two dashes is the time stamp field. This field tells you exactly when someone accessed a file on the server. Because the format of the time field is very specific, the time field can be extracted to perform many different calculations. The format for the time stamp field is as follows:

```
DD/MMM/YYYY:HH:MM:SS OFFSET
```

Right now you are probably thinking, wow, rocket science again. But if you examine the time field a bit at a time, you can begin to get a clear picture of how the time stamp is used. Look again at a sample of the time stamp in an actual entry:

```
pc4.att.net - - [02/Mar/1998:12:37:20 -0800] "GET /
  HTTP/1.0" 304 -
```

Consider these conventions when studying a time stamp:

DD—Refers to a two-digit day designator, such as 02 for the second day of the month.

MMM—Refers to the three-letter designator for the month, such as Mar for March.

YYYY—Refers to a four-digit year designator, such as 1998.

HH—Refers to a two-digit hour designator, such as 08 for 8 A.M. or 23 for 11 P.M.

MM—Refers to a two-digit minute designator, such as 37 for 37 minutes after the hour.

SS—Refers to a two-digit second designator, such as 20.

The only designator that probably doesn't make sense is the OFFSET designator, which indicates the server's offset from GMT (Greenwich Mean Time), Universal Time. Here, the offset is minus eight hours, meaning that the server time is eight hours behind GMT. Although this offset remains the same unless the server time changes according to daylight savings time, the server nevertheless logs it with every entry.

As you will discover later this morning, you can use the time stamp to learn many things about the users visiting your Web site, such as how long they stay on a particular page. If you are really determined, you can even extrapolate the throughput between your server and the remote host, which can ultimately tell you the modem transfer rate that was used.

NOTE *Throughput* refers to the transfer rate between the server and the client computers. By examining throughput, you can gauge the average transfer speed used by visitors to your Web site, which can tell you a great deal about the core visitors to your Web site. Are they coming from the corporate world? Are they dialing up from home? Generally, visitors from the corporate sector have very fast transfer speeds—imagine a T-1 transferring megabytes in seconds—and visitors from the private sector have relatively slow dial-up modem speeds. You will find more on computing transfer speeds and what transfer speeds can tell you a little later this morning.

The HTTP Request Field

The HTTP request field is the fifth field in the common log format. You will use this field to determine three things:

- ✪ The method that the remote client used to request the information
- ✪ The file that the remote client requested
- ✪ The HTTP version that the client used to retrieve the file

The most important item in the HTTP request field is the relative URL of the file requested. By *relative URL*, I mean a URL that is relative only

to your Web server. Relative URLs are interpreted by the server. For example, if you request the file:

```
http://www.tvpress.com/writing/writing2.htm
```

The server will use the relative URL, `/writing/writing2.htm`, to log where the file is found. Similarly, if you use the URL:

```
http://www.tvpress.com/
```

The server will use the relative URL of / and create an entry in the access log similar to this:

```
pc4.att.net - - [02/Mar/1998:12:37:20 -0800] "GET /
   HTTP/1.0" 200 -
```

TIP When you see an entry that ends in a slash, keep in mind that this refers to the default document for a directory, which is typically called index.html, index.htm, or default.html.

Only the most hard-core techies in the group will want to know exactly what the first and last items in the HTTP request field tell us. If this is you, visit **www.tvpress.com/promote/server/** to learn more about these items. To sum it all up, though, the method identifies a specific request type used by the client and is always either GET, POST, or HEAD. The HTTP version item identifies the specific HTTP version used to transfer the file—usually, HTTP/0.9, HTTP/1.0, or HTTP/1.1.

The Status Code Field

The status code field is the sixth field in the common log format. Status codes are diamonds in the rough. From this single code, you can learn whether files were transferred correctly, weren't found, were loaded from cache, and more. The key to status codes is that they are defined in the HTTP specification, making them universal to all Web servers. This means that the status codes used in your server access log are the same as the status codes used in anyone else's server access log.

Status Code Classes

All status codes are three-digit numbers. Because the first digit of the status code indicates the class of the code, you can often tell at a glance what has happened. Table 2.2 shows the general classes for status codes.

TABLE 2.2	GENERAL CLASSES OF STATUS CODES
Code Class	**Description**
1*XX*	Continue/Protocol Change
2*XX*	Success
3*XX*	Redirection
4*XX*	Client error/failure
5*XX*	Server error

In Table 2.2, you can see that status codes fall into five general categories. Because the first category is used rarely and only with HTTP version 1.1, you really only need to remember the other four categories. If you have a status code that begins with 2, the associated file transferred successfully. A status code that begins with 3 indicates that the server performed a redirect. A status code that begins with 4 indicates some type of client error or failure. Finally, a status code that begins with 5 tells you that a server error occurred.

To put this in perspective, look at two entries in the access log:

```
ds.ucla.edu - - [02/Mar/1998:13:38:06 -0800] "GET
  /ns.gif HTTP/1.0" 200 1052

pc4.att.net - - [02/Mar/1998:12:37:20 -0800] "GET /
  HTTP/1.0" 304 -
```

The first entry in the access log has a status code of 200, and the 2, as you now know, indicates a successful transfer. The second entry in the access log has a status code of 304; the 3 indicates a server redirect. Although servers sometimes redirect users to files that have been moved, the redirect usually means that the file has not been modified since it was last requested, and therefore the browser can use a cached version of the file instead of having the server retransfer the file.

Individual Status Codes

To really understand what happens on the server, you will sometimes want to know exactly what a status code means. For this reason, I've taken the most important status codes from the HTTP specification and compiled them in the tables in this section.

A complete list of all the status codes defined in the HTTP 1.1 specification can be found at the companion Web site (**www.tvpress.com/ promote/server/**).

The two most common status codes for successful file transfers are shown in Table 2.3. If you see status code 200, you know that the file transferred successfully and no errors occurred. On the other hand, the status code of 204 indicates that the file was found and transferred but it had no content. This usually tells you that the programmed scripts you use to process data may have created a bad header by mistake.

TABLE 2.3 COMMON STATUS CODES FOR SUCCESS	
Code	**Description**
200	Successful file transfer; file transfer OK
204	Successful file transfer, but file had no content

The two most common redirection codes are shown in Table 2.4. A status code of 302 usually means that the user typed a URL without the trailing slash and the server redirected the request to the proper URL. Thus, if you enter the URL `http://www.tvpress.com`, your server may issue a redirect to `http://www.tvpress.com/`. A status code of 304 tells you that the file was not modified since it was last requested by the client, which allowed the client to load it from cache.

TABLE 2.4 COMMON STATUS CODES FOR REDIRECTION	
Code	**Description**
302	Redirected client to new file; file moved temporarily
304	File not modified; client loaded from cache

Status codes to which you should pay particular attention are those that indicate client error or failure to transfer the file. These status codes are shown in Table 2.5.

TABLE 2.5 COMMON STATUS CODES FOR CLIENT ERROR/FAILURE	
Code	**Description**
400	Invalid request
401	Client not authorized to access file
403	Client forbidden from accessing file or directory
404	File not found

A status code of 400 indicates that the user made an invalid request, which can usually be interpreted as the server not being able to determine what the client tried to request. The status codes of 401 and 403 indicate similar problems and usually mean that the file or directory requested couldn't be accessed due to an access restriction on the server.

Finally, the status code of 404 indicates that the file was not found. If you've browsed the Web, you've probably seen the dreaded 404 many times. Later this morning, under "Gaining Lost Readers from the Error Log," you'll see how to eliminate the 404 - File Not Found error.

You should also pay particular attention to status codes that indicate server errors (see Table 2.6). Suffice it to say that server errors are bad news. Depending on the type of server you use, you may see server errors occasionally. In this case, don't be alarmed. But if you start to see server errors routinely, notify your Web master.

TABLE 2.6 COMMON STATUS CODES FOR SERVER ERRORS	
Code	**Description**
500	Internal server error
502	Bad gateway
503	Service unavailable

The Transfer Volume Field

In the Common Log Format, the last field in the access log is the transfer volume. This field indicates the number of bytes transferred to the client as a result of the request. If a status code other than a success code is used in field six, this field will contain a hyphen (-) or a zero to indicate that no data was transferred.

In this example, 256 bytes were transferred:

```
ps4.att.net - - [02/Mar/1998:14:00:00 -0800] "GET
  /cool.gif HTTP/1.0" 200 256
```

Sometimes, entries that have a status code of 200 will also have a hyphen or zero in the transfer volume field. This usually indicates that the client requested only an HTTP header for the file and not the actual file itself. *HTTP headers* provide information about the data transferred, such as whether it is ASCII text or HTML. Intelligent agents, such as those that verify links in Web pages, often request only a file header and then use the status code returned to determine whether the file exists.

Using Other Server Logs

The access log isn't the only Web server log available. On some servers, you will also find a referrer log and an agent log. The *referrer log* is used to record the URL from which a request comes. This can help you learn exactly how visitors are accessing your Web site. The *agent log* is used to record the type of browser that requests a resource at your Web site.

Although knowing the referring URL and browser type is certainly important, many service providers do not use the referrer log or the agent log. Primarily this is to conserve Web server resources. Before you fault your service provider for not using the extra log files, imagine having to log every request for a file in as many as four different logs. Not only does this eat up file space, it also uses up system resources, such as CPU time.

To reduce the drain on system resources yet retain the valuable information that agent and referrer logs provide, some service providers use what is called a *combined log*. In the combined log, the access, referrer, and agent entries are all logged in a single file. Generally, a referrer field becomes the eighth field and an agent field becomes the ninth field in the access log.

The Referrer Log

The referrer log tells you exactly where a client was before coming to your Web site, which is certainly useful information if you want to see firsthand how people get to your Web site. Entries in the referrer log look like this:

```
http://www.netdaily.com/ -> /ci/w2.htm
```

The URL in the first field of the referrer log indicates the referrer—the site from which the user came. The hyphen and the greater than symbol in the second field are used simply to separate the first and last fields—you can think of them as making up an arrow. The last field in the referrer log is the relative URL on the server that the client requested. Thus, you can translate the log entry as the user going from netdaily.com directly to the file /ci/w2.html in the direction of the arrow.

In the common log file format, no way exists to correlate the entry in the referrer log with entries in the access log. A matching access log entry for the example referrer entry would look something like this, however:

```
pc4.att.net - - [02/Mar/1998:12:37:28 -0800] "GET
  /ci/w2.htm HTTP/1.0" 200 7892
```

Here, you have a request for the page /ci/w2.htm, which could be a match for the entry in the referrer log.

The Agent Log

The agent log tells you the name and version of the browser that requested a file on your server. The values placed in the agent log are taken from the User_Agent field that all browsers supply in the HTTP header accompanying a file request. Although entries in the agent log don't follow a strict format, a general format for entries is as follows:

```
browser name/version (supplemental information)
```

Entries in an actual agent log look like this:

```
Mozilla/4.0 (Windows 95)
aolbrowser/1.1 InterCon-Web-Library 1.2 (Macintosh, 68K)
Lynx/2-4-2 libwww/unknown
```

By examining the agent log, you can determine the browser name, version, and operating system most used by those visiting your Web site. The most common entry is a reference to Mozilla, which is the code name for Netscape Navigator. Watch out, though: If the Mozilla entry also references the keyword compatible or MSIE, the entry is for Microsoft Internet Explorer. The reason for this is that Microsoft Internet Explorer emulates Netscape Navigator under certain circumstances. An agent log entry for Microsoft Internet Explorer may look like this:

```
Mozilla/3.0 (compatible; MSIE 4.0; Macintosh)
```

Together, Netscape Navigator and Microsoft Internet Explorer have about 98 percent of the browser market, which means that most entries in the agent log will pertain to one of these browsers. Beyond Navigator and Internet Explorer, a myriad of other browsers are used by a small percentage of those browsing the Web. Other entries that you might see in the agent log may refer to Opera, a popular third-party browser, or Lynx, a text-only browser.

You may also see entries for search engines that are indexing your Web site. These entries will reference the search engine wandering your site by name, such as Infoseek, MetaCrawler, or WebCrawler.

As you can see, entries in the agent log provide insight into the type of users that visit your site. By examining these entries, you can see the most commonly used browsers, browser versions, and operating systems. This in turn can help you better understand your site's audience and it can also help you decide what features to use within your pages. For example, if 85% of the entries are for Mac computers, you may want to offer extra features for Mac users. Or if 90% of the entries are for Internet Explorer 5.0 and Navigator 5.0, you may want to incorporate more high-level features into your Web pages.

Understanding Other Log File Formats

Now that you know a bit about server log files and their formats, you are ready to move on to the more complex log file formats that you may encounter. These log formats include the *extended log file format* and the *Microsoft IIS log file format*. The good news is that despite the complexities of these formats, the concepts you've learned for the common log file format still apply.

The Extended Log File Format

Many commercial Web servers use the extended log file format. The reason is that this format is completely customizable, which makes it perfect for the diverse needs of businesses. When you customize the log file, you select the fields you want the server to log and the server handles the logging for you.

The key difference between the common format and the extended format is that the extended format gives you much more detailed information. For example, instead of getting just the HTTP status code, the extended format lets you log the status code and the comments related to the status code. With the status code 404, the comments the server logs are usually "File Not Found."

To help you remember how the server is set up, the server tells you specifically what fields are being logged. Although you can select any of the available fields, not all fields will have information available for logging. Thus, if you select a field for which there is no information available, a dash is inserted into the field when it is logged.

The first time you take a look at log entries that use the extended format, you may be a bit confused. The reason for this is that the extended logs record server directives as well as file requests. Because server directives are always preceded by the hash symbol (#), they are easily distinguished from actual file requests.

NOTE   This section is meant to provide an introduction to the extended log format. For detailed information, refer to the W3O Web site (**http://www.w3.org/**) or Microsoft's article called "Customizing W3C Extended Logging" (**http://www.microsoft.com/iis /support/iishelp/iis/htm/core/iiconlg.htm**).

Listing 2.2 shows sample entries from an extended log. Note that as with the common log format, extended log fields are separated with spaces. In the sections that follow, I examine the basic components of these entries, which include field prefixes, field identifiers, and server directives.

Listing 2.2   Sample Entries from an Extended Log

```
#Software: Microsoft Internet Information Server 4.0

#Version: 1.0

#Date: 1998-06-26 16:27:32

#Fields: time c-ip cs-username s-ip cs-method cs-uri-stem cs-
  uri-query sc-status sc-bytes time-taken cs(User-Agent)
  cs(Referer)

16:27:32 192.15.16.8 - 207.149.100.17 GET / - 200 1227 150
  Mozilla/4.02+-+(WinNT;+I+;Nav) -

16:36:23 192.15.16.8 - 207.149.100.17 GET / - 200 1227 150
  Mozilla/4.02+-+(WinNT;+I+;Nav) -
```

Field Prefixes

Each field the server uses has a prefix. These prefixes are summarized in Table 2.7. Basically, all the prefix tells you is how a particular field is used or how the field was obtained for the log entry. For example, the cs prefix tells you the field was obtained from a request sent by the client to the server.

Field Identifiers

Field identifiers detail the type of information a particular field records. To create a named field, the server combines a field prefix with a field identifier. The most commonly used field names are summarized in Table 2.8.

As you take a look at the table, keep in mind that most of these fields relate directly to the fields I've already discussed for the common and combined log file formats. Again, the key difference is that the extended

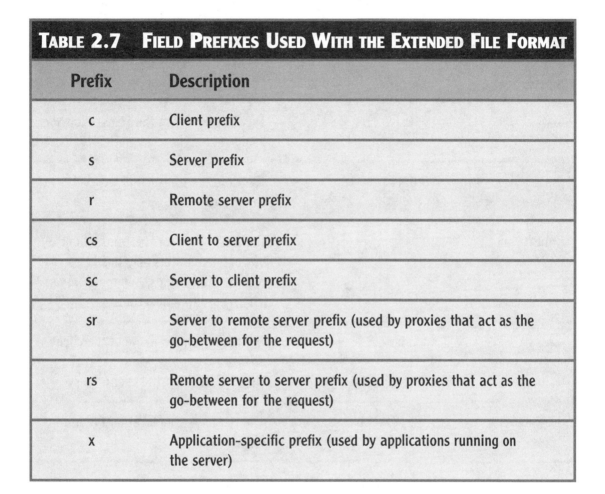

TABLE 2.7	**FIELD PREFIXES USED WITH THE EXTENDED FILE FORMAT**
Prefix	**Description**
c	Client prefix
s	Server prefix
r	Remote server prefix
cs	Client to server prefix
sc	Server to client prefix
sr	Server to remote server prefix (used by proxies that act as the go-between for the request)
rs	Remote server to server prefix (used by proxies that act as the go-between for the request)
x	Application-specific prefix (used by applications running on the server)

format can give you much more detailed information. When you take a look at logs that use the extended format, use the table to help you understand the log entries.

Server Directives

Server directives separate successive sets of requests from a particular user. As shown in Table 2.9, these directives provide many details regarding the Web server and the set of requests being logged.

TABLE 2.8	KEY FIELDS USED WITH THE EXTENDED FILE FORMAT	
Field Name	**Example**	**Description**
date	1998-09-15	The date on which the transaction was completed
time	18:05:00	The time the transaction was completed
time-taken	30	The time taken for the transaction to be completed. Normally this is recorded in seconds, but some servers may record in milliseconds.
c-dns	pc4.att.net	The fully qualified name of the client
c-ip	192.15.16.2	The IP address of the client
cs(Referrer)	http://www.tvpress.com/	The referrer—the location the user came from
cs(User-Agent)	Mozilla/4.02+-+ (WinNT;+I+;Nav)	The user agent or browser making the request
s-method	GET	The HTTP request method
cs-uri	/scripts/adm.dll?KEY=ABC	The file location and query used in the request
cs-uri-query	?KEY=ABC	A query string passed with the file request

Field Name	Example	Description
TABLE 2.8 CONTINUED...		
cs-uri-stem	/scripts/adm.dll	The requested file
cs-username	GREEN\bills	The authenticated name of the user
cs-version	HTTP/1.1	The HTTP version used for the transfer
s-cached	0	Indicates whether a cache hit occurred on the server. A zero in this field indicates the cache wasn't used
sc-bytes	2784	The number of bytes transferred
sc-comment	File Not Found	The comment returned with the status code
sc-status	404	The HTTP status code
s-dns	www.tvpress.com	The fully qualified name of the server
s-ip	207.143.12.8	The IP address of the server

The Microsoft IIS Log File Format

The Microsoft IIS log file format is another log file format you may encounter. As with the extended file format, you are free to select fields you want the server to log. Normally, you do this when you install the server, but your Web server administrator can also update the settings for you.

Although the IIS format uses many of the same fields as the extended file format, these fields are logged in a different way. Additionally, because the

TABLE 2.9 DIRECTIVES USED WITH THE EXTENDED FILE FORMAT	
Directive Name	**Description**
Version	Identifies the version of the extended log file format used
Fields	Specifies the fields as well as the order of the fields recorded in the log file
Software	Identifies the server software that created the log entries
Start-Date	Identifies the date and time the log was started
End-Date	Identifies the date and time the log was finished
Date	Identifies the date and time the entries were made in the log
Remark	Specifies comments

IIS log format gives you no indication of what fields are logged, it is sometimes difficult to determine what a particular field is telling you. Because of this, you may want to ask your service provider if he can switch the server to the extended file format, which is fully supported by IIS.

 NOTE This section provides an introduction to the IIS log format. For detailed information, visit the Microsoft help area for IIS (**http://www.microsoft.com/iis/support/iishelp/iis/htm/core/iiabtlg.htm**).

Listing 2.3 shows sample entries from a log that uses the IIS format. Note that unlike other log formats, the IIS format separates fields using commas.

Listing 2.3   Sample Entries from an IIS-Formatted Log

```
192.15.16.8, -, 5/28/98, 14:00:33, W3SVC, STATS,
   207.149.100.17, 1442, 358, 111, 404, 2, GET, /list.htm,
   Mozilla/2.0 (compatible; MSIE 3.02; Win32), -
192.15.16.8, -, 5/28/98, 14:00:49, W3SVC, STATS,
   207.149.100.17, 291, 364, 25100, 200, 0, GET, /list.htm,
   Mozilla/2.0 (compatible; MSIE 3.02; Win32), -, -,
192.15.16.8, -, 5/28/98, 14:01:33, W3SVC, STATS,
   207.149.100.17, 44063, 361, 954, 200, 0, GET,
   /promote/samp.htm, Mozilla/2.0 (compatible; MSIE 3.02;
   Win32), http://www.tvpress.com/list.htm
192.15.16.8, -, 5/28/98, 14:01:37, W3SVC, STATS,
   207.149.100.17, 161, 400, 409, 200, 0, GET, /book.htm,
   Mozilla/2.0 (compatible; MSIE 3.02; Win32),
   http://www.tvpress.com/promote/samp.htm
```

Regardless of what fields are used with the IIS format, the order of the fields is generally the same as shown in the listing. The key difference is that when you decide not to use a field, it is not logged. The server simply skips the field and writes the next field without leaving a place mark. On the other hand, if you select a field for which there is no information available, a dash is inserted into the field when it is logged.

The fields supported by IIS are shown in Table 2.10. Note that the order of the fields in the table is the general order used by IIS to record fields. However, keep in mind that the actual fields you select can affect the order in which fields are written.

Understanding Visits and Page Views

Understanding how logs are used on your server is the first step to getting a bird's eye view of the big picture for your Web site. Now that you know what the access log looks like, you can use this knowledge to put together the big picture for your Web site. The big picture will tell you how many people are visiting, what pages they are reading, how long they stay at the Web site, and more. You will use the big picture to help you improve and promote your Web site.

TABLE 2.10 FIELDS USED WITH THE IIS FILE FORMAT		
Field Name	**Example**	**Description**
Client IP	192.15.16.2	The IP address of the client
Username	GREEN\bills	The authenticated name of the user
Date	09/15/98	The date on which the transaction was completed
Time	18:05:00	The time the transaction was completed
Service	W3SVC	The name of the Web service logging the transaction
Computer Name	TIGER1	The name of the computer that made the request
Server IP	207.143.12.8	The IP address of the server
Elapsed Time	2508	The time taken for the transaction to be completed in milliseconds
Bytes Received	284	The number of bytes received by the client
Bytes Sent	1752	The number of bytes sent to the client
Status Code	404	The HTTP status code
Windows NT Status Code	0	The error status code from Windows NT
Method Used	GET	The HTTP request method
File URI	/scripts/adm.dll	The requested file
User-Agent	Mozilla/4.02 - (WinNT; I ;Nav)	The user agent or browser making the request
Referrer	http://www.tvpress.com/	The referrer—the location the user came from

Wandering through the Log Files

The access log was meant to be wandered through. After all, it is an ASCII text file. For a Web site that is just getting started, you may find that wandering through the entries looking at the domain name of visitors and the files that they access is a lot of fun. Before your Web site attracts a following, you can often get a very clear picture of who is visiting and what files they view simply by reading the access log every day.

Finding the Access Log

Because the location of the access log is determined when the server is installed, your access log may be in a totally different location than my access log or anyone else's. The best way to find the access log is to ask your service provider or the server administrator where this file is located.

When you start to wander the access log, the advantage of having your own domain becomes clear. For anyone with his or her own domain, the access log will be in a separate file that is easy to search and use. This is true regardless of whether you have your own server or you use someone else's. When multiple domains are served by the same Web server, the log usually has a prefix that indicates the domain, such as `tvpress-access-log` for the access log of **www.tvpress.com**. Otherwise, the access log is usually named `access-log`.

Lots of people publishing on the Web don't have their own domain. If you have an account with a service provider and do not have your own domain, you will share the access log with everyone else using the Web server. For the access log to be meaningful, you will need to extract entries that pertain to your home pages. The part of this section titled "Extracting Information from the Access Log" explains how to do this.

Reading the Access Log

To read the access log, you can use any standard text editor or word processor. Although viewing the file on the Web server is often the easiest option, you can transfer the file from the Web server to your file system and view it locally. To do this, you use FTP (File Transfer Protocol). If you need help with transferring files, be sure to ask your service provider.

Viewing the access log in a text editor can be useful, especially when you are getting started. Keep in mind, however, that the access log can grow rather quickly. Every entry in the access log eats up about 90 bytes of disk space. This means that if a visitor requests a Web page with eight images, the access log will grow by about 810 bytes. Multiply this by a few page requests and a few visitors every day, and you will see that even a Web site with minimal traffic can have a fairly large access log.

Extracting Information from the Access Log

UNIX is one of the most popular Web server platforms. If your service provider uses a UNIX server, you can extract information from the access log using the `grep` command. The basic syntax for this command is as follows:

```
grep what from_where
```

TIP

Mac users, don't despair. The `grep` command is universally popular—so much so that it has been ported to the Mac. For the Mac, this command is called egrep. You can retrieve a copy of `egrep` (egrep.hqx) using one of these URLs:

```
http://mirror.apple.com/Mirrors/00_links.for.anarchie.
    dir/Info-Mac.Archive/text/
```

```
http://massis.lcs.mit.edu/HyperArchive/Archive/text/
```

```
http://sunsite.doc.ic.ac.uk/packages/mac/info-mac
    /_Text_Processing/
```

NOTE

As you will see later this morning, egrep is a more powerful version of grep that allows you to match multiple parameters. After you install egrep, you can perform any of the searches described in this section. Be sure to substitute the keyword `egrep` for `grep` wherever necessary.

Following the basic syntax for grep, you could search the access log for all entries that reference the page `writing.htm` using this command:

```
grep writing.htm access-log
```

Anyone who uses Windows 3.1, Windows 95, or Windows NT can use the DOS `find` command to extract information from files as well. The syntax for `find` is nearly identical to the syntax for `grep`. The key difference is that double quotation marks must surround the search parameter. The basic syntax for the find command is as follows:

```
find "what" from_where
```

Following the basic syntax for find, you can search the access log for all entries that reference the page `writing.htm` using this command:

```
find "writing.htm" access-log
```

To search for multiple items simultaneously, you can use the egrep command. When you use egrep, you use quotation marks to surround the entire query, and the pipe symbol (|) to separate each item that you are looking for, such as:

```
egrep "writing.htm¦writing2.htm" access-log
```

In this example, you are searching the access log for all entries related to writing.htm and writing2.htm. Be sure that you don't put unnecessary spaces around the pipe symbol, because the server may interpret the spaces literally and search only for occurrences that include the spacing that you specify.

NOTE Although you can search for multiple parameters with `egrep` for the Mac, no equivalent exists for the DOS `find` command. A workaround would be to perform consecutive searches of the access log.

Although `grep` and `egrep` usually print their output to the screen, you can redirect the output to a file using the UNIX redirect command (>). To redirect a search to a file called save.txt, you could use this command:

```
grep writing.htm access-log > save.txt
```

DOS understands the redirect command as well. Here is an example that uses the DOS find command and then redirects the results of the search into a text file:

```
find "writing.htm" access-log > save.txt
```

Often, you may simply want to count the number of times a file has been accessed. You do this by directing the output of the grep command through the word count program. The word count program is called wc. You use the pipe symbol to connect the grep command and the wc command, as in this example:

```
grep writing.htm access-log ¦ wc
```

The results that you see will look something like this:

```
7       91      612
```

Forget about the last two numbers and focus on the first number, which is the number of times that the file was accessed.

To count the number of times that a file has been accessed in DOS, you use the /C switch for the find command. The /C switch tells the find command to count the lines in the search result, which gives you the number of entries pertaining to a specific file. You can use the /C switch as follows:

```
find /C "writing.htm" access-log
```

Hits, Hits, and More Hits

Every time a client requests a file from the Web server, an entry goes into the access log. Each file request is considered a hit. As you learned earlier this morning under "Using Web Stats to Understand Your Site's Visitors," the hit is not a very accurate measurement of how many people are visiting your site. This is because recorded hits can be very misleading, especially when you consider that one hit rarely equals one visitor.

Getting Entries from the Log

Listing 2.4 shows a 15-minute slice of entries for an actual access log from the Web site at **www.tvpress.com**. To make the entries easier to follow, I extracted the entries for an entire day and then cut out the entries from 00:00 to about 00:15. The commands that I used to obtain the entries for an entire day are shown in this example:

```
grep "11/Apr/1998" access-log > $HOME/temp.txt
```

Here, the grep command is used to extract all entries containing the string "11/Apr/1998" from a file called access-log. Next, I redirected the output of the grep command to a file in my home directory called temp.txt. To a UNIX computer, the keyword $HOME is generally the same as the full path to your directory on the server.

You could perform a similar operation in DOS with the find command, as follows:

```
find "11/Apr/1998" access-log >
  C:/your_directory/temp.txt
```

You will find this sample access log and other examples online at **www.tvpress.com/promote/examples/**. The file name is access-log.txt.

As you examine the entries in the access log, note that most of the entries are for files ending in the .gif extension, which designates an image file in GIF format. Note also that all of these entries pertain to three specific domains:

- ✪ pc8.att.net
- ✪ at1.vl.com
- ✪ 198.23.25.3

Although you could assume that all these entries pertain to three distinct visitors, this isn't always the case. Consider for a moment that any of these fully qualified domain names could belong to a multiuser computer with lots of users online at any given time. In multiuser environments, it is not uncommon for 25, 50, or even 100 users to be using the same host. That said, determining whether the hits belong to more than three specific visitors is very difficult. For now, I assume that the hits belong to three visitors. Rest assured that I discuss visitors in more detail later this morning. Look for the section titled "Zeroing in on the Visit."

Listing 2.4 Entries from an Access Log

```
pc8.att.net - - [11/Apr/1998:00:01:18 -0700] "GET / HTTP/1.0"
  200 8355
pc8.att.net - - [11/Apr/1998:00:01:25 -0700] "GET /ban2.gif
  HTTP/1.0" 200 1373
pc8.att.net - - [11/Apr/1998:00:01:25 -0700] "GET
  /tvpgis2.gif HTTP/1.0" 200 2809
pc8.att.net - - [11/Apr/1998:00:01:25 -0700] "GET /tvpgis.gif
  HTTP/1.0" 200 7923
pc8.att.net - - [11/Apr/1998:00:01:25 -0700] "GET /bu_off.gif
  HTTP/1.0" 200 926
pc8.att.net - - [11/Apr/1998:00:01:29 -0700] "GET /ban1.gif
  HTTP/1.0" 200 1436
pc8.att.net - - [11/Apr/1998:00:01:25 -0700] "GET /bu_on.gif
  HTTP/1.0" 200 933
pc8.att.net - - [11/Apr/1998:00:01:37 -0700] "GET /tvpgis.gif
  HTTP/1.0" 200 7923
pc8.att.net - - [11/Apr/1998:00:01:37 -0700] "GET /ban5.gif
  HTTP/1.0" 200 1407
pc8.att.net - - [11/Apr/1998:00:01:38 -0700] "GET /ban6.gif
  HTTP/1.0" 200 1452
pc8.att.net - - [11/Apr/1998:00:01:39 -0700] "GET /ban7.gif
  HTTP/1.0" 200 1461
pc8.att.net - - [11/Apr/1998:00:01:40 -0700] "GET /ban8.gif
  HTTP/1.0" 200 1400
pc8.att.net - - [11/Apr/1998:00:01:40 -0700] "GET /ban9.gif
  HTTP/1.0" 200 1265
pc8.att.net - - [11/Apr/1998:00:01:42 -0700] "GET /cbox.gif
  HTTP/1.0" 200 662
pc8.att.net - - [11/Apr/1998:00:01:43 -0700] "GET /bu_on.gif
  HTTP/1.0" 200 926
pc8.att.net - - [11/Apr/1998:00:01:44 -0700] "GET /main5b.gif
  HTTP/1.0" 200 1118
pc8.att.net - - [11/Apr/1998:00:01:45 -0700] "GET /main6b.gif
  HTTP/1.0" 200 1081
```

```
pc8.att.net - - [11/Apr/1998:00:01:46 -0700] "GET /main8b.gif
   HTTP/1.0" 200 1088
pc8.att.net - - [11/Apr/1998:00:01:46 -0700] "GET /main7b.gif
   HTTP/1.0" 200 1101
pc8.att.net - - [11/Apr/1998:00:01:46 -0700] "GET /ban10.gif
   HTTP/1.0" 200 1377
pc8.att.net - - [11/Apr/1998:00:01:47 -0700] "GET /fp97.gif
   HTTP/1.0" 200 5306
pc8.att.net - - [11/Apr/1998:00:01:48 -0700] "GET /banner.gif
   HTTP/1.0" 200 1421
pc8.att.net - - [11/Apr/1998:00:01:49 -0700] "GET /main4b.gif
   HTTP/1.0" 200 1053
pc8.att.net - - [11/Apr/1998:00:01:50 -0700] "GET
   /main10b.gif HTTP/1.0" 200 1027
pc8.att.net - - [11/Apr/1998:00:01:53 -0700] "GET /main9b.gif
   HTTP/1.0" 200 1089
pc8.att.net - - [11/Apr/1998:00:01:55 -0700] "GET /ban4.gif
   HTTP/1.0" 200 1356
pc8.att.net - - [11/Apr/1998:00:01:56 -0700] "GET /main2b.gif
   HTTP/1.0" 200 1113
pc8.att.net - - [11/Apr/1998:00:01:57 -0700] "GET /main3b.gif
   HTTP/1.0" 200 1059
pc8.att.net - - [11/Apr/1998:00:01:58 -0700] "GET /ban3.gif
   HTTP/1.0" 200 1372
pc8.att.net - - [11/Apr/1998:00:01:59 -0700] "GET /mainb.gif
   HTTP/1.0" 200 1081
pc8.att.net - - [11/Apr/1998:00:02:00 -0700] "GET /wpupr.gif
   HTTP/1.0" 200 6376
pc8.att.net - - [11/Apr/1998:00:02:07 -0700] "GET /wpd.gif
   HTTP/1.0" 200 10423
pc8.att.net - - [11/Apr/1998:00:03:28 -0700] "GET /vpjic.html
   HTTP/1.0" 200 7256
pc8.att.net - - [11/Apr/1998:00:03:35 -0700] "GET /jban6.gif
   HTTP/1.0" 200 1508
pc8.att.net - - [11/Apr/1998:00:03:35 -0700] "GET /jban5.gif
   HTTP/1.0" 200 1844
pc8.att.net - - [11/Apr/1998:00:03:35 -0700] "GET /jban3.gif
   HTTP/1.0" 200 1505
pc8.att.net - - [11/Apr/1998:00:03:35 -0700] "GET /jban1.gif
   HTTP/1.0" 200 2134
pc8.att.net - - [11/Apr/1998:00:03:35 -0700] "GET /jban2.gif
   HTTP/1.0" 200 1978
pc8.att.net - - [11/Apr/1998:00:03:35 -0700] "GET /jban4.gif
   HTTP/1.0" 200 1975
```

```
pc8.att.net - - [11/Apr/1998:00:03:40 -0700] "GET /jban8.gif
   HTTP/1.0" 200 2228
pc8.att.net - - [11/Apr/1998:00:03:44 -0700] "GET /jban10.gif
   HTTP/1.0" 200 1701
pc8.att.net - - [11/Apr/1998:00:03:44 -0700] "GET /jban12.gif
   HTTP/1.0" 200 2188
pc8.att.net - - [11/Apr/1998:00:03:48 -0700] "GET
   /jbanner.gif HTTP/1.0" 200 1643
pc8.att.net - - [11/Apr/1998:00:03:48 -0700] "GET /job7.gif
   HTTP/1.0" 200 1139
pc8.att.net - - [11/Apr/1998:00:03:49 -0700] "GET /job8.gif
   HTTP/1.0" 200 1047
pc8.att.net - - [11/Apr/1998:00:03:52 -0700] "GET /job9.gif
   HTTP/1.0" 200 1099
pc8.att.net - - [11/Apr/1998:00:03:53 -0700] "GET /job11.gif
   HTTP/1.0" 200 1124
pc8.att.net - - [11/Apr/1998:00:03:54 -0700] "GET /jban7.gif
   HTTP/1.0" 200 1733
pc8.att.net - - [11/Apr/1998:00:03:56 -0700] "GET /jban11.gif
   HTTP/1.0" 200 1643
pc8.att.net - - [11/Apr/1998:00:03:56 -0700] "GET /job10.gif
   HTTP/1.0" 200 1073
pc8.att.net - - [11/Apr/1998:00:03:56 -0700] "GET /job12.gif
   HTTP/1.0" 200 1119
pc8.att.net - - [11/Apr/1998:00:03:57 -0700] "GET /job3.gif
   HTTP/1.0" 200 1075
pc8.att.net - - [11/Apr/1998:00:04:00 -0700] "GET /job5.gif
   HTTP/1.0" 200 1164
pc8.att.net - - [11/Apr/1998:00:04:01 -0700] "GET /mstats.gif
   HTTP/1.0" 200 6958
pc8.att.net - - [11/Apr/1998:00:04:06 -0700] "GET /job4.gif
   HTTP/1.0" 200 1132
pc8.att.net - - [11/Apr/1998:00:04:08 -0700] "GET /job1.gif
   HTTP/1.0" 200 1154
pc8.att.net - - [11/Apr/1998:00:04:08 -0700] "GET /jicttl.gif
   HTTP/1.0" 200 20288
pc8.att.net - - [11/Apr/1998:00:04:09 -0700] "GET /job2.gif
   HTTP/1.0" 200 1152
pc8.att.net - - [11/Apr/1998:00:04:16 -0700] "GET /job6.gif
   HTTP/1.0" 200 1095
pc8.att.net - - [11/Apr/1998:00:04:19 -0700] "GET /jban9.gif
   HTTP/1.0" 200 1998
at1.vl.com - - [11/Apr/1998:00:04:57 -0700] "GET
   /idn/cissue/resmul.htm HTTP/1.0" 200 396
```

```
pc8.att.net - - [11/Apr/1998:00:05:04 -0700] "GET /vpepc.html
  HTTP/1.0" 200 2741
at1.vl.com - - [11/Apr/1998:00:05:04 -0700] "GET
  /idn/idnttl3.gif HTTP/1.0" 200 4612
pc8.att.net - - [11/Apr/1998:00:05:10 -0700] "GET /epc.html
  HTTP/1.0" 200 501
pc8.att.net - - [11/Apr/1998:00:05:10 -0700] "GET
  /vpepc2.html HTTP/1.0" 200 544
pc8.att.net - - [11/Apr/1998:00:05:10 -0700] "GET
  /ziptour.html HTTP/1.0" 200 526
pc8.att.net - - [11/Apr/1998:00:05:13 -0700] "GET
  /crights.gif HTTP/1.0" 200 5173
pc8.att.net - - [11/Apr/1998:00:05:13 -0700] "GET
  /epubunl2.gif HTTP/1.0" 200 2406
pc8.att.net - - [11/Apr/1998:00:05:19 -0700] "GET /mail.gif
  HTTP/1.0" 200 962
pc8.att.net - - [11/Apr/1998:00:05:29 -0700] "GET /zip2.html
  HTTP/1.0" 200 470
pc8.att.net - - [11/Apr/1998:00:05:34 -0700] "GET
  /vpepc3.html HTTP/1.0" 200 728
at1.vl.com - - [11/Apr/1998:00:05:34 -0700] "GET
  /idn/idnfp.htm HTTP/1.0" 200 7610
pc8.att.net - - [11/Apr/1998:00:05:37 -0700] "GET
  /epubunl2.gif HTTP/1.0" 200 2406
pc8.att.net - - [11/Apr/1998:00:05:43 -0700] "GET /rote.html
  HTTP/1.0" 200 333
pc8.att.net - - [11/Apr/1998:00:05:46 -0700] "GET
  /vpsttl1.gif HTTP/1.0" 200 14361
at1.vl.com - - [11/Apr/1998:00:05:49 -0700] "GET /idn/bg1.gif
  HTTP/1.0" 200 612
at1.vl.com - - [11/Apr/1998:00:05:49 -0700] "GET
  /idn/glnet.gif HTTP/1.0" 200 7425
at1.vl.com - - [11/Apr/1998:00:05:49 -0700] "GET
  /idn/glmail.gif HTTP/1.0" 200 7501
pc8.att.net - - [11/Apr/1998:00:05:53 -0700] "GET /zip3.html
  HTTP/1.0" 200 281
at1.vl.com - - [11/Apr/1998:00:05:56 -0700] "GET
  /idn/site2.gif HTTP/1.0" 200 3097
at1.vl.com - - [11/Apr/1998:00:05:57 -0700] "GET
  /idn/site1.gif HTTP/1.0" 200 1487
pc8.att.net - - [11/Apr/1998:00:06:00 -0700] "GET /wgttl.jpg
  HTTP/1.0" 200 20594
pc8.att.net - - [11/Apr/1998:00:06:02 -0700] "GET
  /vpepc4.html HTTP/1.0" 200 679
```

```
at1.vl.com - - [11/Apr/1998:00:06:07 -0700] "GET /idn/cal.gif
    HTTP/1.0" 200 6713
at1.vl.com - - [11/Apr/1998:00:06:15 -0700] "GET /idn/wpd.gif
    HTTP/1.0" 200 10423
pc8.att.net - - [11/Apr/1998:00:06:18 -0700] "GET
    /epubunl2.gif HTTP/1.0" 304 -
at1.vl.com - - [11/Apr/1998:00:06:18 -0700] "GET
    /idn/wpupr.gif HTTP/1.0" 200 6376
pc8.att.net - - [11/Apr/1998:00:06:35 -0700] "GET
    /vpepc5.html HTTP/1.0" 200 582
at1.vl.com - - [11/Apr/1998:00:06:51 -0700] "GET
    /idn/fp97.gif HTTP/1.0" 200 5306
pc8.att.net - - [11/Apr/1998:00:06:58 -0700] "GET
    /vpepc6.html HTTP/1.0" 200 668
pc8.att.net - - [11/Apr/1998:00:07:31 -0700] "GET /rote2.html
    HTTP/1.0" 200 331
pc8.att.net - - [11/Apr/1998:00:07:34 -0700] "GET
    /vpsttl2.gif HTTP/1.0" 200 14108
pc8.att.net - - [11/Apr/1998:00:07:47 -0700] "GET
    /vpepc5.html HTTP/1.0" 304 -
pc8.att.net - - [11/Apr/1998:00:08:18 -0700] "GET
    /vpepc6.html HTTP/1.0" 304 -
198.23.25.3 - - [11/Apr/1998:00:09:14 -0700] "GET
    /idn/cissue/resmul.htm HTTP/1.0" 200 4516
198.23.25.3 - - [11/Apr/1998:00:09:20 -0700] "GET
    /idn/bg2.gif HTTP/1.0" 200 18079
198.23.25.3 - - [11/Apr/1998:00:09:23 -0700] "GET
    /idn/colttl3.gif HTTP/1.0" 200 1127
pc8.att.net - - [11/Apr/1998:00:09:27 -0700] "GET /zip2.html
    HTTP/1.0" 304 -
198.23.25.3 - - [11/Apr/1998:00:09:29 -0700] "GET
    /idn/resttl2.gif HTTP/1.0" 200 3730
pc8.att.net - - [11/Apr/1998:00:09:32 -0700] "GET
    /vpepc3.html HTTP/1.0" 304 -
pc8.att.net - - [11/Apr/1998:00:09:40 -0700] "GET /rote.html
    HTTP/1.0" 304 -
pc8.att.net - - [11/Apr/1998:00:09:57 -0700] "GET
    /vpsttl1.gif HTTP/1.0" 304 -
pc8.att.net - - [11/Apr/1998:00:10:13 -0700] "GET /rote2.html
    HTTP/1.0" 304 -
pc8.att.net - - [11/Apr/1998:00:10:32 -0700] "GET /jobopp-
    menu.html HTTP/1.0" 200 1297
pc8.att.net - - [11/Apr/1998:00:10:32 -0700] "GET /tvpbanner-
    top.html HTTP/1.0" 200 132
```

```
pc8.att.net - - [11/Apr/1998:00:10:32 -0700] "GET /tvpbanner-
  bot.html HTTP/1.0" 200 607
pc8.att.net - - [11/Apr/1998:00:10:27 -0700] "GET
  /joboppframes.html HTTP/1.0" 200 1592
pc8.att.net - - [11/Apr/1998:00:10:34 -0700] "GET /tvp64.gif
  HTTP/1.0" 200 3231
pc8.att.net - - [11/Apr/1998:00:10:34 -0700] "GET /tvp192.gif
  HTTP/1.0" 200 16648
at1.vl.com - - [11/Apr/1998:00:10:37 -0700] "GET
  /idn/bio/bioerev.html HTTP/1.0" 200 6027
pc8.att.net - - [11/Apr/1998:00:11:04 -0700] "GET
  /jscience.html HTTP/1.0" 200 2508
pc8.att.net - - [11/Apr/1998:00:11:22 -0700] "GET /jintl.html
  HTTP/1.0" 200 2122
pc8.att.net - - [11/Apr/1998:00:12:53 -0700] "GET
  /jdisab.html HTTP/1.0" 200 1197
pc8.att.net - - [11/Apr/1998:00:13:21 -0700] "GET /tvpgis.gif
  HTTP/1.0" 200 7923
pc8.att.net - - [11/Apr/1998:00:13:22 -0700] "GET /tvpgis.gif
  HTTP/1.0" 304 -
198.23.25.3 - - [11/Apr/1998:00:14:39 -0700] "GET
  /idn/idnfp.htm HTTP/1.0" 304 -
```

Examining Log Entries

By looking at individual hits in the log, you can get a better understanding of what is happening on the server. This section follows one of the users through the log. For easy reference, I call this user Joe, as in Joe Web Surfer. Joe's first hit is a request for the top-level home page:

```
pc8.att.net - - [11/Apr/1998:00:01:18 -0700] "GET /
  HTTP/1.0" 200 8355
```

You know this because he requested the file called /, which is the default document in the main directory at the Web site. In examining this hit, Joe entered the URL **http://www.tvpress.com/** into his browser, and the server logged the file request in the access log at `00:01:18`. From the status code `200`, you know that the document was transferred successfully. You also know that `8,355` bytes were transferred. You also know that Joe's domain name in the log files is `pc8.att.net`. This domain name is used for all of Joe's entries.

If you examine the source for the Web page at **www.tvpress.com/**, you will see that it contains many images. Some of these images are displayed when the page is loaded. Other images are hidden and are displayed only when the user performs a specific action, such as moving the mouse pointer over an image linked to another Web page. In all, 32 entries in the access log pertain to this page, as follows:

```
pc8.att.net - - [11/Apr/1998:00:01:18 -0700] "GET / HTTP/1.0"
    200 8355
pc8.att.net - - [11/Apr/1998:00:01:25 -0700] "GET /ban2.gif
    HTTP/1.0" 200 1373
pc8.att.net - - [11/Apr/1998:00:01:25 -0700] "GET
    /tvpgis2.gif HTTP/1.0" 200 2809
pc8.att.net - - [11/Apr/1998:00:01:25 -0700] "GET /tvpgis.gif
    HTTP/1.0" 200 7923
pc8.att.net - - [11/Apr/1998:00:01:25 -0700] "GET /bu_off.gif
    HTTP/1.0" 200 926
pc8.att.net - - [11/Apr/1998:00:01:29 -0700] "GET /ban1.gif
    HTTP/1.0" 200 1436
pc8.att.net - - [11/Apr/1998:00:01:25 -0700] "GET /bu_on.gif
    HTTP/1.0" 200 933
pc8.att.net - - [11/Apr/1998:00:01:37 -0700] "GET /tvpgis.gif
    HTTP/1.0" 200 7923
pc8.att.net - - [11/Apr/1998:00:01:37 -0700] "GET /ban5.gif
    HTTP/1.0" 200 1407
pc8.att.net - - [11/Apr/1998:00:01:38 -0700] "GET /ban6.gif
    HTTP/1.0" 200 1452
pc8.att.net - - [11/Apr/1998:00:01:39 -0700] "GET /ban7.gif
    HTTP/1.0" 200 1461
pc8.att.net - - [11/Apr/1998:00:01:40 -0700] "GET /ban8.gif
    HTTP/1.0" 200 1400
pc8.att.net - - [11/Apr/1998:00:01:40 -0700] "GET /ban9.gif
    HTTP/1.0" 200 1265
pc8.att.net - - [11/Apr/1998:00:01:42 -0700] "GET /cbox.gif
    HTTP/1.0" 200 662
pc8.att.net - - [11/Apr/1998:00:01:43 -0700] "GET /bu_on.gif
    HTTP/1.0" 200 926
pc8.att.net - - [11/Apr/1998:00:01:44 -0700] "GET /main5b.gif
    HTTP/1.0" 200 1118
pc8.att.net - - [11/Apr/1998:00:01:45 -0700] "GET /main6b.gif
    HTTP/1.0" 200 1081
pc8.att.net - - [11/Apr/1998:00:01:46 -0700] "GET /main8b.gif
    HTTP/1.0" 200 1088
```

```
pc8.att.net - - [11/Apr/1998:00:01:46 -0700] "GET /main7b.gif
   HTTP/1.0" 200 1101
pc8.att.net - - [11/Apr/1998:00:01:46 -0700] "GET /ban10.gif
   HTTP/1.0" 200 1377
pc8.att.net - - [11/Apr/1998:00:01:47 -0700] "GET /fp97.gif
   HTTP/1.0" 200 5306
pc8.att.net - - [11/Apr/1998:00:01:48 -0700] "GET /banner.gif
   HTTP/1.0" 200 1421
pc8.att.net - - [11/Apr/1998:00:01:49 -0700] "GET /main4b.gif
   HTTP/1.0" 200 1053
pc8.att.net - - [11/Apr/1998:00:01:50 -0700] "GET
   /main10b.gif HTTP/1.0" 200 1027
pc8.att.net - - [11/Apr/1998:00:01:53 -0700] "GET /main9b.gif
   HTTP/1.0" 200 1089
pc8.att.net - - [11/Apr/1998:00:01:55 -0700] "GET /ban4.gif
   HTTP/1.0" 200 1356
pc8.att.net - - [11/Apr/1998:00:01:56 -0700] "GET /main2b.gif
   HTTP/1.0" 200 1113
pc8.att.net - - [11/Apr/1998:00:01:57 -0700] "GET /main3b.gif
   HTTP/1.0" 200 1059
pc8.att.net - - [11/Apr/1998:00:01:58 -0700] "GET /ban3.gif
   HTTP/1.0" 200 1372
pc8.att.net - - [11/Apr/1998:00:01:59 -0700] "GET /mainb.gif
   HTTP/1.0" 200 1081
pc8.att.net - - [11/Apr/1998:00:02:00 -0700] "GET /wpupr.gif
   HTTP/1.0" 200 6376
pc8.att.net - - [11/Apr/1998:00:02:07 -0700] "GET /wpd.gif
   HTTP/1.0" 200 10423
```

By putting the image hits together with the page hit, you can see how long Joe's browser took to finish loading the page. The first request had a time stamp of

```
[11/Apr/1998:00:01:18 -0700]
```

The last request for this page had a time stamp of

```
[11/Apr/1998:00:02:07 -0700]
```

By calculating the difference between the time stamps, you can see that 49 seconds elapsed between the first file request and the last file request. To see how long the page actually took to load completely, you need to figure out how long the final image took to load. Based on previous entries in the log, say that the final image took nine seconds to load, which puts the total load time for the page at 58 seconds.

On the Web, 59 seconds is a lifetime. Fortunately for this visitor, the page has a lot of text and most of the graphics are at the bottom of the page. Next, Joe selected the link to the Internet Job Center at **http://www.tvpress.com/vpjic.html**. The entry in the log for this hit is this:

```
pc8.att.net - - [11/Apr/1998:00:03:28 -0700] "GET
   /vpjic.html HTTP/1.0" 200 7256
```

Here, Joe selected a hypertext link that brought him to the page called `vpjic.html`. Although Joe didn't enter the actual URL, you know that the URL to the page is **http://www.tvpress.com/vpjic.html**. The server logged the file request in the access log at `00:03:28`. The status code `200` tells you that the document was transferred successfully. You also know that `7,256` bytes were transferred.

By examining the time difference between the previous page request and this page request, you can learn how long Joe stayed on the top-level home page. The top-level home page was requested at

```
[11/Apr/1998:00:01:18 -0700]
```

The page for the Internet Job Center was requested at

```
[11/Apr/1998:00:03:28 -0700]
```

This information shows that Joe spent 2 minutes and 10 seconds on the home page. Granted, part of this time was probably spent waiting for graphics to load, but the total page viewing time is still meaningful, especially if the page has a lot of text.

The top-level page for the Internet Job Center is a graphics-intensive page with very little text that isn't part of a graphic image. The next 27 entries in the access log pertain to graphics in this page:

```
pc8.att.net - - [11/Apr/1998:00:03:35 -0700] "GET /jban6.gif
   HTTP/1.0" 200 1508
pc8.att.net - - [11/Apr/1998:00:03:35 -0700] "GET /jban5.gif
   HTTP/1.0" 200 1844
```

```
pc8.att.net - - [11/Apr/1998:00:03:35 -0700] "GET /jban3.gif
   HTTP/1.0" 200 1505
pc8.att.net - - [11/Apr/1998:00:03:35 -0700] "GET /jban1.gif
   HTTP/1.0" 200 2134
pc8.att.net - - [11/Apr/1998:00:03:35 -0700] "GET /jban2.gif
   HTTP/1.0" 200 1978
pc8.att.net - - [11/Apr/1998:00:03:35 -0700] "GET /jban4.gif
   HTTP/1.0" 200 1975
pc8.att.net - - [11/Apr/1998:00:03:40 -0700] "GET /jban8.gif
   HTTP/1.0" 200 2228
pc8.att.net - - [11/Apr/1998:00:03:44 -0700] "GET /jban10.gif
   HTTP/1.0" 200 1701
pc8.att.net - - [11/Apr/1998:00:03:44 -0700] "GET /jban12.gif
   HTTP/1.0" 200 2188
pc8.att.net - - [11/Apr/1998:00:03:48 -0700] "GET /jbanner.gif
   HTTP/1.0" 200 1643
pc8.att.net - - [11/Apr/1998:00:03:48 -0700] "GET /job7.gif
   HTTP/1.0" 200 1139
pc8.att.net - - [11/Apr/1998:00:03:49 -0700] "GET /job8.gif
   HTTP/1.0" 200 1047
pc8.att.net - - [11/Apr/1998:00:03:52 -0700] "GET /job9.gif
   HTTP/1.0" 200 1099
pc8.att.net - - [11/Apr/1998:00:03:53 -0700] "GET /job11.gif
   HTTP/1.0" 200 1124
pc8.att.net - - [11/Apr/1998:00:03:54 -0700] "GET /jban7.gif
   HTTP/1.0" 200 1733
pc8.att.net - - [11/Apr/1998:00:03:56 -0700] "GET /jban11.gif
   HTTP/1.0" 200 1643
pc8.att.net - - [11/Apr/1998:00:03:56 -0700] "GET /job10.gif
   HTTP/1.0" 200 1073
pc8.att.net - - [11/Apr/1998:00:03:56 -0700] "GET /job12.gif
   HTTP/1.0" 200 1119
pc8.att.net - - [11/Apr/1998:00:03:57 -0700] "GET /job3.gif
   HTTP/1.0" 200 1075
pc8.att.net - - [11/Apr/1998:00:04:00 -0700] "GET /job5.gif
   HTTP/1.0" 200 1164
pc8.att.net - - [11/Apr/1998:00:04:01 -0700] "GET /mstats.gif
   HTTP/1.0" 200 6958
pc8.att.net - - [11/Apr/1998:00:04:06 -0700] "GET /job4.gif
   HTTP/1.0" 200 1132
pc8.att.net - - [11/Apr/1998:00:04:08 -0700] "GET /job1.gif
   HTTP/1.0" 200 1154
pc8.att.net - - [11/Apr/1998:00:04:08 -0700] "GET /jicttl.gif
   HTTP/1.0" 200 20288
```

```
pc8.att.net - - [11/Apr/1998:00:04:09 -0700] "GET /job2.gif
   HTTP/1.0" 200 1152
pc8.att.net - - [11/Apr/1998:00:04:16 -0700] "GET /job6.gif
   HTTP/1.0" 200 1095
pc8.att.net - - [11/Apr/1998:00:04:19 -0700] "GET /jban9.gif
   HTTP/1.0" 200 1998
```

By reviewing the entries for the Internet Job Center page, you can see that the total loading time is about 54 seconds. The next page request comes at 00:05:04, when Joe requests the page shown in this log entry:

```
pc8.att.net - - [11/Apr/1998:00:05:04 -0700] "GET /vpepc.html
   HTTP/1.0" 200 2741
```

When you determine the time difference between the page requests, you see that Joe spent 1 minute and 36 seconds at the Internet Job Center page. Although this may not seem like a long time, the top-level page for the Internet Job Center is really just a graphical doorway to the job center's resources, such as the page at vpepc.html.

As you continue to follow Joe through the Web site, you see lots of page hits in rapid succession. The primary reason for this is that vpepc.html is a frame-enhanced page with three frames. The loading of the frames is logged with these entries:

```
pc8.att.net - - [11/Apr/1998:00:05:10 -0700] "GET /epc.html
   HTTP/1.0" 200 501
pc8.att.net - - [11/Apr/1998:00:05:10 -0700] "GET
   /vpepc2.html HTTP/1.0" 200 544
pc8.att.net - - [11/Apr/1998:00:05:10 -0700] "GET
   /ziptour.html HTTP/1.0" 200 526
Graphic images in those three frames are logged with these
   entries:
pc8.att.net - - [11/Apr/1998:00:05:13 -0700] "GET
   /crights.gif HTTP/1.0" 200 5173
pc8.att.net - - [11/Apr/1998:00:05:13 -0700] "GET
   /epubun12.gif HTTP/1.0" 200 2406
pc8.att.net - - [11/Apr/1998:00:05:19 -0700] "GET /mail.gif
   HTTP/1.0" 200 962
```

The page at vpepc.html also uses client pull to create a rolling slide show. Client pull is a technology that allows you to tell a browser to load a specific file at a specific time. All these entries in the log are for slides—pages and their images in the slide show:

```
pc8.att.net - - [11/Apr/1998:00:05:29 -0700] "GET /zip2.html
   HTTP/1.0" 200 470
pc8.att.net - - [11/Apr/1998:00:05:34 -0700] "GET
   /vpepc3.html HTTP/1.0" 200 728
pc8.att.net - - [11/Apr/1998:00:05:37 -0700] "GET
   /epubunl2.gif HTTP/1.0" 200 2406
pc8.att.net - - [11/Apr/1998:00:05:43 -0700] "GET /rote.html
   HTTP/1.0" 200 333
pc8.att.net - - [11/Apr/1998:00:05:46 -0700] "GET
   /vpsttl1.gif HTTP/1.0" 200 14361
pc8.att.net - - [11/Apr/1998:00:05:53 -0700] "GET /zip3.html
   HTTP/1.0" 200 281
pc8.att.net - - [11/Apr/1998:00:06:00 -0700] "GET /wgttl.jpg
   HTTP/1.0" 200 20594
pc8.att.net - - [11/Apr/1998:00:06:02 -0700] "GET
   /vpepc4.html HTTP/1.0" 200 679
pc8.att.net - - [11/Apr/1998:00:06:18 -0700] "GET
   /epubunl2.gif HTTP/1.0" 304 -
pc8.att.net - - [11/Apr/1998:00:06:35 -0700] "GET
   /vpepc5.html HTTP/1.0" 200 582
pc8.att.net - - [11/Apr/1998:00:06:58 -0700] "GET
   /vpepc6.html HTTP/1.0" 200 668
pc8.att.net - - [11/Apr/1998:00:07:31 -0700] "GET /rote2.html
   HTTP/1.0" 200 331
pc8.att.net - - [11/Apr/1998:00:07:34 -0700] "GET
   /vpsttl2.gif HTTP/1.0" 200 14108
pc8.att.net - - [11/Apr/1998:00:07:47 -0700] "GET
   /vpepc5.html HTTP/1.0" 304 -
pc8.att.net - - [11/Apr/1998:00:08:18 -0700] "GET
   /vpepc6.html HTTP/1.0" 304 -
pc8.att.net - - [11/Apr/1998:00:09:27 -0700] "GET /zip2.html
   HTTP/1.0" 304 -
pc8.att.net - - [11/Apr/1998:00:09:32 -0700] "GET
   /vpepc3.html HTTP/1.0" 304 -
pc8.att.net - - [11/Apr/1998:00:09:40 -0700] "GET /rote.html
   HTTP/1.0" 304 -
pc8.att.net - - [11/Apr/1998:00:09:57 -0700] "GET
   /vpsttl1.gif HTTP/1.0" 304 -
pc8.att.net - - [11/Apr/1998:00:10:13 -0700] "GET /rote2.html
   HTTP/1.0" 304 -
```

When you examine the hits for the slide show, note the status code 304 that appears in later entries. Here, Joe's browser is requesting a file, but because the file hasn't been modified since it was last viewed, the browser loads the file from its file or memory cache.

Joe spends quite a bit of time viewing the slide show before moving on. Joe accessed the slide show at 00:05:04 when he followed the link to `vpepc.html`; not until 00:10:27 did he move on to a new area of the Web site. Thus, the total time spent viewing the slide show was 5 minutes, 23 seconds.

The next page request is logged with this entry:

```
pc8.att.net - - [11/Apr/1998:00:10:27 -0700] "GET
  /joboppframes.html HTTP/1.0" 200 1592
```

If you view the entry without understanding how the site is organized, you miss the fact that there is no way to get from the slide show to the job opportunities page at the Internet Job Center. So what happened?

Well, Joe probably pressed the Back button in his browser's menu (older browsers don't move back through frames) and jumped back to the top-level page of the Internet Job Center. Because this page was completely loaded from cache, no log entry occurred. The job opportunities page is another frame-enhanced page, so the next three requests for HTML documents pertain to this single page:

```
pc8.att.net - - [11/Apr/1998:00:10:32 -0700] "GET /tvpbanner-
  top.html HTTP/1.0" 200 132
pc8.att.net - - [11/Apr/1998:00:10:32 -0700] "GET /tvpbanner-
  bot.html HTTP/1.0" 200 607
pc8.att.net - - [11/Apr/1998:00:10:32 -0700] "GET /jobopp-
  menu.html HTTP/1.0" 200 1297
```

These pages contain only two graphics:

```
pc8.att.net - - [11/Apr/1998:00:10:34 -0700] "GET /tvp64.gif
  HTTP/1.0" 200 3231
pc8.att.net - - [11/Apr/1998:00:10:34 -0700] "GET /tvp192.gif
  HTTP/1.0" 200 16648
```

NOTE If you examine the original log entries, you will see that the request for the `joboppframes.html` page is logged after the requests for the frames that are a part of the page. The reason for this is that Joe's browser got ahead of itself and started loading the pages before it finished with the main page.

The left-side frame in the job opportunities page acts as a menu. When you click on links in the side frame, pages are loaded into the main frame to the right. The log entries show that Joe selected three of the menu options and that two images were associated with the last option. Note that the last image was loaded from the browser's cache:

```
pc8.att.net - - [11/Apr/1998:00:11:04 -0700] "GET
   /jscience.html HTTP/1.0" 200 2508
pc8.att.net - - [11/Apr/1998:00:11:22 -0700] "GET /jintl.html
   HTTP/1.0" 200 2122
pc8.att.net - - [11/Apr/1998:00:12:53 -0700] "GET
   /jdisab.html HTTP/1.0" 200 1197
pc8.att.net - - [11/Apr/1998:00:13:21 -0700] "GET /tvpgis.gif
   HTTP/1.0" 200 7923
pc8.att.net - - [11/Apr/1998:00:13:22 -0700] "GET /tvpgis.gif
   HTTP/1.0" 304 -
```

Because the menu pages contain links to job-related Web sites and the log shows no more entries for this user, it is safe to assume that Joe followed one of the links and wandered off into cyberspace. Looking back, you can see that this user really put the Web site to the test. The log shows about 100 hits for this particular user. By figuring the time difference between the first hit at 00:01:18 and the last hit at 00:13:22, you can see that Joe spent more than 12 minutes browsing the Web site.

Although individual hits aren't good indicators of a site's popularity, groups of hits do provide insight into what is happening at your Web site. The first few times that you read the access log, you may want to take the time to really understand what you see. To do this, you can use the techniques I've used in this section. After you gain a clearer picture of what is happening at your Web site, you probably won't want to spend much time reviewing individual entries in the log, which is why later parts of this section focus less on individual entries and more on the bigger picture. You'll also be happy to know that software is available that tracks stats for you. I discuss these programs on Saturday afternoon in the section titled "Transforming the Numbers into Meaningful Data."

Assessing Page Views

Another statistic that Web publishers often track is the page view. A *page view* is an entry in the access log that belongs to a document file, such as a Web page. When you search the log for page views, you get a more accurate picture of the popularity of your Web site and the resources that people find interesting. You can use this information to help you determine how to market and promote your Web site. Tracking page views can also be an enlightening experience, especially when you discover that the most visited pages aren't the pages that you expected to be the most popular.

Obtaining Page Views

Most page views at a Web site pertain to requests for HTML documents. You can extract page views for Web pages from the access log using commands similar to these:

```
grep .htm access-log
```

or

```
find ".htm" access-log
```

Here, I searched for document files ending in the .htm extension. Because grep and find use pattern matching, these commands also return entries for file names that end in the .html extension.

Unfortunately, a search for document files ending in the .htm and .html extensions misses page accesses for default documents in directories. As you may remember, default documents are logged as / or `directory_name/`. Because / is used to designate directories within the file system, however, you need to find a way to search exclusively for default documents. To do this, you follow the / with a space, such as:

```
grep "/ " access.log
```

To put the search for HTML documents and default documents together, you need to use the egrep command in UNIX, such as:

```
egrep ".htm¦/ " access-log > save2.txt
```

NOTE The character following the .htm file extension is the pipe symbol (|), not an L. The space between the slash and the quotation mark is important. If you do not use the space, you will get matches every time an entry has a directory path.

In DOS, you can perform a similar search using a clever workaround. The first step is to perform the search for files ending in the .htm extension and then put the results in a file:

```
find ".htm" access-log > save2.txt
```

Then you search the access log for default documents and append the results to the end of the same file:

```
find "/ " access-log >> save2.txt
```

TIP The append command (>>) works in both DOS and UNIX.

If you perform the egrep or find search against the access-log.txt file, your results will be similar to those shown in Listing 2.5.

Listing 2.5   Page Views in the Access Log

```
pc8.att.net - - [11/Apr/1998:00:01:18 -0700] "GET / HTTP/1.0"
    200 8355
pc8.att.net - - [11/Apr/1998:00:03:28 -0700] "GET /vpjic.html
    HTTP/1.0" 200 7256
at1.vl.com - - [11/Apr/1998:00:04:57 -0700] "GET
    /idn/cissue/resmul.htm HTTP/1.0" 200 396
pc8.att.net - - [11/Apr/1998:00:05:04 -0700] "GET /vpepc.html
    HTTP/1.0" 200 2741
pc8.att.net - - [11/Apr/1998:00:05:10 -0700] "GET /epc.html
    HTTP/1.0" 200 501
pc8.att.net - - [11/Apr/1998:00:05:10 -0700] "GET
    /vpepc2.html HTTP/1.0" 200 544
pc8.att.net - - [11/Apr/1998:00:05:10 -0700] "GET
    /ziptour.html HTTP/1.0" 200 526
pc8.att.net - - [11/Apr/1998:00:05:29 -0700] "GET /zip2.html
    HTTP/1.0" 200 470
```

```
pc8.att.net - - [11/Apr/1998:00:05:34 -0700] "GET
   /vpepc3.html HTTP/1.0" 200 728

at1.vl.com - - [11/Apr/1998:00:05:34 -0700] "GET
   /idn/idnfp.htm HTTP/1.0" 200 7610

pc8.att.net - - [11/Apr/1998:00:05:43 -0700] "GET /rote.html
   HTTP/1.0" 200 333

pc8.att.net - - [11/Apr/1998:00:05:53 -0700] "GET /zip3.html
   HTTP/1.0" 200 281

pc8.att.net - - [11/Apr/1998:00:06:02 -0700] "GET
   /vpepc4.html HTTP/1.0" 200 679

pc8.att.net - - [11/Apr/1998:00:06:35 -0700] "GET
   /vpepc5.html HTTP/1.0" 200 582

pc8.att.net - - [11/Apr/1998:00:06:58 -0700] "GET
   /vpepc6.html HTTP/1.0" 200 668

pc8.att.net - - [11/Apr/1998:00:07:31 -0700] "GET /rote2.html
   HTTP/1.0" 200 331

pc8.att.net - - [11/Apr/1998:00:07:47 -0700] "GET
   /vpepc5.html HTTP/1.0" 304 -

pc8.att.net - - [11/Apr/1998:00:08:18 -0700] "GET
   /vpepc6.html HTTP/1.0" 304 -

198.23.25.3 - - [11/Apr/1998:00:09:14 -0700] "GET
   /idn/cissue/resmul.htm HTTP/1.0" 200 4516

pc8.att.net - - [11/Apr/1998:00:09:27 -0700] "GET /zip2.html
   HTTP/1.0" 304 -

pc8.att.net - - [11/Apr/1998:00:09:32 -0700] "GET
   /vpepc3.html HTTP/1.0" 304 -

pc8.att.net - - [11/Apr/1998:00:09:40 -0700] "GET /rote.html
   HTTP/1.0" 304 -

pc8.att.net - - [11/Apr/1998:00:10:13 -0700] "GET /rote2.html
   HTTP/1.0" 304 -

pc8.att.net - - [11/Apr/1998:00:10:32 -0700] "GET /jobopp-
   menu.html HTTP/1.0" 200 1297

pc8.att.net - - [11/Apr/1998:00:10:32 -0700] "GET /tvpbanner-
   top.html HTTP/1.0" 200 132

pc8.att.net - - [11/Apr/1998:00:10:32 -0700] "GET /tvpbanner-
   bot.html HTTP/1.0" 200 607

pc8.att.net - - [11/Apr/1998:00:10:27 -0700] "GET
   /joboppframes.html HTTP/1.0" 200 1592

at1.vl.com - - [11/Apr/1998:00:10:37 -0700] "GET
   /idn/bio/bioerev.html HTTP/1.0" 200 6027

pc8.att.net - - [11/Apr/1998:00:11:04 -0700] "GET
   /jscience.html HTTP/1.0" 200 2508

pc8.att.net - - [11/Apr/1998:00:11:22 -0700] "GET /jintl.html
   HTTP/1.0" 200 2122
```

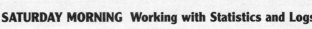

```
pc8.att.net - - [11/Apr/1998:00:12:53 -0700] "GET
  /jdisab.html HTTP/1.0" 200 1197
198.23.25.3 - - [11/Apr/1998:00:14:39 -0700] "GET
  /idn/idnfp.htm HTTP/1.0" 304 -
```

Understanding Page Views

Like the hit, the page view can be a misleading statistic, especially if you interpret page views literally. For example, if you access a frame-enhanced page with three frames, four page views are generated. These entries from the access log are an example of a single page request generating multiple page views:

```
pc8.att.net - - [11/Apr/1998:00:05:04 -0700] "GET /vpepc.html
  HTTP/1.0" 200 2741
pc8.att.net - - [11/Apr/1998:00:05:10 -0700] "GET /epc.html
  HTTP/1.0" 200 501
pc8.att.net - - [11/Apr/1998:00:05:10 -0700] "GET
  /vpepc2.html HTTP/1.0" 200 544
pc8.att.net - - [11/Apr/1998:00:05:10 -0700] "GET
  /ziptour.html HTTP/1.0" 200 526
```

Still, when you want to determine the popularity of a Web site, the page view is definitely a more accurate statistic than the hit. Tracking page views can help you learn which areas of your Web site are the most popular, and after you determine the most popular pages, you can direct your energies to those pages. Although this certainly doesn't mean that you should abandon areas of your site that don't generate steady traffic, you will want to rethink your Web publishing strategy.

If you think about it, focusing your time and resources on the most popular areas of your Web site makes sense. After all, there are only so many hours in a week. Determining the most popular pages at your Web site can also help you promote your Web site to the world (more on this on Saturday afternoon under "Transforming the Numbers into Meaningful Data").

Tracking page views requires time and patience, but the rewards are well worth the effort, especially when you discover whether people truly enjoy your Web site or are just racing through in their quest to find the best of the Web. Earlier in this section, I tracked Joe Web Surfer through the access log. Joe's visit lasted about 12 minutes and took him to many different pages at the Web site. In each of the areas Joe visited, he stayed a reasonable length of time, so you can assume that he not only browsed but read. Based on this assumption, it is fairly safe also to assume that Joe liked what he saw.

When you examine page views at your Web site, look for indicators that can tell you whether people liked what they saw. As you examine page views, some of the questions that you can ask yourself include:

- ✪ How long did the average visitor stay?
- ✪ How many pages did the visitor access at the site?
- ✪ Did the visitor stay long enough on a page to take in what he or she saw?

Tips for Tracking Page Views

Savvy Web advertisers will ask you how many page views your site gets rather than zeroing in on hits. Tracking page views for a Web site with a single focus is easy; all you need to do is perform daily, weekly, or monthly searches against the access log for page requests. Then, you total the requests to come up with the magic number that you can display at your Web site or give to a would-be advertiser.

One way to total page views is to send the output of `grep` or `egrep` to the word count program, `wc`. After running this command, the result that you see on your screen is the total number of page accesses for the period covered by the log:

```
egrep ".htm¦/ " access-log ¦ wc
```

NOTE   As stated previously, the result that you see will have three different numbers. Forget about the last two numbers and focus on the first number, which is the number of times that the file was accessed.

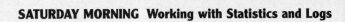

In DOS, you can perform a similar search using two different calls to the find command with the /C switch, and then adding the results:

```
find /C ".htm" access-log
find /C "/ " access-log
```

Although the previous examples total the page views for the entire Web site, you won't know the specific areas of the Web site that are generating the bulk of the traffic. One way to make tracking page views in different areas of a Web site easier is to create subdirectories in your Web site's structure for document files that belong to the various resources, such as /job/, for your site's job-related area, and /writing/, for your site's writing-related area. You should also place image files in a directory called images.

If you use subdirectories, you can count page views for each area at your Web site, using commands such as these:

```
grep /job/ access-log ¦ wc
```

or

```
find /C "/writing/" access-log
```

If you don't use subdirectories, you can use egrep or multiple finds to search for all the document files of a particular area. For a small Web site with a few pages, this type of search is not that difficult, but as your site grows, you will really wish that you had created subdirectories. An example of searching for multiple pages in the access log and then totaling the result follows:

```
egrep "job1.html¦jobintl.html¦jobres.html¦topjob.html"
  access-log ¦ wc
```

Here, I searched for four specific Web pages in the access log and then counted the results to determine the total number of page views. If you use stats tracking software, the program will do this for you. However, it is essential that you understand how the program comes up with the numbers it does. The better you understand how stats are obtained, the better your chances of understanding the Big Picture and the Big Picture is what you promote to people who want to advertise on your Web site.

Zeroing In on the Visit

The most meaningful Web site statistic is the visit. A *visit* is a collection of hits and page views that pertain to a specific person who requested files from your Web site. Thus, when you count visits, you are counting the number of people who stopped by your Web site.

Putting Visits Together

Although visits are the most important Web site statistic, tracking visits isn't easy without defining exactly what is and isn't a visit. One way to count visits is to tally every distinct domain name in the access log. Although the number that you came up with certainly would be a summary of all the domains in the log, it wouldn't necessarily be an accurate picture of all the visits to your Web site.

As I stated earlier, a domain name could pertain to a multiuser host with 25, 50, or even 100 users. Yet, even if you could eliminate the possibility of the multiuser host, is it fair to count all accesses by the same user as a single visit? What if the user accessed the Web site 50 different times over a period of 30 days? Are these considered 50 visits or just 1 visit?

Well, there's a big difference between someone shopping at your store 1 time and 50 times, so there is certainly a big difference between someone visiting a Web site 1 time and 50 times. In all fairness, you need to limit the scope of visits to a specific time period, such as all consecutive file requests that are separated by no more than 30 minutes. Following this, you would say that if a person browsed your site for 5 minutes one day and 15 minutes the next day, you have two different visits. On the other hand, if a person browsed your site for 10 minutes, went away, and then came back 15 minutes later, you have a single visit.

Tracking Visits

The best way to track visits in the access log is with tracking software. You'll learn all about tracking software this afternoon. Tracking software

also counts visits by limiting the scope of visits to specific time frames. For now, though, I show you how to put together visits on your own.

When I examined Joe's visit, I showed you that you can track individual visits in the log quite easily. As long as the domain pertains to a single-user host, all you need to do is find the domain name that you want to track, and then extract all the hits for that domain. When you track individual visits, you are mostly interested in the summary information, such as:

- How long did the person visit?
- What page did the person start on?
- What areas did the person visit?
- How long did the person stay in each area?
- What was the total number of hits for this visitor?
- What was the total number of page views for this visitor?

A summary of Joe's visit would look something like this:

Minimum length of visit:
12 minutes, 4 seconds

Start page:
/

Main pages visited and duration:
/—2 minutes 10 seconds
`vpjic.html`—1 minute, 36 seconds
`vpepc.html`—5 minutes, 28 seconds
`joboppframes.html`—2 minutes, 50 seconds

Total hits:
97

Total page views:
27

If you wanted to search for all the hits for `at1.v1.com`, you could use this command:

```
grep at1.v1.com access-log > save.txt
```

This command would create a file called save.txt containing all the hits for `at1.v1.com`. Using a text editor, you could open the file for viewing and examine the hits. Keep in mind that you would want to look at the hits only for the specific date that you are analyzing.

Using the techniques discussed previously in the section titled "Examining Log Entries," you could put together a picture of the visit for `at1.v1.com`. The summary for this visit looks something like this:

Minimum length of visit:
> 5 minutes, 40 seconds

Start page:
> /idn/cissue/resmul.htm

Main pages visited and duration:
> /idn/cissue/resmul.htm—37 seconds
> idnfp.htm—5 minutes 3 seconds
> /idn/bio/biorev.html—unknown

Total hits:
> 13

Total page views:
> 3

The last visit in the access log is for the host at IP address 198.23.25.3. The summary for this visit looks something like this:

Minimum length of visit:
> 5 minutes, 25 seconds

Start page:
> /idn/cissue/resmul.htm

Main pages visited and duration:
/idn/cissue/resmul.htm—5 minutes 25 seconds
idnfp.htm—unknown

Total hits:
5

Total page views:
2

Getting the Big Picture

Although the three sample visits in the access log may not seem like much, you can use the statistics gathered to gain a clearer understanding of the big picture for this Web site. The big picture takes into account all visits to the Web site during a specific period of time, such as the 15-minute time slice used in this section.

When you put together the big picture, you must ask yourself many important questions. The answers to these questions will help you understand who is visiting your Web site and why. The main questions that you will want to ask include:

- What was the total number of visitors for this time period?

- What was the length of the average visit?

- What was the average duration of a page view?

- What was the average number of page views per visitor?

- What was the average number of hits per visitor?

- What domain classes and geographic areas are represented (percentages)?

When you examine the logs over a periods of days or weeks, you will want to ask these additional questions:

- What are the busiest hours of the day?
- What are the busiest days of the week?
- What are the most requested pages?
- What are the most common last pages requested?

Right about now, you may be wondering why you would want some of these statistics. Before I answer that question, go back to the three visits in the access log and put together the big picture for these visits. When you answer the main questions, you come up with stats that look like this:

Visitor count:

3

Duration of analysis:

15 minutes

Length of the average visit:

7 minutes, 3 seconds

Average duration of page view:

2 minutes 54 seconds

Average number of page views per visitor:

10.67

Average number of hits per visitor:

38.3

Domain classes and geographic areas:

50% Net

50% Com

NOTE   Throwing out the IP address helps to make the domain class statistic more concrete and meaningful. Because correlating IP addresses to actual domains is difficult, most tracking software will do the same thing.

With these stats in hand, you can now answer the all-important questions concerning who is visiting and why. The list that follows provides descriptions that can help you make sense out of the stats you've gathered so far. Keep in mind that these are generalities meant to get you started thinking about how you can use these stats to promote your Web site and to make your Web site a better place to visit.

- **Visitor count:** Tells you how many people are visiting. You can use this to gauge the true popularity of your Web site. Whereas a new or low-traffic Web site may get 5 to 100 visitors a day, a popular Web site may get 5,000 to 10,000 visitors a day.

- **Length of the average visit:** This is an indicator of whether people are really reading pages at your Web site or just browsing. It can also be an indicator of whether people like what they see. The longer the average visit, the more information the visitor is finding and reading.

- **Average duration of page view:** This can be an indicator of whether people are reading or just browsing. When you examine this statistic, you also need to keep in mind the length and style of pages that you have at your Web site. Are they highly textual, highly graphical, or both?

- **Average number of page views per visitor:** Generally, the more pages people view, the happier they are, and if people are viewing many pages at your Web site, they are finding information that interests them. When you count page views, you need to keep in mind the setup of your pages. Do you use frame sets that result in multiple page views? Do you use client pull to create slide shows?

- **Average number of hits per visitor:** Over time, you can use this information to estimate the number of visitors without having to wander through the logs.

- **Domain classes and geographic areas:** This can tell you where people visiting your Web site live and work, which is great information to have if you want to attract advertisers.

✪ **Busiest hours of the day:** Tells you the time of day when most people visit your Web site. This statistic can help you plan daily updates, promotion campaigns, and advertising.

✪ **Busiest days of the week:** Tells you the day of the week when most people visit your Web site. This statistic can also help you plan weekly updates, promotion campaigns, and advertising.

✪ **Most requested pages:** Tells you the pages that visitors find the most interesting and/or useful. Can be used to tailor your Web site to visitors' needs and to help you determine which pages should receive most of your attention.

✪ **Most commonly requested last pages:** Can help you spot trends and bad pages. If the last page requested has lots of links to external Web sites, this statistic tells you that this is the point from which most visitors are leaving. If the last page requested doesn't have links to external Web sites, you may want to examine the page in question.

Hits, page views, and visits are the statistics that you will use to promote your Web site to the world and to make your Web site more effective. Hits are generated whenever files are requested, meaning that a single page request can generate many hits in the access log. Because hits can be a misleading statistic, you can look to page views to give you a more accurate picture of the areas of your Web site that are attracting an audience. When you want to determine how many people are stopping by your Web site, the visit is the statistic that you will use. Finally, hits, page views, and visits come together to help you create the big picture for your Web site.

Take a Break

After pouring your time and resources into a Web site, do you really want to risk losing people who visit your Web site but don't get to where they expected? Not really, especially when every visitor is someone who could help spread the news about your terrific Web site. The next part of this section covers how to gain readers who otherwise would have been lost because of bad links at your site or bad references from other sites.

But before you dive in, take a break! You deserve it. Grab yourself a cup of coffee or tea. Afterward, fire up your browser and surf over to one of my favorite places on the Web, the Web Learning Center (**http://www.weblearningcenter.com/**). While you are there, drop into a forum and post a question, or better yet, give a fellow cybernaut a hand by answering a question.

Gaining Lost Readers from the Error Logs

Don't lose visitors once they've found a doorway into your slice of cyberspace. Nothing stops would-be visitors dead in their tracks like an error. They see errors as brick walls and often race off as quickly as they can click the mouse. How many times have you seen the dreaded `404 - File Not Found`? Did you hang around the Web site that you tried to access, or did you just click your browser's Back button and head off in some other direction?

Errors are often the result of bad links in your Web pages or bad references to your pages from other Web sites. When it comes to finding and fixing bad links in your pages, you have total control and can easily track down the problems—if you know how. When it comes to bad references to your pages at your Web site, you may think that finding and fixing these problems is beyond your control. Nothing could be further from the truth, however. You can fix errors regardless of their source, and you're about to find out how.

Errors: We All Hate Them

We all hate errors, yet we've grown so accustomed to them that they seem like an everyday part of the quest to browse the Web. Stop and think for a moment about your reaction when you encounter an error like the one shown in Figure 2.5. Your reaction, be it restrained contempt or outright indignation, is mirrored thousands of times around the world every day.

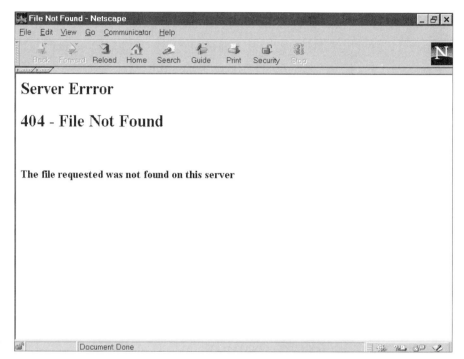

Figure 2.5

The dreaded 404 -
File Not Found error

After the initial outrage at hitting a dead end in cyberspace passes, what is your next reaction? Most of the time, you probably click on your browser's Back button to return to the site that sent you to the wrong address. Or perhaps you enter a new URL into the browser and head off into another direction. The person who is persistent enough to puzzle through the error, trying to figure out another way to get at the information using the bad URL, is rare. As a result, just about every time that your server displays an error, you lose a visitor—maybe forever.

When you are trying to increase traffic at your Web site, the last thing you want to do is lose visitors. Thus, one of the keys to increasing and maintaining traffic to your Web site is to reduce errors and help readers find their way, which is exactly what you're about to learn.

Understanding Web Server Errors

Web servers record errors in two different log files. File requests that result in errors are recorded in the access log. A more detailed description of the error is also recorded in the error log.

Access Log Errors

Any time that an error is related to an entry in the access log, you will find a status code that describes the error. As you learned earlier in this session under "Using Web Stats to Understand Your Site's Visitors," status codes indicate the general type of error and fall into one of these categories: success, redirection, client error, and server error.

In error tracking for your Web site, the client error status codes are the most helpful. A typical error recorded in the access log looks like this:

```
pc8.att.net - - [11/Apr/1998:00:01:00 -0700] "GET
   /home.htm HTTP/1.0" 404 -
```

Here, the status code 404 indicates that the file was not found. Other status codes for client errors are shown in Table 2.11. Note that the status codes 405–415 are defined in the HTTP 1.1 specification and are not part of the older HTTP specifications.

The Error Log

The error log provides a running record of just about everything that happens on the server. Entries in the error log are placed on a single line with a time stamp and a short descriptive statement that explains what actually occurred. Unfortunately, the common log format for time stamps does not apply to the error log, which means that some servers may use a different format for the time stamp in the error log.

The File Not Found error is the most common error that you will find in the error log. Other types of errors recorded in the error log include lost connections and time-outs.

TABLE 2.11 STATUS CODES FOR CLIENT ERROR	
Code	Description
400	Invalid request
401	Not Authorized
402	Payment required
403	Forbidden
404	File not found
405	Method not allowed
406	Not acceptable
407	Proxy authentication required
408	Request time-out
409	Conflict
410	Unsupported media type

Error: File Not Found

The File Not Found error is a very common occurrence in the error log. A typical error log entry for this error looks like this:

```
[11/Apr/1998:00:01:02 -0700] access to
  /usr/www/docs/tvpress/home.htm failed

for pc8.att.net, reason: File does not exist
```

Here, the server records that the host `pc8.att.net` requested the file home.htm but the file was not found. The server maps the requested URL, **http://www.tvpress.com/home.htm**, to the actual directory on the server containing the file, which in this case is /usr/www/docs/tvpress/. Note also that the entry was placed on two lines so that it would fit on the page.

NOTE The best way to see the format of time stamps for your error log is to examine some of the entries. Keep in mind that the error log is an optional log, which means that your server may or may not be configured to use one.

Error: Lost Connection

Whenever the connection from the server to the client is broken, the server records a Lost Connection message in the error log. Although a lost connection may sound like a bad thing, more often than not the user is to blame for this type of error. Any time that you click on the Stop button in the middle of a transfer, you cause the server to lose the connection and, in turn, the server records the lost connection in the error log. Similarly, if you click on the Back button or exit your browser during the loading of a page, the server loses the connection to your browser and records the lost connection in the error log.

A server loses connection at one of two key times, as follows:

✪ Just after the request has come in and before the server has processed the request

✪ After the request has been processed and during the file transfer

When the server loses the connection just after the request comes in, the server records a Request Connection Lost message. When the server loses the connection during the file transfer, the server records a Send Connection Lost message. A Lost Connection error looks like this:

```
[11/Apr/1998:05:05:05 -0700] request lost connection to
  client pc8.att.net
```

Error: Time-Out

A less-common error for the server to record is a time-out. If the server has to wait too long for a client to respond, the server will break the open connection and log a time-out. The length of time that the server waits before timing out is the time-out rate. Typically, this rate is set high so that the server doesn't issue a time-out inadvertently. A time-out error looks like this:

```
[11/Apr/1998:05:05:35 -0700] time out to client
  pc8.att.net
```

Here, the connection time-out rate has elapsed. The server breaks the open connection to the client and logs the time-out in the error log.

Administrative Messages

Servers use the error log to record much more than errors. In the error log, you will also find administrative messages. These messages record server startup, server shutdown, and other server status changes. Here's an example of an administrative message:

```
[11/Apr/1998:00:01:02 -0700] HTTPd: starting as httpd -
  d /usr/www/
```

In this example, the administrative message records the start of the main Web server process, HTTPd—the process that handles Web server transactions.

Finding Trouble Spots in the Logs

Errors are frustrating for everyone. Wouldn't it be great to have a way to fix errors? Well, there are ways to fix errors, and you start with the logs to find trouble spots. These are three major trouble spots that can cause you to lose potential visitors forever:

- Missing files
- Lost connections
- Server time-outs

Because the server records a time stamp and the domain information for client-related requests and errors, tracking trouble spots in the logs is fairly straightforward. You can use grep or find to extract errors from the access log based on the status code that you are looking for, such as 404. Then, if you want to get a better description of the error, look for the matching entry in the error log.

NOTE Keep in mind that the server doesn't necessarily record access log and error log entries simultaneously. For this reason, there may be a few seconds' difference between the access log time stamp and the error log time stamp.

Missing Files

The most common errors are those that relate to files that the server can't find. Contrary to what you might think, the Web publisher is to blame for this error more often than the user is, and I'll readily admit that I am guilty of causing the dreaded 404 - File Not Found error.

What Causes the File Not Found Error?

Bad links are a key reason for the File Not Found error. When you create a Web page, you add hypertext links that relate to pages at your Web site as well as other Web sites. Although all your links may work perfectly when you first create your Web site, things change over time. You update pages. You move pages to different locations. You combine some pages. You delete other pages.

Unfortunately, every time that you move or delete Web pages, you may unwittingly start an avalanche of errors. Joe, who bookmarked one of the pages that you moved or deleted, can't get to the page anymore. Mary, who created a page showing links to her favorite Web sites, now has several invalid links that point to your Web site. Worse, the search engines with which you registered indexed your Web site; and now, hundreds of people who look for resources like yours can't find your pages anymore.

How Are Missing Files Logged?

In the access log, files that the server can't find are recorded with entries that look like this:

```
at1.vl.com - - [11/Apr/1998:23:59:00 -0800] "GET
  /samp.htm HTTP/1.1" 404 -
```

The corresponding entry in the error log looks something like this:

```
[11/Apr/1998:23:59:00 -0800] access to
  /usr/www/docs/tvpress/samp.htm failed
```

```
for at1.vl.com, reason: File does not exist
```

In this example, the server could not find the file called samp.htm. The server recorded the failed request in the access log and then recorded a description of the error in the error log.

How Can You Find File Problems?

You can search for the File Not Found error in the access log using grep or find. Because the status code may not be a unique element in the access log, you may want to surround the search string in quotation marks and include spacing, as in these examples:

```
grep " 404 " access-log > save.txt
```

or

```
find " 404 " access-log > save.txt
```

NOTE As discussed earlier, grep is a UNIX command and find is a DOS command. Mac users may be able to search using the egrep command, which must be installed on your system.

I recommend searching for problem files in the logs weekly for large sites or sites that change frequently, and at least monthly for other sites. If you've never checked for problem files, now is a good time.

How Can You Fix File Problems?

After you have compiled a list of files that the server couldn't find, use the list to help you find trouble spots at your Web site. Start by printing the list. Next, compare the file names on the list to the actual files on your server. If you find a file that is on the list and available on your server, use your browser to try to retrieve the file from the server. Be sure to use the same URL that the user entered. If the file loads without problems, cross the file off the list and move on to the next file on the list. Here, there was probably an intermittent problem with the user's Internet connection, which doesn't necessarily mean that anything is wrong on your server.

If the file doesn't load in your browser, check the file name. Does the file name on the server exactly match the URL that you entered? Most servers are case sensitive, meaning that the mixture of uppercase and lowercase letters must match exactly. When you find a naming problem, you have a bad reference in one of your Web pages that you need to fix. The easiest way to find the problem page—and possibly other pages that contain the bad reference—is to search your Web directories using the `grep` or `egrep` command for the bad reference.

A bad reference to a Web page called `welcome.htm` that should have been referenced as `welcome.html` could be fixed as follows:

- Change to the directory containing your Web pages. If you have multiple document directories, examine each in turn.

- Use `grep` or `egrep` to search for references to the file name `welcome.htm`, such as `grep welcome.htm *`

- Record the list of file names containing the bad reference.

- Edit the files and correct the bad references.

NOTE Some Web page editors allow you to find and replace links in multiple pages using a single command. For example, with HomeSite by Allaire, you can tell the editor the name of the link you want to replace and which pages you want to replace the link in.

Additionally, you can find the specific file that contains the bad reference by looking for the previous Web page accessed by the user. To do this, find the error in the access log and then move back through earlier entries in the log. Usually, the first page access that you find prior to the error is the page containing the error. I say *usually*, because with framed documents, a group of Web pages may have been loaded simultaneously. In such a case, you would need to examine each of the documents that is a part of the frame-enhanced page.

If you don't have a naming problem, you may have a permission problem. On UNIX Web servers, the directory and the file must have specific permissions before readers can access your files. Generally, the directory needs to be executable and the file needs to have read access. If you don't know how to check or set file permissions, ask your Internet service provider.

Next, highlight all the files that don't relate to Web pages or other document files, such as references to image files. Most likely, the highlighted list of files points to broken references in your Web pages. Fix these references either by updating the related page or by moving the file to where it is supposed to be.

Now that you've narrowed the list a bit, look for URLs that belong to files that you've moved or deleted. When you find a reference to a file that you moved, jot down the new name of the file. When you find a reference to a file that you deleted, make a note to yourself that the file was deleted.

Because users are looking for these files and you want to build rather than lose readership, you will want to redirect these lost visitors to the new location of the resource. Alternatively, you can create a placeholder document with the old URL, telling visitors that the resource is no longer available and then redirecting them to another area of your Web site. For details on how to redirect users to new locations, see the upcoming section titled "Redirecting Lost Readers."

Although the remaining files on your list should pertain to true errors on the part of the user or someone else, you don't want to discard the list just yet. Take a look at the list one more time and ask yourself whether any patterns exist. For example, one of my resource pages is located at `http://www.tvpress.com/idn/`. I found that some users were requesting the page `http://www.tvpress.com/idn.htm`. I don't know why they were looking for this page, but they did it often enough that it seemed worthwhile to create a placeholder page. The job of the placeholder page was to direct lost visitors to the resource for which they were looking.

Lost Connections

Lost connections are often the result of impatient users not wanting to wait for your page, its graphics, and other multimedia files to finish loading. Consequently, if you find a page that has lots of lost connections related to it, you may want to examine the page and change it so that it either loads quicker or follows sound design techniques that allow the visitor to use or peruse the page before it finishes loading.

Interestingly enough, lost connections are recorded in the access log with a status code of 200. As you may recall, this status code means that the document was successfully retrieved. Well, here's what happens and why lost connections are recorded with a success code: The server finds the referenced file and correlates the success with the status code of 200. When the connection is lost, the server completes the entry in the access log and then records the lost connection in the error log.

If you have pages with lots of text, graphics, or multimedia, you may want to periodically check for lost connections. To do this, search the error log for entries containing the keywords "`lost connection`." When you find entries for lost connections, try to match those entries to specific entries in the access log.

Use the time stamp to help you find candidate entries—those with matching or similar time stamps. Next, examine the actual bytes transferred for those entries. If the number of bytes transferred for an entry is less than the byte size of the file, you can be sure that you've found the corresponding entry in the access log. For example, although the byte size of the file home.htm is 9672 bytes, the server recorded that 956 bytes were transferred in this entry:

```
pc8.att.net - - [11/Apr/1998:00:01:00 -0700] "GET
  /home.htm HTTP/1.0" 200 956
```

The corresponding entry in the error log is as follows:

```
[11/Apr/1998:00:01:00 -0700] send lost connection to
  client pc8.att.net
```

TIP If you don't have access to the error log, you can still look for lost connections. To do this, look for file accesses logged with the incorrect file size, as outlined previously.

Unfortunately, sometimes the connection is lost after the server completely transfers the file but before the client completely processes the data. When the server loses the connection after completing the transfer, the bytes transferred will match the byte size of the file. In this case, you may not be able to determine the cause of the error and should just move on to the next item on the list.

Time-Outs

Although time-outs are rather rare on Web servers, this coverage would be incomplete without at least mentioning how to spot them. A time-out is sort of like the server getting impatient with the client and wanting to move on. You probably won't see time-outs unless you have large multimedia or compressed files that are retrieved using the standard Web file transfer protocol, HTTP.

Unfortunately, if your server uses an older version of the transfer protocol, you can find time-outs only if you have access to the error log. Further, matching access and error log entries for time-outs is not practical if the access log has no corresponding entry. For this reason, you won't be able to determine the specific files that are causing the time-out.

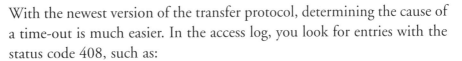

With the newest version of the transfer protocol, determining the cause of a time-out is much easier. In the access log, you look for entries with the status code 408, such as:

```
at1.vl.com - - [11/Apr/1998:23:59:00 -0800] "GET
  /samp.mpeg HTTP/1.1" 408 -
```

If you see time-outs frequently for the same file, you may want to tell your Internet service provider about the problem. Although the service provider should be able to set the time-out ratio higher, the service provider may also tell you that the byte size for the offending file is unreasonably large. In the latter case, you may want to break the large file into several parts.

Redirecting Lost Readers

As you learned earlier in this section, every time that you move or delete a Web page, you can start an avalanche of errors. Anyone who has bookmarked the page that you changed will get an error. Anyone who has created a link to the page from his or her own Web site will be unwittingly directing people to a dead end. Anyone who uses a search engine to find resources may also get a retrieval containing references to the pages that you've changed.

The result is that lots of people who otherwise would have visited your wonderful niche of cyberspace get lost. They hit the proverbial brick wall and run off in some other direction. And they may never return. When a user gets all the way to your Web site through the maze of cyberspace, do you really want to risk losing that user because of something that you can fix?

To remedy this situation, you should create a placeholder document. The key to the placeholder document is that it takes the place of a Web page or other document file that you moved or deleted, and then redirects the user to a different location at your Web site. If you have a list of documents that you've moved or deleted, why not create a few placeholder documents right now? Every visitor counts.

TIP

The way to avoid brick walls and placeholder documents altogether is to plan out your Web site before you build it. The simplest planning rule is to give each area of your Web site its own directory to start with, and to make the default document for this directory the home page for the area. Unfortunately, in the real world, most Web publishers (myself included) don't like to plan things out before they dive in, which means that they should use placeholder documents to help direct traffic whenever necessary.

Redirection Basics

The technique that you use to redirect visitors can be as simple as the one shown in Figure 2.6. Here, you tell visitors that the resource has been moved or deleted. Next, you provide them with the URL of the new resource or an escape route to another location at your Web site.

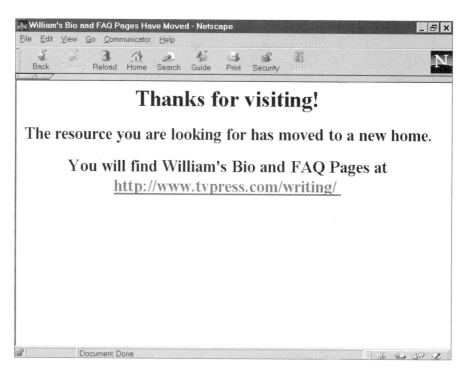

Figure 2.6

Helping lost readers find their way makes sense.

The source for the redirection page is shown as Listing 2.6. In the examples area of the book's Web site (**www.tvpress.com/promote/examples/**), you will find the source code in the file stanek.htm.

Listing 2.6   Redirecting the User

```
<HTML>
<HEAD>
<TITLE>William's Bio and FAQ Pages Have Moved</TITLE>
</HEAD>
<BODY BGCOLOR="#ffffff">
<DIV ALIGN=CENTER>
<H1>Thanks for visiting!</H1>
<H2>The resource you are looking for has moved to a new
    home.</H2>
<H2>You will find William's Bio and FAQ Pages at
<A HREF="http://www.tvpress.com/writing/">
http://www.tvpress.com/writing/
</A>
</H2>
</DIV>
</BODY>
</HTML>
```

More Redirection Techniques

Another technique for redirecting visitors is to automate the redirection with client pull technology. With client pull, you insert an instruction in the Web page that tells the visitor's browser to retrieve a new document after a specified amount of time has elapsed. Thus, the visitor can get to the new location of a resource or be redirected to any location on your Web site without having to do anything. Most browsers are capable of using client pull.

The HTML tag that you will use to redirect the visitor's browser is the <META> tag, which can be used only in the HEAD element of your Web page. You will use the HTTP-EQUIV attribute of the <META> tag to tell the browser that you want to refresh the browser window. You will use the

CONTENT attribute of the <META> tag to tell the browser two things: how long to wait and what document to load.

An example of the <META> tag is:

```
<META HTTP-EQUIV="Refresh" CONTENT="5;
    URL=http://www.tvpress.com/">
```

Here, the HTTP-EQUIV attribute is assigned the keyword Refresh, which tells the browser that you want to prepare to refresh the current window. The CONTENT attribute has two parts separated by a semicolon and a space. The 5 tells the browser to wait five seconds before refreshing the browser window. The next part of the CONTENT attribute tells the browser the URL of the page that you want to load into the refreshed window. The URL must have the full path specified, including the http://.

Figure 2.7 shows an example page that redirects the visitor to a new location at a Web site. As you see, the page still has an informative and helpful

Figure 2.7

Why not use client pull to redirect the user?

explanation of what happened. Just in case the user's browser doesn't support the technology, the appropriate links are placed on the page as well.

The markup for the sample page is shown as Listing 2.7. Online, you will find the source code in the file idn.htm.

Listing 2.7 Automating the Redirection

```
<HTML>
<HEAD>
<TITLE>Internet Daily News Has Moved</TITLE>
<META HTTP-EQUIV="Refresh" CONTENT="2; URL=http://www.net-
  daily.com/">
</HEAD>
<BODY BGCOLOR="#0000ff" text="#ffff00" link="#fffbf0"
vlink="#808000" alink="#ff0000">
<DIV ALIGN=CENTER>
<P>
   <A HREF="http://www.netdaily.com/">
   <IMG SRC="idnttl3.gif" ALT="Internet Daily News Logo">
   </A>
</P>
<H1>
   <A HREF="www.netdaily.com">A free newspaper serving over
   25,000 daily!</A>
</H1>
<H2>Our front page has moved. Please update your links to
<A HREF="http://www.netdaily.com">http://www.netdaily.com</A>
</H2>
</DIV>
</BODY>
</HTML>
```

Redirection Using Your Web Server

Although the basic redirection techniques work well, more and more Web servers are starting to support automatic redirection. With automatic redirection, the server takes over and maps the old URL to the new one, which makes the redirection fairly transparent to the user. For example, you could tell the server to map all requests to www.tvpress.com/fun/ to www.tvpress.com/summer/ or even www.fun.com.

Most commercial Web servers support URL redirection. You'll find that Microsoft IIS and Netscape Enterprise make this task fairly easy to accomplish. However, you'll need access to the Web server's administration tools, which you may not have if you use a service provider.

No More 404 — File Not Found

The typical errors servers report are meaningless to most people, and even the people who know what the status codes mean probably would much rather have a helpful pointer than an error that says 404 - File Not Found. Fortunately, ways to fix it are available so that the nondescriptive and meaningless errors reported by servers go the way of the dinosaur. This section shows you how to eliminate this error message for good.

Earlier, you learned that status codes are recorded with entries in the access log. Status codes are also used by the server to determine which error documents to display.

When the Web server software was installed, the technician who set up the server defined specific parameters that told the server how to report errors and which error documents to display. Because the default error documents are rarely replaced, chances are good that visitors to your Web site see errors like the one shown previously in Figure 2.5. You can confirm this by entering an invalid URL that refers to your Web site, such as:

```
http://www.your_server.com/nothingatall.html
```

If your server reports a vague error message, don't worry; this can be changed by defining new error documents. On most servers, regardless of operating system, you can define the documents to retrieve when an error occurs. For example, with Microsoft IIS, you can tell the server the name and location of the page you want to load when a certain error occurs.

With the thought of eliminating the dreaded 404 - File Not Found error forever, take a chance and talk to the head technician or Web master who

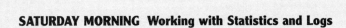

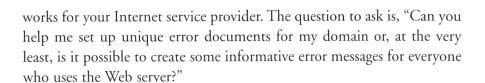

works for your Internet service provider. The question to ask is, "Can you help me set up unique error documents for my domain or, at the very least, is it possible to create some informative error messages for everyone who uses the Web server?"

A Few Last Words on Errors

Errors are show stoppers. Don't let people who want to visit your site think that what they are looking for is gone. Every visitor counts, especially when you are trying to increase traffic to your Web site. But the reason for fixing trouble spots goes well beyond preventing the loss of someone trying to find your Web site. You need to do everything within your power to build a steady readership. To attract and maintain an audience over the long haul, you need to maintain your site and provide readers with lifelines when you move or delete files.

Although all this talk about the access log and the error log is certainly useful, you may sometimes want to gather stats without having to dig through the server log files. Also, sometimes server logs simply aren't available. For this reason, the next part of this session looks at ways for you to obtain stats without using server logs.

Simple Ways to Obtain Stats without Server Logs

The whole idea behind gathering stats is to put together the big picture for your Web site. When you want to get a clear idea of exactly who is visiting and why, nothing beats the detailed records that you can gather from the access log. But log files aren't the only way to gather stats for your Web site. In this session, I examine ways to gather stats that don't require server logs.

Tracking Stats without Logs

Server logs files are invaluable when it comes to tracking stats and understanding the traffic to your Web site. Anytime you track stats without the server log files, you risk missing the big picture completely. For this reason, the techniques that I discuss in this morning's session may be best used to supplement the stats you are tracking in the log file rather than completely replace gathering stats from the logs. Supplementing the stats that you track using server log files with the techniques discussed in this session gives you additional avenues for obtaining stats and getting feedback from visitors. If you have access to server log files, however, I recommend skipping this section altogether.

Still, sometimes you may prefer to forget about the logs and look at alternative ways to track stats. Although alternatives are your only option to gather stats if you are truly locked out of the log files, you may also want to consider using alternatives to log files when you have a very small Web site or a limited collection of home pages. Specifically, if you publish fewer than five Web pages, such as a home page with links to three other related pages, you should strongly consider tracking stats without server logs.

Although many techniques to track stats without server logs are available, this session focuses on the ones that you can implement right now, such as:

✪ Counters to track hits or page views

✪ Guest books to learn more about visitors and to get feedback from visitors

When you deal with counters and guest books, you usually have to work with CGI scripts. A script is a program that runs on the server and processes information submitted by users. The *Common Gateway Interface* (CGI) is a standard that allows scripts to act as gateways—that is, interfaces—between a browser and the server.

Scripts are executed in one of two ways: automatically, when a page containing a reference to the script is loaded; or only at a specific time, such as when a user submits a form containing a reference to the script. On most Web servers, CGI scripts can be executed only if they are in a specific directory. Usually, this directory is called cgi-bin.

If you do not have your own domain, the cgi-bin directory that you will use is often located at /usr/cgi-bin. If you have your own domain, the cgi-bin directory that you will use is usually located within your public directory for Web documents, such as:

```
your_home_dir/public_html/cgi-bin
```

or

```
your_home_dir/www/cgi-bin
```

 NOTE To confirm the directory that you need to use for CGI scripts, ask your Internet service provider or read the FAQ pages at the service provider's Web site. You'll also need to know the directory path to the Perl scripting language, such as:

```
/usr/local/bin/perl
```

Introducing Counters

A *counter* is a script that you place in a Web page to tell you and other visitors how many times the page or files related to a page have been accessed. Counters can be configured to track hits, page views, and other statistics. The exact behavior of a counter depends on the programming in the script. Some counters are fairly advanced and tell you many different things about the hits and page views. Other counters are very basic and simply tally the number of hits or page views.

Although having a fancy counter that gives you lots of stats may seem great, a basic counter that will tally page views is usually just what the doctor ordered. Whether the counter displays text values or a graphical representation of the value is a matter of personal preference. Keep in mind that the primary reason you use the counter is so that you can gather stats for your Web site.

All over the Web, you will find counter scripts that people have written and made available for others to use for free. With so many great choices, selecting a counter script for your Web site can be difficult. To narrow the field to a manageable number that you can implement right now, I chose a counter to use as an example.

Installing a Counter, Step-by-Step

The script that I chose for this section is called TextCounter. TextCounter is a CGI script written in Perl. Before you can use this script, you need to know:

⚙ Whether the server allows Perl scripts to run

⚙ Whether the server is configured to use server-side includes

TIP Perl (Practical Extraction and Reporting Language) is a programming language used to create scripts that run on servers. Perl is a terrific language for working with text. When you execute a Perl script or include the contents of a page directly in another page, you use a technology called server-side includes. Most servers support server-side includes (SSI).

Provided that the answer to both of these variables is yes, you will be able to install and use the script. The other information that you need to know before you get started is as follows:

⚙ The file path to the directory that you can use for scripts, such as `C:\wwwroot\cgi-bin`.

⚙ The URL path to the directory for scripts, such as `..\cgi-bin`.

Downloading and Unarchiving the Script

After you have all the information you need to get started, you are ready to download the script. You will find the source for the script at:

`http://worldwidemart.com/scripts/textcounter.shtml`

Fire up your browser and jaunt over to Matt Wright's Script Archive using the URL provided. This page has links to several different compressed versions of the TextCounter script. Select the script archive labeled:

`textcounter.zip`

This will take you to the download page. The script name and compression type should be set for you already. If so, all you need to do is click on the form button labeled "Download Selected File" to start the file transfer to your PC. On your PC, use an unzip utility such as PKUNZIP to extract the archive. If you don't have an unzip utility, visit the utilities area of the Web site for this book so that you can find a site to download an unzip utility. You will find the utilities area at **http://www.tvpress.com /promote/utilities/**.

NOTE If you use a DOS unzip utility, the 8 + 3 naming convention for file names will apply, meaning that the file name will look something like textco~1.zip. On my PC, PKUNZIP complained that it couldn't extract the archive, yet the files came out just fine. I also noted that the file name had changed to Counter.pl, so I moved the file to counter.pl (all lowercase).

After you unzip the archive, you will find a directory called textcounter and a directory called data. The textcounter directory will contain the following files:

- ❖ README: A file containing the installation instructions

- ❖ counter.pl: The Perl script for the counter

- ❖ convert.pl: A script for converting file names from version 1.2 to version 1.2.1 of the counter

NOTE In the examples, I assume that you don't have a previous version of the counter script. Thus, I do not discuss how to use the convert.pl script.

Editing the Script

Now you need to edit the script in your text editor or word processor. Start by changing the directory path information if necessary. If your server's Perl directory is not at /usr/local/bin/perl, you need to change the directory path referenced in the first line of the program. For example, if Perl is located at /usr/bin/perl, you would change the first line of the program to #!/usr/bin/perl.

Each Web page that uses the counter will use a separate data file to store and retrieve the current tally of page views. The following variable in the script tells the server where to look for these data files:

$data_dir

You'll find the $data_dir variable in the Variables section. You make the variable assignment at the very top of the script. Set the value of the $data_dir variable to a valid directory on your server. My Web directory path is /home/william/www, so I set the $data_dir variable to this value:

$data_dir = "/home/william/www/data/";

Save the file. You're done with the modification. Although you can configure lots of optional variables, the default settings work just fine.

Installing the Script on the Server

You are now ready to transfer the file to the server. Use whatever tool you normally use for file transfers, such as FTP. Be sure to move the script to the directory designated for CGI scripts, which is typically /usr/cgi-bin. Afterward, make sure the directory and the script can be executed. Typically, you do this by setting properties for the directory and the script.

Now that you've installed the script, you can create the data directory. Be sure that the directory is accessible and that files placed in the directory can be executed. If you are unsure how to do this, ask your service provider or check its list of Frequently Asked Questions (FAQ).

Testing and Using the Script

The final step is to update one of your Web pages to call the script and display the page view count. Although updating all of your pages to use

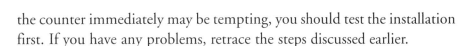

the counter immediately may be tempting, you should test the installation first. If you have any problems, retrace the steps discussed earlier.

Keep in mind that most counters are displayed as one of the last elements on a Web page. Thus you probably want to add the counter to the latter portion of your Web page. The line to call the script looks like this:

```
<!--#exec cgi="/URL/path/to/scripts/counter.pl"-->
```

Be sure to substitute the relative URL path to CGI scripts on your server, such as:

```
<!--#exec cgi="/cgi-bin/counter.pl"-->
```

or

```
<!--#exec cgi="../cgi-bin/counter.pl"-->
```

If the script is installed correctly, the counter displays a message similar to this one in your Web page:

```
00001 hits since July 4, 1997
```

If you have problems, the primary culprits are these: the location of the data directory and the permissions on the data directory. Ensure that the data directory is located within your Web directory. Furthermore, you should ensure that the permissions on the data directory are set properly.

Figure 2.8 shows an example of a Web page that uses the TextCounter script. The source for this Web page is available as Listing 2.8. Online, you will find this file saved as count_samp.htm. Look for this file at **www.tvpress.com/promote/examples/**. Click on the option for Chapters 6-10.

Introducing Guest Books

Guest books give publishers a way to obtain information about visitors as well as vital feedback about the site. You can think of guest books as cyberspace versions of the traditional guest books that were popular in the quaint inns of yesteryear. Guest books used by inns were popular because anyone visiting the inn could see who had visited previously. Guest books used on the Web are popular for much the same reason.

Most guest books ask visitors for personal information, such as full name, e-mail address, and country or state of residence. Guest books also invite visitor comments, and it is this vital feedback that gives publishers insight into exactly what people think about the Web site.

An example guest book is shown in Figure 2.9. This guest book from the Internet Daily News Web site allows visitors to create an entry in the guest book and also allows them to join a mailing list for readers of the newspaper.

Like counters, guest books are quite popular, so many guest book scripts are available. In the next section, you will find step-by-step instructions for installing a guest book script written in Perl.

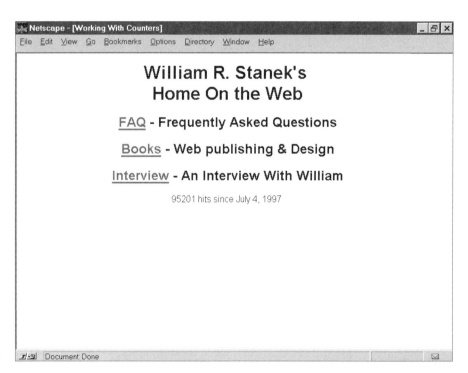

Figure 2.8

Using the
TextCounter script

Listing 2.8   A Sample Page with a Counter

```html
<HTML>
<HEAD>
<TITLE>Working With Counters</TITLE>
</HEAD>
<BODY BGCOLOR="#FFFFFF">
<DIV ALIGN=CENTER>
<H1>William R. Stanek's <BR>Home On the Web</H1>
<H2><A
  HREF="http://www.tvpress.com/writing/writing.htm">FAQ</A>
- Frequently Asked Questions</H2>
<H2><A
  HREF="http://www.tvpress.com/writing/writing2.htm">Books</A>
- Web publishing & Design</H2>
<H2><A
  HREF="http://www.tvpress.com/writing/writing3.htm">Inter-
  view</A>
- An Interview With William</H2>
<!--#exec cgi="/cgi-tvpress/counter.pl"-->
</DIV>
</BODY>
</HTML>
```

Installing a Guest Book, Step-by-Step

The script that I have chosen for this section is called Guestbook. The
author of this script is Matt Wright. Before you can use this script, you
need to know these facts:

- ✿ Whether the server allows Perl scripts

- ✿ Whether the server is configured to use server-side includes

 NOTE As stated previously, don't worry about the terminology. Simply ask your Internet service
provider whether the server is configured to use CGI and server-side includes.

Provided that the answer to both of these variables is yes, you will be able
to install and use the script. The other information that you need before
you get started is as follows:

⚙ The directory that you can use for scripts

⚙ The URL path to the directory for scripts

Downloading and Unarchiving the Script

After you have all the information that you need to get started, you are ready to download the script. You will find the source for the script at:

`http://www.worldwidemart.com/scripts/guestbook.shtml`

This page contains links to several different versions of the Guestbook script. Select the script archive labeled:

`guestbook.zip`

This will take you to the download page. The script name and compression type should be set for you already. If so, all you need to do is click on the form button labeled Download Selected File to start the file transfer

Figure 2.9

A guest book at
Internet Daily News

to your PC. On your PC, use an unzip utility such as PKUNZIP to extract the archive.

NOTE If you use a DOS unzip utility, the 8 + 3 naming convention for file names will apply, meaning that the file names will look something like guestbo~1.zip. On my PC, PKUNZIP complained that it couldn't extract the archive, yet the files came out just fine. I also noted that the file names had changed to GUESTBOO.PL, GUESTLOG.HTM, ADDGUEST.HTM, and GUESTBOOK.HTM.

After you unzip the archive, you will find five files in the current directory:

- ✪ README: a file containing the installation instructions

- ✪ guestbook.pl: the Perl script for the guest book

- ✪ addguest.html: the guest book form that visitors can use to add an entry

- ✪ guestbook.html: the actual page that displays the guest book entries

- ✪ guestlog.html: a page for displaying entries without comments

Updating the HTML Pages for the Guest Book

Because the original guest book pages were rather generic, I've created new pages for you to use. These pages are ready to go with minimal modification, and you will find them in the folder for this session on the companion Web site.

The addguest.html Page

The main page for adding entries to the guest book is called addguest.html (see Figure 2.10). The source for this page is shown in Listing 2.9. The add guest form that you see in this page is designed so that it can be put into any page at your Web site. You just need to type the markup from the line that reads "Begin Copy" to the line that reads "End Copy" into the markup in your Web page.

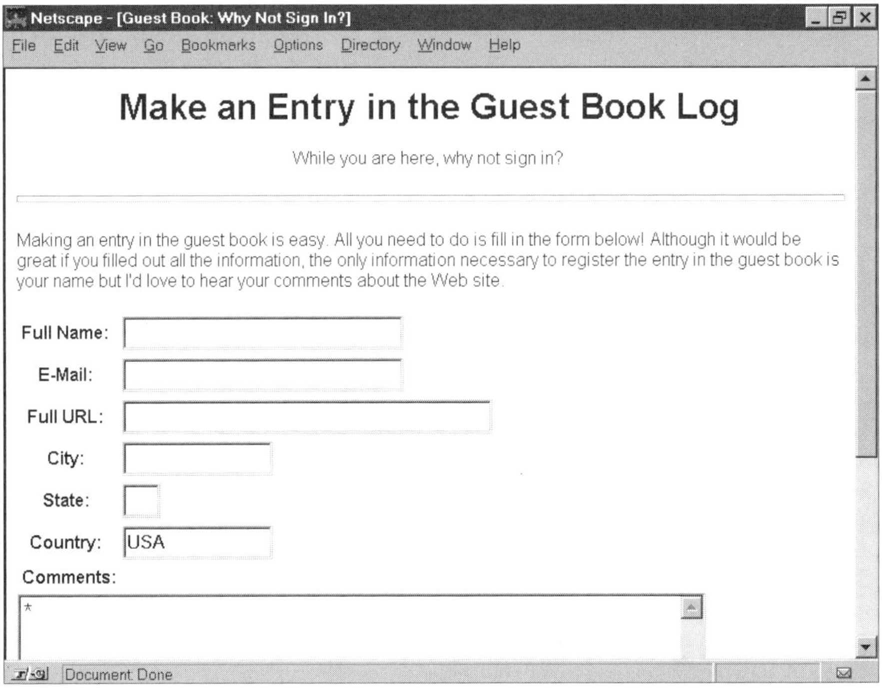
Netscape - [Guest Book: Why Not Sign In?]
File Edit View Go Bookmarks Options Directory Window Help
Make an Entry in the Guest Book Log
While you are here, why not sign in?
Making an entry in the guest book is easy. All you need to do is fill in the form below! Although it would be great if you filled out all the information, the only information necessary to register the entry in the guest book is your name but I'd love to hear your comments about the Web site.
Full Name:
E-Mail:
Full URL:
City:
State:
Country:
USA
Comments:
Document: Done

Figure 2.10

A Web page for adding entries in the guest book

Hypertext links at the bottom of the addguest.html page are meant to link to your home page and the guest book. Check these links to ensure that they are valid for your Web site. If they are, the only modification that you need to make is in the line that calls the script. Currently, this line reads as follows:

```
<FORM METHOD=POST ACTION="http://www.your_isp.com/cgi-
  bin/guestbook.pl">
```

Update the `ACTION` attribute so that it points to the correct location of the Guestbook script on your server. Save the page after you make the changes.

Listing 2.9   The addguest.html Page

```
<HTML>
<HEAD>
<TITLE>Guest Book: Why Not Sign In?</TITLE>
</HEAD>
<BODY BGCOLOR="#FFFFFF" LINK="#FF0000" VLINK="#FF0000">
<!-- Begin Copy -->
<H1 ALIGN=CENTER>Make an Entry in the Guest Book Log</H1>
<P ALIGN=CENTER>While you are here, why not sign in?</P>
<HR SIZE=5>
<P>Making an entry in the guest book is easy.
All you need to do is fill in the form below!
Although it would be great if you filled out all
the information, the only information necessary to
register the entry in the guest book is your name
but I'd love to hear your comments about the Web site.</P>
<FORM METHOD=POST ACTION="http://www.your_isp.com/cgi-
  bin/guestbook.pl">
<TABLE CELLPADDING=1 CELLSPACING=1>
<TR><TH>Full Name:</TH>
<TD><INPUT TYPE=TEXT NAME=realname SIZE=30></TD></TR>
<TR><TH>E-Mail:</TH>
<TD><INPUT TYPE=TEXT NAME=username SIZE=30></TD></TR>
<TR><TH>Full URL:</TH>
<TD><INPUT TYPE=TEXT NAME=url SIZE=40></TD></TR>
<TR><TH>City: </TH>
<TD><INPUT TYPE=TEXT NAME=city SIZE=15></TD></TR>
<TR><TH>State:</TH>
<TD><INPUT TYPE=TEXT NAME=state SIZE=2></TD></TR>
<TR><TH>Country:</TH>
<TD><INPUT TYPE=TEXT VALUE=USA NAME=country SIZE=15></TD></TR>
<TR><TH>Comments:</TH>
<TD> </TD></TR>
</TABLE>
<TEXTAREA NAME=comments COLS=60 ROWS=4>*</TEXTAREA>
<P><INPUT TYPE=SUBMIT VALUE="Sign the Guest Book">
```

```
<INPUT TYPE=RESET>
</FORM>
<!-- End Copy -->
<HR>
<P><A HREF="/">Home Page</A> ¦¦ <a href="guestbook.html">
Guest Book </a></P>
<P>Guest book script created by Matt Wright.</P>
</BODY>
</HTML>
```

The guestbook.html Page

The page for displaying entries in the guest book is called guestbook.html (see Figure 2.11). The source for this page is shown in Listing 2.10. You shouldn't need to make any changes to this page.

Figure 2.11

The main guest
book page

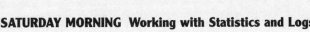
Listing 2.10 The guestbook.html Page

```
<HTML>
<HEAD>
<TITLE>Guest Book: Who's Been Visiting?</TITLE>
</HEAD>
<BODY BGCOLOR="#FFFFFF" LINK="#FF0000" VLINK="#FF0000">
<DIV ALIGN=CENTER>
<H1>Welcome to the Guest Book Log</H1>
<H2>See Who's Been Visiting </H2>
<P>While you are here, <a href="addguest.html">fill out</A>
 the guest book and stay awhile.</P>
</DIV>
<HR SIZE=5>
<!--begin-->
<HR>
<P><A HREF="../">Back to My Home Page</A></P>
<P>Guest book script created by Matt Wright.</P>
</BODY>
</HTML>
```

The guestlog.html Page

The page for displaying guest book summaries and errors is called guest-
log.html (see Figure 2.12). The source for this page is shown in Listing
2.11. You shouldn't need to make any changes to this page.

Listing 2.11 The guestlog.html Page

```
<HTML>
<HEAD>
<TITLE>Guest Book: Summary</TITLE>
</HEAD>
<BODY BGCOLOR="#FFFFFF" LINK="#FF0000" VLINK="#FF0000">
<DIV ALIGN=CENTER>
<H1>Guest Book Visitor Summary</H1>
<P>NOTE: This page summarizes the entries by date and domain.
```

```
<BR>Because this page also shows errors,
it is not intended to be read by visitors.</P>
</DIV>
<HR SIZE=5>
<!--begin-->
<HR>
```

Editing the Script

Now that you've unarchived the GuestBook script, you need to edit the script in your text editor or word processor. Start by changing the directory path for Perl information if necessary. If your server's Perl directory is not at `/usr/local/bin/perl`, you need to change the directory path referenced in the first line of the program. For example, if Perl is located at `/usr/bin/perl`, you would change the first line of the program to read as follows:

```
#!/usr/bin/perl
```

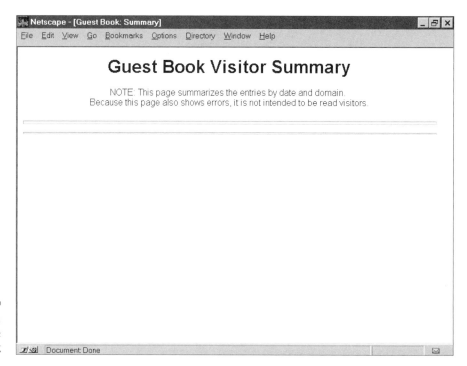

Figure 2.12

The summary and error page for the guest book

On your Web server, you will store the script in the directory for CGI scripts and the guest book pages in the directory for Web pages. Before you do this, you need to set the following variables in the script:

`$guestbookurl`	The absolute URL to the guest book log page at your Web site
`$guestbookreal`	The actual file path to the page that displays the guest book entries
`$guestlog`	The actual file path to the summary version of the guest book
`$cgiurl`	The URL path to the guestbook.pl script
`$date_command`	The path to the date command

You will find the variable assignments at the very top of the script. Start by assigning a value to the `$guestbookurl` variable. The value that you assign to the `$guestbookurl` variable is the absolute URL to the guest book log page at your Web site, such as:

```
$guestbookurl =
  "http://www.your_isp/~you/guestbook.html";
```

Next, assign a value to the `$guestbookreal` variable. This variable tells the Guestbook script the actual file path to the guest book log page. My home path is /home/william and my Web documents are in the directory www, so I set the `$guestbookreal` variable to this value:

```
$guestbookreal = "/home/william/www/";
```

Now set the `$guestlog` variable. The value for this variable is the actual file path to the summary version of the guest book, such as:

```
$guestlog = "/home/william/public_html/guestlog.html";
```

The next variable is the URL to guestbook.pl. Enter the full URL path to this script, such as:

```
$cgiurl = "http://www.tvpress.com/cgi-bin/guestbook.pl";
```

Finally, if the path to the date program on your Web server isn't /usr/bin/date, you need to set the $date_command variable. For example, if the date program on your server is at /usr/date, you would set the $date_command variable as follows:

```
$date_command = "/usr/date";
```

Save the file. You're done with the modification. Although you can configure many optional variables, the default settings work just fine.

Installing the Script and Pages on the Server

You are now ready to transfer the Guestbook script and the associated Web pages to the server. Use whatever tool you normally use for file transfers, such as FTP. Be sure to move the script to the directory designated for CGI scripts, which is typically /usr/cgi-bin. Afterward, make sure the directory and the script can be executed. Typically, you do this by setting properties for the directory and the script.

Now that you've installed the script, you can move the Web pages for the guest book to your directory for Web pages. Next, set the guestbook.html and guestlog.html files so that users have read and write access to these files.

Testing and Using the Guest Book

The final step is to test the guest book. Enter the full URL to the add guest.htm page at your Web site and try to make an entry. If you have any problems, retrace the steps discussed earlier. Otherwise, you now have a terrific way to find out who is visiting and get feedback.

Fail Safe: A Guest Book That Anyone Can Use

You may wonder whether there is a quick and easy way to get information from visitors without the hassles of CGI, and the answer is my universal guest book. The universal guest book takes advantage of the mailto: action that you can assign to HTML forms. When you use the mailto: action, the contents of the form are mailed directly to you.

Implementing the Universal Guest Book

You can implement the universal guest book by adding a form to any of your Web pages that references the `mailto:` action. The value that you assign to the `mailto:` action is your e-mail address, such as: `director @tvpress.com`.

When you use the universal guest book, try to keep it simple and be sure to use the ENCODING type text/plain. This encoding type tells the reader's browser to send the contents of the form as plain text. Listing 2.12 shows an example guest book that asks users to fill in their full name, city, state, and country. You will find this listing online saved as `guest.htm`. Look in the examples area at **http://www.tvpress.com/promote/examples/**.

If you want to use this example, just modify the e-mail address and paste the markup into a Web page. When the form is submitted, the visitor's entry will be mailed directly to you.

Listing 2.12 A Universal Guest Book

```html
<HTML>
<HEAD>
<TITLE>The Universal Guest Book</TITLE>
</HEAD>
<BODY BGCOLOR="#FFFFFF">
<H3>Sign the Guestbook</H3>
<FORM method="POST" ACTION="mailto:you@your_domain.com"
ENCODING="text/plain">
<TABLE>
<TR><TH>Your Name:<TR><TD><INPUT NAME="YourName" SIZE="25">
<TR><TH>City:<TR><TD><INPUT NAME="email" SIZE="25">
<TR><TH>State &amp; Country<TR><TD><INPUT NAME="Address"
  SIZE="25">
<TR><INPUT TYPE="SUBMIT" VALUE="SIGN GUEST BOOK"><INPUT
  TYPE="RESET">
</TABLE>
</FORM>
</BODY>
</HTML>
```

Wrapping Up and Looking Ahead

Understanding how logs are used on your server is the first step to getting a bird's eye view of the Big Picture for your Web site. The most important log is the access log. The entries in the access log provide just about everything you need to determine who visits your site and why.

Once you have the Big Picture, don't forget to keep the pages and links at your site up to date. Every visitor counts, especially when you are trying to increase traffic to your Web site. But the reason for fixing trouble spots goes well beyond preventing the loss of someone trying to find your Web site. You need to do everything within your power to build a steady readership. To attract and maintain an audience over the long haul, you need to maintain your site and provide readers with lifelines when you move or delete files.

Although all this talk about the access log and the error log is certainly useful, you may sometimes want to gather stats without having to dig through the server log files. Using a counter, you can track hits or page view stats. Using a guest book, you can track domain information and get feedback from visitors.

In the next part of the book (Saturday afternoon), you learn how to use your site's stats to attract visitors and to make your Web site a better place to visit.

Putting the Motion in Promotion

✿ Transforming the Numbers into
Meaningful Data

✿ Capitalizing on Search Engine
Fundamentals

✿ Registering with the Top Search
Engines on the Planet

✿ Submitting Your Web Site to the
Top Guides, Lists, and Directories

Saturday morning covered how to unlock the secrets of the server log files and how to use the logs to obtain key Web site stats such as number of hits, page views, and visits. Together, these stats help you unravel the big picture for your Web site. You also saw how to use the error logs to clear up the trouble spots at your Web site and gain readers you otherwise would have lost. Finally, you learned about gathering stats without using server logs.

This afternoon, you learn how to put the stats to work. You start by summarizing the stats and transforming them into meaningful data. Then, you use the stats to make your Web site a better place to visit and to find your niche in the wonderful world of cyberspace. Enhancing your Web site based on what the stats tell you and using your Web site's niche to your advantage are key ingredients that will help you attract the masses.

This afternoon, you'll also delve into the rich array of resources available on the Web to help you get your site noticed. Rather than present you with a hodgepodge of hit-or-miss choices, I put my countless hours of research and experience into these pages to bring you what I consider the best. This way, you can maximize your time.

Transforming the Numbers into Meaningful Data

All the data that you've gathered so far is great, but to make it useful, you need to transform the raw statistics into meaningful data. You can create meaningful data by either rolling up your sleeves and digging in or using tracking software that does the job for you.

When you track stats by hand, you get to see all the data first-hand, which gives you a keener sense of exactly what is happening at your Web site. Tracking stats by hand isn't difficult, but it is somewhat time consuming because you have to slog through the server logs.

When you track stats using tracking software, the software compiles the stats for you. You have to choose the type and format of reports that are compiled from the stats, however.

Tracking Day-to-Day Traffic by Hand

When you track day-to-day traffic by hand, the stats on which you want to focus are hits and page views. Your primary means of gathering stats is the access log. If the server logs aren't available, you can also use counters to gather stats. The best types of counters are those that count page views.

In this section, I show you additional techniques that you can use to summarize Web site stats. Use these techniques in addition to those discussed in the Saturday Morning session under "Understanding Visits and Page Views." The reason to summarize stats is to gain a better understanding of your Web site's big picture. As stated in this morning's session, the big-picture questions that you can answer when you track hits and page views are the following:

✪ **Most requested pages:** Tells you the pages that visitors find the most interesting or useful. Can be used to tailor your Web site to visitors' needs and help you determine which pages should get most of your attention.

- ⚙ **Average duration of page view:** Can be an indicator of whether people are reading or just browsing. When you examine this statistic, you also need to keep in mind the length and style of pages that you have at your Web site. Are they highly textual, highly graphical, or both?

- ⚙ **Domain classes and geographic areas:** Can tell you where people visiting your Web site live and work. Great information to have if you want to attract advertisers.

- ⚙ **Busiest hours of the day:** Tells you the time of day most people visit your Web site. This statistic can help you plan daily updates, promotion campaigns, and advertising.

- ⚙ **Busiest days of the week:** Tells you the day of the week that most people are visiting your Web site. This statistic can also help you plan weekly updates, promotion campaigns, and advertising.

- ⚙ **Most commonly requested last pages:** Can help you spot trends and bad pages. If the last page requested contains lots of links to external Web sites, this statistic tells you that this is the point of departure for most visitors. If the last page requested doesn't have links to external Web sites, you may want to examine the page in question.

Summarizing Hits

Each entry in the access log represents a hit. Usually, when you look at hits, you will want only summary data, such as how many hits are in the access log right now. Summary data provides you with an overview of the activity at your Web site.

Searching the Logs

As covered under "Understanding Visits and Page Views" in this morning's session, you can track day-to-day stats using the find or grep command. The find command is available at the DOS prompt on all

Windows-based systems. You can use the find command to search through the server log files and to count hits and page views, such as:

```
find "overview.html" access-log > save.txt
```

Here, the find command is used to search for all entries that reference the page overview.html. The results of the find search are put into a file called save.txt. Entries in the save.txt file are complete lines and look exactly like those in the access log:

```
pc8.att.net - - [11/Apr/1998:00:01:18 -0700] "GET /
  HTTP/1.0" 200 8355

pc8.att.net - - [11/Apr/1998:00:01:25 -0700] "GET
  /ban2.gif HTTP/1.0" 200 1373
```

As discussed earlier, you can use the grep command to search the server log files on UNIX systems. Although the grep command originated on UNIX platforms, an extended version of grep, called egrep, is available for the Macintosh. In this example, the grep command is used to search for all page views for the file overview.html:

```
grep overview.html access-log
```

Getting the Stats

Regardless of whether you use find or grep, these commands match the keyword for which you are looking to entries in a named file, such as access-log or tvpress-access-log. The results of the search are printed to the screen by default but are preferably directed to a file that you can read or search later.

To count the number of hits in the access log at any given time, search for a string that is common to all entries in the access log. Because all log entries have the bracket character ([), you can summarize hits as follows:

```
find /C "[" access-log
```

or

```
grep "[" access-log ¦ wc
```

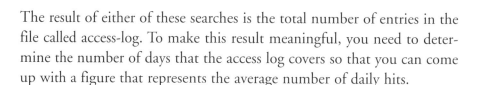

The result of either of these searches is the total number of entries in the file called access-log. To make this result meaningful, you need to determine the number of days that the access log covers so that you can come up with a figure that represents the average number of daily hits.

Making Sense of the Numbers

The entries in your access log could cover a few days or a few months. Most access logs are archived monthly. This means that last month's log is usually moved to an archive directory or compressed using ZIP, GZIP, or some other compression utility that saves space on the file system. Although you would expect the log to be archived on a specific day of the month, this isn't always the case. Often, the log is archived when it grows to a specific size, such as 10 megabytes.

If the old log files are available in the same directory, you can look at the date on the last month's log file to determine when it was archived. The time difference between the most recently archived log and the current date tells you the number of days that the current log represents.

Another way to determine the number of days that the log covers is to examine the access-log file directly. Loading the file into a text editor usually isn't practical, however, because the file size may be several megabytes. On a UNIX system, you can use the head or pg commands to look at the beginning of the file:

```
head access-log
```

or

```
pg access-log
```

On a Windows system, you can use the more command to ensure that you see entries one page at a time. At the DOS prompt, enter the usual search information and then redirect the output through the more command with the pipe symbol (|). After you record the time stamp on the first entry, press Ctrl+C to end the search. An example of using the more command is as follows:

```
find "[" access-log ¦ more
```

To determine the average daily hits to your Web site, divide the hit count by the number of days the log covers, such as:

```
3502 / 30
```

The average number of hits can help you estimate how much traffic your Web site is generating without your having to wade through the logs or using Web site tracking software. If you look for hits related to specific days, you also can tell busy days from slow days without digging deeper into the logs. You'll learn more about summarizing hits for specific days in the next section.

Tallying Page Views by Hand

A page view is an important statistic because it tells you how many times a particular Web page has been accessed. You can use this statistic to determine the popularity of each individual page at your Web site.

Adopting a Schedule

Whenever you track page views by hand, you should do so on a regular basis, such as daily, weekly, or monthly. I recommend gathering stats daily at first, and then moving to a weekly or monthly schedule when you get into a solid routine that makes tracking stats seem like second nature. Next, make a list of the Web pages you want to track. Although you may want to track all pages at your Web site, tracking page views for individual Web pages isn't always practical. For this reason, you may want to select only the top-level pages at your site, such as your home page or the main page for a uniquely focused area at your Web site.

When you want to track stats on a regular basis, you can use to your advantage the time stamp that all access log entries have. To track stats daily, you search for all references to a specific date, such as:

```
grep "11/Apr/1998" access-log > $HOME/temp.txt
```

To track stats weekly, you repeat the daily search for each day of the week, such as:

```
grep "14/Apr/1998" access-log > $HOME/temp.txt
grep "15/Apr/1998" access-log >> $HOME/temp.txt
grep "16/Apr/1998" access-log >> $HOME/temp.txt
grep "17/Apr/1998" access-log >> $HOME/temp.txt
grep "18/Apr/1998" access-log >> $HOME/temp.txt
grep "19/Apr/1998" access-log >> $HOME/temp.txt
grep "20/Apr/1998" access-log >> $HOME/temp.txt
```

NOTE The append command (>>) tells grep and find to add the results to a specified file. Keep in mind that grep is a UNIX command and find is a DOS command. Mac users can use a command called egrep but must install this on their system. For more details on these commands, look in the Saturday Morning session under "Understanding Visits and Page Views."

To track stats monthly, you search for the month string, such as:

```
find "Apr/1998" access-log >> save.txt
```

Checking Individual Page Views

After you extract page views for a particular time period, you can summarize the stats relating to each page. To do this, search the file that you just created for each page individually and count the number of entries. The /C option of the find command lets you count the number of entries for each page:

```
find /C "overview.html" save.txt
```

On UNIX systems, you will use the wc command to count the number of entries for each page:

```
grep overview.html save.txt ¦ wc
```

Because typing the commands repeatedly can be tedious, you can create a batch file to help automate the tracking process. The batch file can contain the initial search through the access log as well as searches for each page that you want to track.

Say that you want to track stats for these pages on a daily basis:

/—Your home page

vpbg.htm—Your background page

/writing/—A top-level page

You need to create a file containing the appropriate commands to check the stats for these pages. The most important thing to remember is to update the search parameters, such as the date you are looking for, before you run the batch file. After you edit and save the batch file, you can run it to check the stats.

On a UNIX platform, your batch file contains these commands:

```
grep "11/Apr/1998" /www/logs/access-log > $HOME/temp.txt
echo "Home Page Count: "
grep " / " temp.txt ¦ wc
echo "Background Page Count: "
grep "vpbg.htm" temp.txt ¦ wc
echo "Writing Area Count: "
grep "/writing/ " temp.txt ¦ wc
```

NOTE When you examine the example, note the reference to the directory /www/logs. If your access log is not in this directory, you need to enter the actual directory path for your system. Note also the use of the echo command to display descriptive text during the search. Don't let all these commands confuse you; just practice using the commands and change the examples to meet your needs.

After you create and save the file, change the mode of the file so that you can execute it. If the file name is stat_track, you can change the mode as follows:

```
chmod 755 stat_track
```

Here, 755 is used to set the mode of the file, with each digit having a specific meaning. The first digit sets the mode for the file owner. The 7 says that the owner can read, write, and execute the file. The second digit sets the mode for the group the owner is a member of. The 5 says that members of this group can read and execute the file. The third digit sets the mode for all other users. The 5 says that other users can read and execute the file.

As long as you are in your home directory, you run the batch file from the command prompt by typing:

```
stat_track
```

The output from this batch file looks like this:

```
Home Page Count:
152
Background Page Count:
43
Writing Area Count:
28
```

Here, the page views for /, vpbg.htm, and /writing/ are 152, 43, and 28, respectively. Although the name of the batch file on a UNIX system isn't restricted, your batch file on a Windows-based computer should end with the .bat extension, such as track.bat. Based on the previous example, the batch file for a Windows-based system looks like this:

```
find "11/Apr/1998" access-log > save.txt
find /C " / " save.txt
find /C "vpbg.htm" save.txt
find /C "/writing/ " save.txt
```

NOTE If your access log is not in the same directory as the batch file, you need to enter the actual directory path for your system. Again, don't allow these commands to confuse you. Practice using the commands and work through the examples.

If you save the file as track.bat, you run it from the DOS prompt by typing:

```
track
```

The output from this batch file looks like this:

```
D:\>find "11/Apr/1998" access-log > save.txt
D:\>find /C " / " save.txt
————— save.txt: 29
D:\>find /C "vpbg.htm" save.txt
————— save.txt: 13
D:\>find /C "/writing/ " save.txt
————— save.txt: 2
```

Here, the page views for /, vpbg.htm, and /writing/ are 29, 13, and 2, respectively.

Tracking Software

Although tracking stats by hand definitely gives you a sense that you have hands-on control over your Web site and its destiny, you can find software that will handle the task of tracking stats for you. You will find that most of the commercial tracking software comes with all the bells and whistles that you would expect. If you have a few hundred dollars, stats programs are good investments. Still, the freeware and shareware tracking solutions available are really quite good and ideally suited to the needs of the average Web publisher.

Why Use Tracking Software?

Tracking software is great for tracking hits, page views, and the nebulous visit. Because tracking software makes it possible to track visits, you can use tracking software to obtain all the pieces of the big picture for your Web site. From Saturday morning's work, you know that the big picture helps you answer these questions related to your site's traffic:

- What was the total number of visitors for this time period?
- What was the length of the average visit?
- What was the average duration of a page view?
- What was the average number of page views per visitor?
- What was the average number of hits per visitor?
- What domain classes and geographic areas were represented (percentages)?
- What were the busiest hours of the day?
- What were the busiest days of the week?
- What were the most requested pages?
- What were the most common last pages requested?

Helping you answer these questions with limited fuss is what tracking software is all about. Still, working with tracking software requires a trade-off. Everything that tracking software does is based on your server log files. You need to configure the software to access your Web server and retrieve the log files. You also need to be patient with the software while it searches through the logs and extracts the information for which you are looking. The larger your log's files, the longer and harder the tracking software has to work to get the stats.

At first glance, tracking software may seem to potentially save you a lot of time, but that isn't always the case. It took me an entire day to obtain, install, configure, and test tracking software for my Web server. The result of that initial eight-hour investment is that the software runs automatically and the reports are generated weekly. Every week, I spend 45 to 60 minutes reviewing and analyzing the reports. Making configuration changes to the software takes about an hour, and afterward, I can retrieve different types of reports.

For desktop tracking software, you have to transfer the server logs to your PC. On a weekly basis, I download the server's log files for a moderately active Web site. The download time using a 28.8 Kbps modem takes just over two hours. After the logs are on my PC, the tracking software usually optimizes the data—a process that takes me anywhere from 15 to 30 minutes. Next, I have to generate individually each of the reports that I want to see—a process that takes 5 to 15 minutes per report on my PC. Then, I spend 15 to 20 minutes reviewing and recording the data.

To see how tracking stats by hand compares to using tracking software, I also examined the amount of time that I spend tracking stats by hand. On a daily basis, I looked at hits and page views for each of four major areas at my Web site as well as total hits and page views for the entire Web site. It takes me about five minutes to obtain the necessary stats when I type the commands by hand, but only a few seconds to update and run a batch file with the same commands. Afterward, I spend 20 to 25 minutes summarizing, analyzing, and recording the stats.

As you can see, the main reason to use tracking software isn't always to save time. Rather, the main reason to use tracking software is that the software does most of the work for you and allows you to analyze the log files in great detail.

TIP Because this book is designed to be used in a weekend, the ins and outs of installing and using the various tracking software packages is beyond the scope of this book. As you will see when you start to use tracking software, you can spend an entire day just getting a good feel for the software. That said, this book would not be complete without a fairly comprehensive discussion on tracking software, which you will find in the sections that follow. Supplementing this discussion is a list of tracking software programs and their locations on the Web. That list is on the Web site for this book, at **www.tvpress.com /promote/utilities/**.

An Overview of Tracking Software

Most tracking software creates graphical representations of the traffic at your Web site. Graphs and charts are great for helping you understand the activity at your site without having to dig through the numbers. A

summary of visits using a graph is shown in Figure 3.1. The software that I used to create the graph is called net.Analysis Desktop.

Other tracking software summarizes your site's traffic using completely text-based means, which doesn't necessarily mean that the results lack graphs and charts. Graphs can be created using text characters, such as the dash or plus sign.

As a matter of fact, Analog 2.0 from the University of Cambridge Statistical Laboratory generates a daily report graph using only text. The daily report graph summarizes page views by representing a set amount of pages with a plus sign. An example of this daily report is shown in Listing 3.1.

NOTE   Analog 2.0 is created by Steve Turner from the University of Cambridge Statistical Laboratory. This software is free, and versions of Analog 2.0 are available for just about every operating system, including DOS, Windows 3.1/95/NT, Mac, and most UNIX systems. You can obtain Analog 2.0 by visiting **http://www.statslab.cam.ac.uk/~sret1/analog/**.

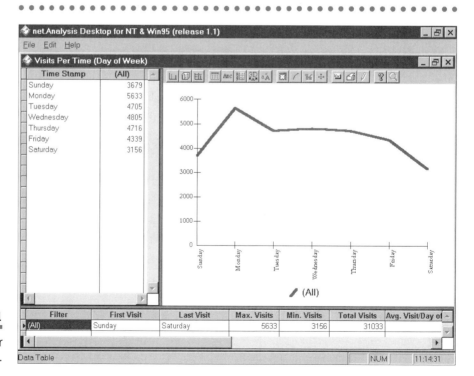

Figure 3.1

Graphs are great for summarizing stats.

Listing 3.1   A Daily Report from Analog 2.0

```
Daily Report
— — — — — —


Each unit (+) represents 100 requests for pages, or part
  thereof.


      date: pages:
— — — —   — —
  1/Apr/97:   2396:  +++++++++++++++++++++++
  2/Apr/97:   1968:  ++++++++++++++++++++
  3/Apr/97:   1996:  ++++++++++++++++++++
  4/Apr/97:   1619:  ++++++++++++++++
  5/Apr/97:   1057:  ++++++++++

  6/Apr/97:   1302:  ++++++++++++++
  7/Apr/97:   2167:  ++++++++++++++++++++++
  8/Apr/97:   2003:  +++++++++++++++++++++
  9/Apr/97:   1777:  ++++++++++++++++++
 10/Apr/97:   1858:  +++++++++++++++++++
 11/Apr/97:   1939:  ++++++++++++++++++++
 12/Apr/97:   1424:  ++++++++++++++

 13/Apr/97:   3723:  ++++++++++++++++++++++++++++++++++++++
 14/Apr/97:   4200:  ++++++++++++++++++++++++++++++++++++++++++
 15/Apr/97:   4319:  +++++++++++++++++++++++++++++++++++++++++++++
 16/Apr/97:   3867:  +++++++++++++++++++++++++++++++++++++++++
 17/Apr/97:   3279:  +++++++++++++++++++++++++++++++++++
 18/Apr/97:   2482:  +++++++++++++++++++++++++
 19/Apr/97:   1957:  ++++++++++++++++++++

 20/Apr/97:   1952:  ++++++++++++++++++++
 21/Apr/97:   2570:  +++++++++++++++++++++++++++
```

Tracking Software on the Server and on the Desktop

Beyond graphics or text-based representations of the data compiled by
tracking software are two other categories of tracking software:

✪ Tracking software that runs on your desktop PC

✪ Tracking software that runs on the server

Tracking Software That Runs on Your Desktop PC

Tracking software can run from your desktop PC. Unlike tracking software installed on a server, desktop tracking software generally does not run automatically. This means that you are responsible for starting the software, telling it to retrieve the access log for the server, and then compiling the types of reports that you want to see.

net.Analysis is an example of tracking software that runs on your desktop. When you start net.Analysis, the first thing that you must do is retrieve the current log file, which net.Analysis calls importing the file. Your modem speed and the size of the log file determine how long retrieving the log file takes, from a few minutes to several hours.

After retrieving the log file, the tracking software examines the file and optimizes it. The optimization process typically involves removing or commenting out references to image files as well as indexing the file for quicker searching later. Your CPU speed and memory determine how long the optimization takes. The final step is when you tell the software what type of reports you want to generate.

Most tracking software that runs on your desktop isn't free. Still, you can usually obtain free trial versions of the software by visiting the developer's Web site. Desktop tracking software that you may want to try includes:

✪ WebTrends Log Analyzer (**www.webtrends.com**)

✪ Marketwave HitList Professional (**www.marketwave.com**)

✪ net.Analysis Desktop (**www.netgen.com**)

Tracking Software That Runs on a Remote Server

Most tracking software is installed as an add-on for a remote server. The job of server-based tracking software is to help automate the tracking process. Generally, you automate the tracking process by telling the soft-

ware to periodically read in the log files and compile them for your reports. Server-based software can also allow users to remotely create and compile reports. In this way, you run resource-intensive processes on a server and not on your desktop PC.

I use the term "remote server" rather than "Web server" because most commercial tracking software shouldn't be run on the Web server itself. Running the software on the Web server may block access to your Web site. The reason is that the software typically uses all of the available server resources. Thus, you may need a separate server machine specifically for stats.

That said, there are exceptions to every rule, and Analog 2.0 is one of them. Analog 2.0 is designed to run directly on a Web server and uses limited server resources to make this work. When you install Analog 2.0, you configure the software to generate specific types of reports at designated intervals, such as every week. From then on, Analog 2.0 generates the specified reports automatically. If you later decide that you want a different set of reports, you need to reconfigure the software. Fortunately, the whole process of reconfiguring the software and generating new reports takes only a few minutes.

You should ask your Internet service provider whether it has already selected some type of tracking software that you can use, or whether installing your own tracking software is okay. Most Internet service providers already have tracking software installed on their Web servers. To access this software, you usually just need to ask. If your Internet service provider doesn't have tracking software installed on the server, you may want to point your provider in the direction of Analog 2.0, which is arguably the most versatile tracking software anywhere that doesn't cost a dime.

Other good choices that you'll want to tell your ISP about include:

- ✪ MKStats: Extremely versatile and free for noncommercial use. MKStats uses Perl. (**http://www.mkstats.com/**)

- ✪ wwwstat: Fairly versatile freeware that also uses Perl. (**http://www.ics.uci.edu/pub/websoft/wwwstat/**)

- ✿ gwstat: a freeware stats program that builds on wwwstat and lets you generate graphs. (**http://dis.cs.umass.edu/stats/gwstat.html**)

- ✿ HitList Commerce and Enterprise: Commercial tracking software designed for heavy-duty use. (**http://www.marketwave.com/**)

- ✿ WebTrends Professional: Commercial Tracking software for the pros. (**http://www.webtrends.com/**)

Finally, You Know What Pages Are Popular; Now What?

Regardless of whether you track your site's stats by hand or use tracking software, the result is that you now have a better understanding of who is visiting your Web site and why. You should also have answers to many of the big-picture questions. These answers can help you make your Web site a better place to visit and will also help you increase traffic to your Web site.

Right about now, you are probably wondering why I keep saying that you can use the stats to make your Web site a better place to visit as well as to increase traffic to your Web site. After all, the title of the book is *Increase Your Web Traffic In a Weekend, Revised Edition,* not *Make Your Web Site a Better Place to Visit In a Weekend.*

The simple truth is that the long-term success of your Web site is based upon understanding your site's good points and bad points. By understanding your site's good points, you learn how to market the Web site to the world. By understanding your site's bad points, you learn what you need to do to fix the problems. If you don't fix the problems at your Web site, you may lose readers just as fast as you find new ones.

The steps to follow to make your Web site a better place to visit include:

- ✿ Directing users to popular areas

- ✿ Cleaning up unused pages

- ✿ Avoiding dead-ends

- ✿ Fixing errors

After you take a close look at your Web site, you can move on to the next step, which is to find your niche in cyberspace and formulate a plan that uses your niche to market your Web site to the world.

Directing Users to Popular Areas

Every road sign you can add to the Web makes cyberspace just a little bit more enjoyable, so why not create a few road signs that direct users to popular areas at your Web site? Your road signs don't need to be extravagant. You can use plain-old text to create links to other pages at your Web site, but you need to tell visitors that those other pages exist.

Obviously, you don't want to tell visitors about every single Web page you've published. Instead, you want to direct users to the popular areas of your Web site by creating links to the top-level page within the specific areas that you want to promote. The idea here is that people visiting your sports information page, for example, may also be interested in your sports equipment page. They can't get to the sports equipment page if you don't tell them it exists, however.

Say that your site's stats show that seven pages at the Web site get the most traffic. The URLs for these pages are these:

- **http://www.cooldays.com/**—your main home page
- **http://www.cooldays.com/summer/**—a page that promotes summertime activities
- **http://www.cooldays.com/summer/water-skiing.html**—a page within the summertime activities area that covers water skiing
- **http://www.cooldays.com/summer/surfing.html**—a page within the summertime activities area that covers surfing
- **http://www.cooldays.com/equipment/**—a page that discusses where you can look on the Web to get the best bargains in sports equipment
- **http://www.cooldays.com/equipment/forsale.html**—a page that lets people post ads to sell their sports equipment

○ **http://www.cooldays.com/equipment/tips.html**—a page that provides tips for getting the best value for your money when you buy sports equipment

When you examine the seven most visited pages, you see that three specific areas of the Web site are getting the most traffic:

○ The main home page

○ The summertime activities area

○ The sports-equipment area

The home page is the place to toot your horn about the main areas at your site, but you also need to do so on the top-level pages within the site. Although you may think that most visitors start on the site's home page, this isn't always true. In fact, most people probably start their visit on some other page. For this reason, you should tell anyone visiting the

Figure 3.2

Directing visitors to the sports equipment area

summertime activities area that you have this wonderful sports-equipment area, and vice versa.

By promoting both areas, you increase page views at your site and let readers know that your site really does have a lot to offer. On the Web page at **http://www.cooldays.com/summer/**, you add a clear road sign that directs visitors to the sports equipment area (see Figure 3.2). The markup for the road sign is as follows:

```
<HR SIZE=5>
<H3><A HREF="http://www.cooldays.com/equipment/">Sports Equip-
    ment</A></H3>
<UL>
<LI>Find the best bargains on the Web
<LI>Read tips for buying sports equipment that will save you
    a bundle
<LI>Get great deals on used equipment or post your own for
    sale ad
</UL>
```

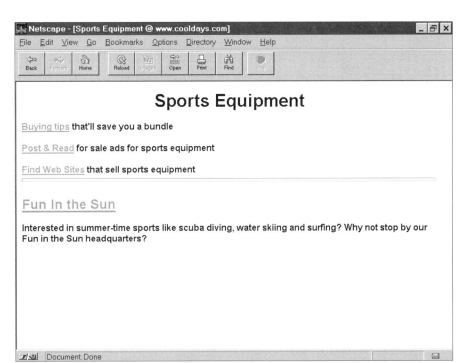

Figure 3.3

Directing visitors to the summertime activities area

Then, on the Web page at **http://www.cooldays.com/equipment/**, you add another road sign that directs visitors to the summertime activities area (see Figure 3.3). The markup for the road sign is as follows:

```
<HR SIZE=5>
<H3><A HREF="http://www.cooldays.com/summer/">Fun In the
  Sun</A></H3>
<P>Interested in summer-time sports like scuba diving,
water skiing and surfing? Why not stop by
our Fun in the Sun headquarters?
```

Cleaning Up Unused Pages

After studying your Web site to see how you can direct traffic to popular areas, you should take a hard look at pages that rarely get visitors. Although your first impulse may be to delete the page or stop updating the page, this may not be the right solution. Rather than remove or neglect the page, you should ensure that other pages at your Web site have clear road signs that tell people what the page is all about. You may also want to consider combining the information on this page with information on another page.

Say that your site's stats show two pages at the Web site rarely receive visitors. The URLs for these pages are as follows:

- **http://www.cooldays.com/summer/background.html**—a background page for the summertime activities area

- **http://www.cooldays.com/summer/scuba/deepwater.html**—a page that promotes deep-water scuba diving

After examining the background page, you may discover that you can summarize the information and place it directly on the top-level page for the summertime activity area. In this way, visitors to this area of the Web site get a quick summary without having to visit the background page. By adding the information to the top-level page, you make the area a better place to visit.

Next, you look at the page that promotes deep-water scuba diving. Your scuba diving pages are broken down into three categories: fresh water, salt

water, and deep water. Although the fresh water and salt water scuba pages get lots of visitors, the deep-water page rarely gets a visitor. The problem here may be organizational; perhaps your top-level page needs to explain that deep water refers to deep-sea scuba diving with submersibles and that you also feature video from the Galapagos undersea expedition.

Avoiding Dead Ends

Dead ends are show stoppers. All your Web pages should end with links that lead back to a main page, the previous page, or the next page in a series of pages. Links at the bottom of a Web page are subtle reminders that the Web site has more to offer. By adding appropriate links to the bottom of your Web pages, you can make navigating your Web site easier, thereby increasing traffic to your Web site. Remember, if readers visit your sports-related Web site, they are interested in sports, so why not help them find the information they are looking for?

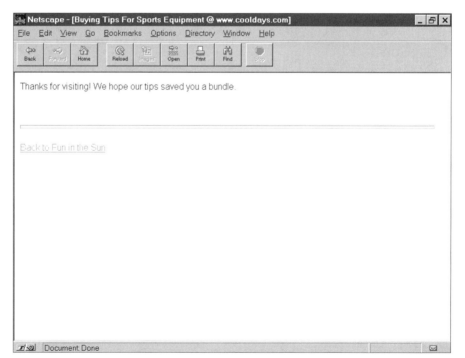

Figure 3.4

Avoiding dead ends with a basic link

Links at the bottom of a Web page can be as basic as the one shown in Figure 3.4. The markup for the link is as follows:

```
<HR SIZE=5>
<P><A HREF="/summer/">Back to Fun in the Sun</A></P>
```

You can also use mini-menus that tell readers about other areas of your Web site, such as the one shown in Figure 3.5. The markup for this mini-menu is as follows:

```
<HR SIZE=5>
<P><A HREF="/">Our Home Page </A> ¦¦
<A HREF="/summer/">Fun in the Sun</A> ¦¦
<A HREF="/equipment/">Sports Equipment</A></P>
```

Another form of dead end is a page that causes the reader to lose interest in your Web site. For example, a page full of errors or inconsistencies may make the reader think that the rest of your Web site isn't worth visiting. For this reason, you may want to look for pages that are often the last page that people visit, and see whether they need updating.

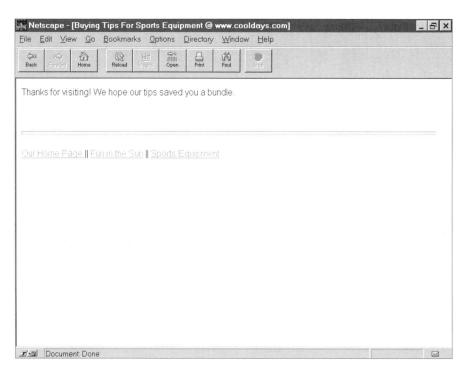

Figure 3.5

Avoiding dead ends by ending the page with a mini-menu

A Last Look at Error Correction

Whenever you have bad references in your Web pages, you risk losing visitors. If you haven't taken the time to examine the errors in the server log's files, you may want to do so now. Refer to the Saturday Morning session under "Gaining Lost Readers from the Error Logs" for help with this.

Understanding Your Niche

After tracking your site's stats, you should have a clearer understanding of the resources that attract visitors to your Web site. These resources help define your niche in cyberspace. Understanding your niche and using it to your advantage are the keys to success when you try to promote your Web site to the world. By taking the time to learn exactly why people visit your Web site, you save yourself a barrel full of heartaches.

Before they started tracking their stats, the creators of www.cooldays.com thought that the underwater video sequences they published online were the main events at their Web site. As it turned out, the Web pages covering deep-sea scuba diving were the least visited. Although you could say that the problem was poor organization, it turns out that the Web site had lots of other things to offer visitors.

Thus, although the creators of the Web site started out to build a resource for scuba divers, they ended up with a Web site that covered many different water sports, including water skiing and surfing. They also created a wonderful guide to buying sports equipment online. Looking back, they saw that their niche covered two different areas: resources for anyone who loved water sports; and resources for buying and selling sports equipment online.

Unfortunately, the site's banners and logos promoted the site as "A great place for anyone who loves scuba diving." Worse, the developers of the site used this same slogan whenever they had an opportunity to promote the Web site. When they registered with search engines, they hyped their great scuba-diving center and forgot about the other areas. When they traded links with other sites, they told the publisher to be sure to tell

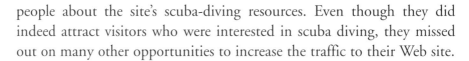

people about the site's scuba-diving resources. Even though they did indeed attract visitors who were interested in scuba diving, they missed out on many other opportunities to increase the traffic to their Web site.

As you can see, the creators of www.cooldays.com should have taken the time to put together a better picture of their Web site before they started promoting their site as a great place for anyone who loves scuba diving. A better description of their Web site would have been this:

A terrific site for anyone who loves water sports! We have tons of resources covering scuba diving, water skiing, surfing, and many other water sports. We also have a terrific guide to sites that sell sports equipment. Our buying tips may save you a bundle.

The creators of www.cooldays.com could also create separate descriptions for each popular area at the Web site. This would allow them to promote the Web site as a whole and each area separately. For example, the next time they register in a search engine, they could use the combined description and then register each area separately as well. You'll learn all about search engines in the next section, "Capitalizing on Search Engine Fundamentals."

Before you continue, create descriptive blurbs for your Web site. Start by identifying the most popular areas at your Web site, and then use the subjects that these areas cover to come up with a brief description that identifies your site's niche. Afterward, create separate descriptions for each popular area at your Web site.

Capitalizing on Search Engine Fundamentals

Finding Web sites would be nearly impossible without sites that let you quickly and easily search for information. These so-called search engines provide a service that puts all the resources of the Web within reach. Search engines allow Web publishers to register their Web pages so that the pages will be added to the list of resources the search engine knows about. Search engines allow Web users to find the pages listed in the

search engine using keywords and phrases that identify the information that the users want to find.

Although search engines are one of the primary means of getting your site noticed by users around the world, few people truly understand how search engines work. That is, people rarely get the most out of the search engine and often waste their time and resources when they register their site with search engines. In this part of this session, you will learn how search engines do what they do and how you can make the most of the techniques that search engines use to index and reference your Web site.

Millions of Users Are but a Search Away

More than 100 million people are just a click away from your Web site. They just need to follow the references that lead to you. The only problem is that your Web site probably doesn't show up in the results retrieved by the search engine they are using, and on the rare occasion when the results show your site, the information that users need to make the decision to visit your site is lacking. At that point, they head off to some other site. Day in and day out, this scenario plays out at the hundreds of search engines on the Web. The result is that your Web site doesn't get the level of traffic it deserves.

Because few people truly understand how search engines work, Web publishers often get frustrated when they try to attract visitors using search engines. Usually, the Web publisher will register the site with a few search engines and then sit back and wait for the visitors to come. When the visitors don't come, the publisher then registers with more search engines. Eventually, the publisher may even turn to commercial services that promise to bring visitors to the Web site.

Search engines are one of the least understood Internet tools, and any time there is a lack of understanding, someone out there is going to try to make a buck at your expense. You'll find services trying to sell you the Holy Grail for hundreds of dollars. These services tell you that they will register your site with every search engine available; get your site listed in the top 10 search results every time; or trick search engines into display-ing your site more often. To all that, I say: Don't buy what they're selling unless you've got money to burn. Instead, take the time to learn how search engines work and use this information to get your site noticed by millions of Web users.

Indexers, Spiders, Crawlers, and Other Web Beasties

In the early days of the Web, search engines were simple tools for finding information using indexes. Much like the index of your favorite computer book, the purpose of the index was to make finding information possible by using keywords. Rather than the page references used in traditional indexes, Web indexes had hypertext links that you could click on to access the information at Web sites around the world.

Over the years, search engines evolved. Today, the best search engines are complex applications that use advanced techniques to put millions of Web pages at the fingertips of Web users. Often, these advanced search engines have descriptive names that hint at the techniques the search engine uses to index Web pages, such as *spider* or *crawler*.

Working with Search Engines

No matter what label you use to identify a search engine, the fundamen-tal purpose of a search engine is generally to index Web sites in a way that allows people to use keywords to find Web pages that interest them. To do this, search engines rely on a computer called an indexer, spider, or crawler to ferret out the pages at your site and then create indexed references to those pages in the search engine's database. After the pages are indexed in the search engine's database, anyone can use the front-end search process to find the pages.

If you jaunt over to Infoseek at **www.infoseek.com/**, you will find that the main page has an area called New Search. As shown in Figure 3.6, New Search contains an input field for entering keywords or phrases you

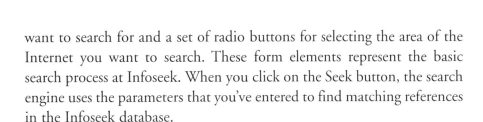

want to search for and a set of radio buttons for selecting the area of the Internet you want to search. These form elements represent the basic search process at Infoseek. When you click on the Seek button, the search engine uses the parameters that you've entered to find matching references in the Infoseek database.

When you search using the keywords "Internet Daily News" and click on the Web radio button, you get a list of results like those shown in Figure 3.7. Typically, the results of a search are displayed according to their relevance to the search parameters that you entered. Here, the probability that the first listing is a match is 100 percent. The probability that the second listing is a match is 81 percent.

When you see a probability of 90 to 100 percent, the search engine believes the document is a very strong match for your search. Generally, the probability of a match is based on the number of times your search

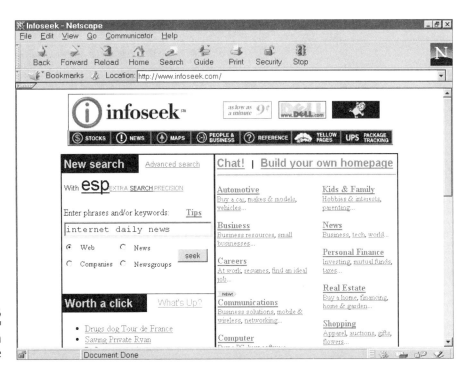

Figure 3.6

Using a search engine

words occur in the associated document, the position of the words within the document, and several other factors.

Most search engines display references to the top 10 or 20 pages that match your search parameters. Successive groups of matching pages are also available, but you have to follow a link to another results page. At Infoseek, you can click on the Next 10 link found at the top and bottom of the results page to see additional pages that might be matches for your search.

Often, the matching pages are described using the page title and a brief description taken from the page itself. Most commercial search engines allow you to customize the search and results displayed. The search engine at Infoseek lets you customize the search in many different ways. You can show or hide summary information; elect to display results in sets of 10, 20, 30, 40, or 50 pages; and a whole lot more.

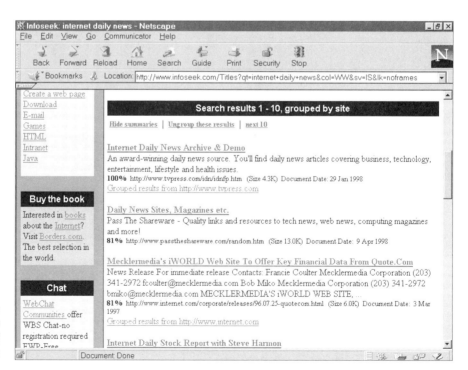

Figure 3.7

The results of a search

Comparing Search Engines and Directory Lists

Search engines and directory lists are very different. When you look for information with a search engine, you use keywords. When you look for information at a directory listing, you search by following links to pages within the directory site. Your search starts by clicking on a broad category, such as entertainment, and you eventually drill down to a very specific subject, such as movie reviews. One of the best known directory lists is Yahoo! (**www.yahoo.com**).

When you visit the Yahoo! home page (shown in Figure 3.8), you are greeted by a listing of the top-level categories of information available at the site. Under the top-level categories are more focused categories of information. If you select the News and Media category, you end up on the page shown in Figure 3.9. As you can see, this page shows many different broad categories of news. By selecting another link, you can get to a more narrowly focused category, such as business news or technology news.

Figure 3.8

A directory site is very different from a search site.

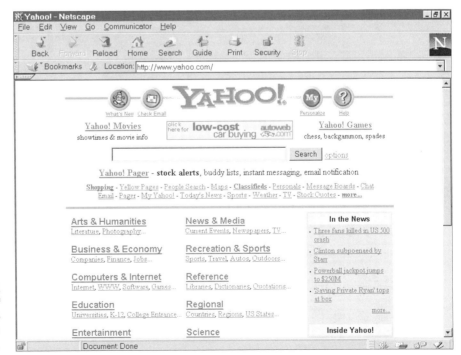

Yahoo! also makes use of a search engine. Whereas the Lycos (**www.lycos.com**) search engine lets you search the Web, the Yahoo! search engine finds pages within Yahoo!'s own Web site that contain references to the information you seek. In this way, you can find information faster, without having to spend time following links from a broad category to a narrowly focused category. Directory lists are covered extensively later in this session under the heading, "Submitting Your Web Site to the Top Guides, Lists, and Directories."

Search Engine Fundamentals

Although we've come to think of search engines as giant applications that find information, a search engine is really three different applications that work together to find and retrieve information. These are the applications:

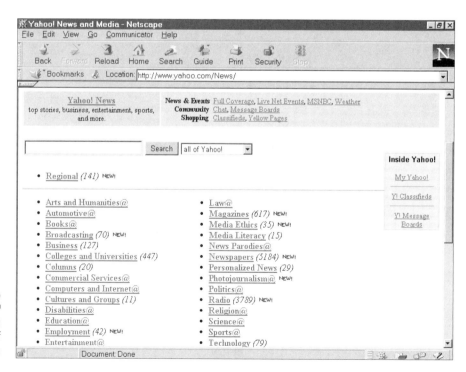

Figure 3.9

Accessing a broad category of information

- ✪ **An indexer:** The back-end application that finds and indexes pages for inclusion in a database; other names for this type of application include *spider*, *crawler*, and *robot.*

- ✪ **A database:** The application that stores the indexed references to Web pages.

- ✪ **A query interface:** The application that handles the queries submitted by users.

Search engines can't find or index your Web site without a little help, which is why people register their sites with search engines. Another way for a search engine to find your Web site is through a link to one of your pages from someone else's site. After a search engine finds your Web site, the search engine uses the links within your pages to find additional pages at your Web site. In this way, the search engine crawls through your Web site one link at a time and adds the information from your Web site into its database.

What Do Search Engines Look For?

Search engines don't store all the data in your pages. Instead, search engines create indexed references to your pages. Most of the time, such an indexed reference contains the following information:

- ✪ **Page title:** From the TITLE element of your Web page

- ✪ **Page URL:** The absolute URL to your Web page

- ✪ **Summary description:** A description taken from the page itself

- ✪ **Keyword list:** A list of keywords taken from the page itself; accompanied by a relevancy index that explains how relevant each indexed word is to other indexed words and, often, how relevant the indexed words are to the page title as well

Although most search engines create indexed references to your Web pages, just about every search engine gathers this information from different areas of your Web page. Whereas one search engine may gather the summary description for your page from the first few hundred characters,

another search engine may look for common words or phrases in the page to use in the summary description.

The various search engines use the summary information in different ways as well. Some search engines make all the information available to user queries. Other search engines store all of the information categories, yet user queries are performed only against specific categories of data, such as the page title and keyword list.

What Does the Indexed Reference Look Like for a Real Web Page?

To get a better understanding of what indexers do, I give you a look at a real Web page and point out what an indexed reference for the page looks like. Figure 3.10 shows the page in a Web browser. The source for the page is shown in Listing 3.2.

As you examine the sample Web page, note the title and the use of the <META> tag to describe the page and identify keywords. Also note that the page contains lots of text.

Listing 3.2   A Sample Web Page

```
<HTML>
<HEAD>
<TITLE>Writer's Gallery: Resources for Writers and
   Readers</TITLE>
<META NAME=description" CONTENT="Writer's Gallery is a place
   for anyone who loves the written word. You'll find links to
   hundreds of writing-related resources as well as new works
   of fiction published at our site.">
<META NAME="keywords" CONTENT="writing, reading, write, read,
   book, author, story, fiction, nonfiction, literary, mythol-
   ogy, medieval, biblical, renaissance, library, Dante,
   Dickens, Faulkner, Shakespeare, news, world news, enter-
   tainment news, business news, current events, publishing,
   dictionary, encyclopedia, bookshelf">
</HEAD>
<BODY BGCOLOR="#000080" text="#ffff00" link="#fffbf0"
vlink="#808000" alink="#ff0000">
```

```
<IMG SRC="wgttl2.jpg" ALT="Writer's Gallery" BORDER=0
  ALIGN=LEFT>
<CENTER>
<H1>A place for anyone who loves the written word!</H1>
<H3>Over 250 New Resources!</H3>
</CENTER>
<FONT SIZE=-1><P><A HREF="vpspons.html">We're looking for
  sponsors.</A>
<P>Brought to you by the Original Virtual Press — Fine Pub-
  lications, Community Service and Much More Since March,
  1994.
If you'd like more information about <A HREF="vpbg.html">The
Virtual Press</A> or would like to post information to the
Writer's Gallery:  Send e-mail to <A
  HREF="mailto:wg@tvpress.com">wg@tvpress.com</A></FONT></P>


<P><IMG SRC="bboard.gif" ALIGN="BOTTOM" ALT="* ATTN *">Put a
  bookmark here.
Come back and visit!</P>
<BR CLEAR=ALL>
<H2><A HREF="vpwfeat.html">Writer's Gallery Features</A></H2>
<P>Find hundreds of zines, thousands of books and links to
all good things related to writing!  </P>
<H2><A HREF="vpwlite.html">Writer's Gallery Literary
  Resources</A></H2>
<P>If you need a literary reference look here.  From Greek
mythology to the Renaissance.  From medieval to biblical.
From the 9th century to the 19th century.  This page covers
it all.</P>
<H2><A HREF="vpwauth.html">Writer's Gallery Great
  Authors</A></H2>
<P>If  you are looking for information on great writers from
history, look here.  You'll find information on writers from
Dante, Dickens, Faulkner, Shakespeare and more!</P>
<H2><A HREF="wcurrent.html">Writer's Gallery Guide to Current
  Events</A></H2>
<H3><A HREF="http://tvpress.comhttp://www.tvpress.com/idn/"
  TARGET="_parent">
Internet Daily News</A> ¦¦ <A HREF="wcurrent.html#usnews">US
  News</A> ¦¦
<A HREF="wcurrent.html#worldnews">World News</A> ¦¦
```

```
<A HREF="wcurrent.html#busnews">Business News</A> ¦¦
<A HREF="wcurrent.html#entnews">Entertainment News</A> ¦¦
<A HREF="wcurrent.html#finnews">Finance News</A></H3>


<H2><A HREF="vpwcomp.html">Writer's Companions</A></H2>
<P>Dictionaries, encyclopedias & more!  All the reference
 works you wish were on your bookshelf.</P>
<H2><A HREF="vpwresou.html">Writer's Resources</A></H2>
<P>A comprehensive resource list for writers!  The Writer's
 Resource includes Virtual Libraries, Meta Indexes, Web Data-
  bases and more!  Dozens of them . . . </P>
<H2><A HREF="vpnewgp.html">Newsgroups for Writers</A></H2>
<P>Looking for a great way to meet fellow writers?
Join a discussion group!</P>
<H2><A HREF="vppubl.html">Who's Who in Publishing on the
  WWW&#153;</A></H2>
<P>Find publishers on the Web</P>
<H2><A HREF="vpwart.html#art">Art</A></H2>
<P>Interested in finding art resources?  Try these
  resources.</P>
<H2><A HREF="vpwart.html#movies">Movie &amp; Industry
Information</A></H2>
<P>Movie reviews & great movie information</P>
<HR SIZE=4>


<FORM METHOD="POST" ACTION="mailto:wg@tvpress.com">
<P>Help us grow add a link to Writer's Gallery!</P>
<P><TEXTAREA NAME="writer's galery links" COLS="40" ROWS="1">
</TEXTAREA></P>
<P>Please describe the link.</P>
<P><TEXTAREA NAME="writer's galery description" COLS="40"
  ROWS="1">
</TEXTAREA></P>
<P><INPUT TYPE="SUBMIT"> <INPUT TYPE="RESET"></P>
</FORM>
<HR SIZE=4>
<P>Questions or comments pertaining to the TVP Web site can
  be directed to
<A HREF="mailto:webmaster@tvpress.com">
<IMG SRC="mail.gif" ALIGN="MIDDLE" ALT="*e-mail*">
```

```
webmaster@tvpress.com</A></P>
<P>This page, and all contents, are <A HREF="vpcopy.html">
Copyright (C) by The Virtual Press, USA.</A>
</P>
</BODY>
</HTML>
```

When different search engines index this Web page, they come up with different results. For search engine A, an indexed reference to the page could look like this:

- ✿ **Page title:** Writer's Gallery: Resources for Writers and Readers

- ✿ **Page URL: http://www.tvpress.com/vpwg.html**

- ✿ **Summary description:** A place for anyone who loves the written word! Over 250 new resources! We're looking for sponsors.

Figure 3.10

A sample Web page from the Writer's Gallery

○ **Keyword list:** Author, biblical, books, bookshelf, business news, comment, community, companion, current events, database, entertainment news, events, finance news, gallery, Greek mythology, history, index, industry, information, library, literary, medieval, movie, mythology, news, newsgroup, press, publication, question, reference, renaissance, resource, service, sponsor, virtual, word, world news, writer, writer newsgroup, writing, written word

Here, the search engine takes most of the information that it needs directly from the body of the Web page. Because of this, each word in the page is weighed for relevancy and inclusion in the keyword list. You learn more about relevancy later in this session. Also, note that the summary description for this page is truncated at a preset number of characters, which means that the last sentence isn't complete in this case.

For search engine B, an indexed reference to the page could look like this:

○ **Page title:** Writer's Gallery: Resources for Writers and Readers

○ **Page URL: http://www.tvpress.com/vpwg.html**

○ **Summary description:** Writer's Gallery is a place for anyone who loves the written word. You'll find links to hundreds of writing-related resources as well as new works of fiction published at our site.

○ **Keyword list:** Author, biblical, book, bookshelf, business news, current events, Dante, Dickens, dictionary, encyclopedia, entertainment news, Faulkner, fiction, fiction works, library, literary, medieval, mythology, news, nonfiction, publishing, read, reader, reading, renaissance, resource, Shakespeare, story, world news, write, writer, writing, written word

Here, the search engine obtains the page description from the <META> tag and then combines the keyword information provided in the <META> tag with words used in the page to come up with a keyword list. Although this technique may seem unusual, many search engines that take advantage of meta-information combine the description and keywords that you provide with information taken from the body of the page.

NOTE •
Don't worry, I cover more about the <META> tag and meta-information later in the session. Look for the heading, "Getting the Most from Keywords and Meta-Information."
• •

For search engine C, an indexed reference to the page could look like this:

- **Page title:** Writer's Gallery: Resources for Writers and Readers
- **Page URL: http://www.tvpress.com/vpwg.html**
- **Summary description:** A place for anyone who loves the written word! Over 250 new resources! We're looking for sponsors.

Here, the search engine only makes use of the page title and a summary description obtained from the first 100 characters of text found in the page. Although the streamlined entries in the database aren't desirable for the publisher, the search engine designers probably chose this format because it drastically reduces the size of the database, which in turn reduces overhead and speeds up database queries.

What Happens After Your Web Site Is Indexed?

Indexing a Web site is not a one-time deal. After the search engine initially indexes your site, your site is usually scheduled for reindexing at periodic intervals. By reindexing Web sites, search engines keep up with the ever-changing face of the Web. That said, not all search engines automatically reindex your site, and some search engines reindex your Web site so infrequently that you end up with outdated references.

Additionally, the way that a search engine reindexes your Web site may not be what you expect. Some search engines simply check to see whether the page still exists but don't update the actual reference to the Web page. Other search engines check the page header to see whether the page has changed, so if you changed text at the bottom of the page, the search engine won't reindex the page. Still other search engines use the modification date on the page to determine whether the page should be reindexed. The search engine then either reindexes the page immediately or schedules the page for reindexing at a later date.

Another problem with search engines is that pages you deleted months ago may still be listed. Although some search engines let you remove outdated references from the database, the best way to solve these and other problems that you may encounter is to periodically resubmit your Web site to the search engine. For problems related to pages that you've moved to different locations, you may also want to use placeholder documents and the redirection techniques examined in the Saturday Morning session under "Gaining Lost Readers from the Error Logs." In this way, you direct readers from the old page to the new page, and eventually the search engine picks up on this and updates the references to your Web site.

Boosting Visits with Ordinary Descriptions

To a search engine, text is the most important part of the page. Search engines use ordinary text to describe the page, to build the keyword list, and to determine the relevance of the page to particular subjects. Although search engines may treat text in different ways, they share some common themes concerning how text is indexed and referenced.

Understanding Summary Descriptions

Whenever results are displayed by a search engine, the main thing that sells your page to the reader is the summary description, which usually comes from the first 100 to 200 characters in the Web page. When you look at your Web pages to see what the description may look like, be sure to include all text in headers, paragraphs, and other text elements on the page.

Because some search engines have very specific parameters for obtaining the summary description, text at the top of the page is usually given more weight than text at the bottom of the page. Thus, if you have a short description at the top of your page followed by several graphic elements, tables, or linked lists, the search engine may not use text from the later sections of the page. By understanding this, you can see why some page descriptions are really short and others fill out the full 100 to 200 characters used by the search engine.

To help get your Web site noticed, create clear summary statements for your key Web pages, which includes the home page and top-level pages at your Web site. The summary statement should be the first text element in the page, perhaps directly following your graphical banner. If you keep the summary statement short but descriptive, it usually flows well with the rest of the page.

 TIP Whenever possible, try to end your summary statement with proper punctuation. Believe it or not, a few search engines look for complete statements. Phrases without punctuation are considered ambiguous, and phrases with punctuation are considered relevant.

Understanding Relevancy

The position of text in your Web page often determines its relevancy. Because of the variations in how search engines use text, relevancy is one of the hardest search engine terms to pin down. In general terms, the relevancy of text describes:

- How a word relates to other words
- The proximity of one word to another
- The position of the word within the page
- Whether the word is presented as part of a complete statement
- How many times the word is used in the page

The concept of relevancy explains why some of the techniques that publishers use to get their pages listed at the top of search results lists have little effect, and also explains why a technique may work for one search engine and not for others. In the end, the varying definition of relevancy makes optimizing your Web pages for each and every search engine almost impossible. In fact, you'd probably be wasting your time if you tried to optimize your Web pages for all the search engines.

Have you ever come across a Web page that repeated a word over and over again? Well, the publisher was probably trying to get the page listed as the top choice when a user searched using this keyword. Although this technique may have worked for a particular search engine, most other search engines would have completely ignored the repeated use of the word, which caused the page to appear lower in their search results lists.

Have you ever come across a Web page that used phrases that didn't seem to fit in the Web page, yet there the phrases were just the same? Here, the publisher was probably trying to get the page to show up when someone searched for a hot topic, such as news, entertainment, or sports. Again, this technique may have worked for a particular search engine, but other search engines would have given the entire page lower relevancy because it was full of ambiguous phrases and didn't seem to have a common thread.

Rather than haphazardly repeat keywords or use ambiguous phrases in your Web page, use sound organizational techniques that bolster the relevancy of your page's theme. Focus your attention on your home page as well as your top-level pages first. When you look at your home page or top-level page, ask yourself these questions:

- ✪ Is the subject of the page clear?

- ✪ Can I weave the main subject(s) of the page throughout the main text in such a way that it builds relevancy?

- ✪ Does the page build the relationship between the main subject and related topics?

- ✪ Can I add descriptions to lists of links to clearly define what the link points to?

- ✪ Are the statements made in the page clear and complete?

- ✪ Can I transform ambiguous phrases into clear statements that relate to the main theme of the page?

Using Page Titles to Your Advantage

A good page title will bring visitors to your Web site. Most search engines display Web pages according to their titles, making the page title one of the most important elements for bringing visitors to your Web site. Additionally, your browser displays the title prominently at the top of its window, and when you bookmark a page, the title is used to differentiate the page from other pages that you've marked.

Beyond its job of grabbing the reader's attention, the title also plays an important role in determining the relevancy of the Web page to the reader's search parameters. Specifically, the keywords in the title often receive greater emphasis than other keywords on the page.

The best titles describe the subject of the page in a clear and meaningful way. Instead of a title that says, "Welcome to my home page," use a title that says "Bill's Home Page: Find Sports Memorabilia, Sports Records, & Player Stats." In this way, search engines that use the page title to determine relevance will have a clear understanding of the page's subject and the most important keywords.

Getting Your Frame-Enhanced or Graphics-Intensive Page Noticed

Pages with frames, scripts, and lots of graphics present special problems to publishers and search engines. With frame-enhanced pages, the main document usually contains only references to the files that a browser loads into each frame. With scripts, the code is in the place of the all-important text at the top of the page. With graphics-intensive pages, the text on the page is limited.

Although some search engines are smart enough to understand and properly handle frame-enhanced pages, scripts, and graphics-intensive pages, such search engines are more the exception than the rule. Fortunately, you can get your page noticed without eliminating frames, scripts, or your wonderful graphics. You use meta-information to do this. The next section provides more details on the <META> tag.

Getting the Most from Keywords and Meta-Information

Meta-information is data that is included in a Web page header but is hidden from the reader. Usually, meta-information contains instructions or special notes for Web clients, such as your browser or the indexer used by a search engine. To provide meta-information to a Web client, you use the <META> tag. The information that you can provide to search engines with the <META> tag includes a very specific description of the page as well as additional keywords for the page.

Working with Meta-Information

Before you add meta-information to your Web pages, you should know that not all search engines make use of the <META> tag. A search engine that doesn't use the meta-information simply ignores the information. Additionally, most of the search engines that use meta-information still index the entire contents of your Web page. Thus, you use the <META> tag to give search engines additional information, not to replace the information that they've already gathered from the Web page.

You use the following two main attributes when you use the <META> tag:

- ❂ NAME: Used to describe the type of meta-information that you are providing, such as NAME="description" or NAME="keywords"

- ❂ CONTENT: Used to supply the actual meta-information, such as the description of your Web page or a list of keywords for the Web page

You can add a description to your page using meta-information as follows:

```
<META NAME="description" CONTENT="Writer's Gallery is a place
  for anyone
who loves the written word. You'll find links to hundreds of
writing-related resources as well as new works of fiction
published at our site.">
```

You can add a keyword list to your page using meta-information as follows:

```
<META NAME="keywords" CONTENT="writing, reading, write, read,
book, author, story, fiction, nonfiction, literary,
mythology, medieval, biblical, renaissance, library, Dante,
Dickens, Faulkner, Shakespeare, news, world news,
entertainment news, business news, current events,
publishing, dictionary, encyclopedia, bookshelf">
```

In a Web page, the meta-information is always added to the page header inside the <HEAD> and </HEAD> tags, as in this example:

```
<HTML>
<HEAD>

<TITLE>Writer's Gallery: Resources for Writers and
   Readers</TITLE>

<META NAME="description" CONTENT="Writer's Gallery is a place
for anyone who loves the written word. You'll find links to
hundreds of writing-related resources as well as new works of
fiction published at our site.">

<META NAME="keywords" CONTENT="writing, reading, write, read,
book, author, story, fiction, nonfiction, literary,
mythology, medieval, biblical, renaissance, library, Dante,
Dickens, Faulkner, Shakespeare, news, world news,
entertainment news, business news, current events,
publishing, dictionary, encyclopedia, bookshelf">

</HEAD>
<BODY>
 . . .
</BODY>
</HTML>
```

Using Meta-Information in Your Web Page

The description of your page in the <META> tag is every bit as important as the summary description in the main text of the page. The advantage to describing a page in the <META> tag is that you provide the exact description that you want to use, rather than have the search engine

extrapolate the description from the main text of the page. A good <META> tag description summarizes the main selling points of the page in 200 characters or less. Because some search engines use page descriptions that are fewer than 200 characters, try to put the most relevant information first.

When it comes to finding your Web page in a search engine, a <META> tag keyword list gives your Web page a definite edge over a page that doesn't use meta-information. The main thing to remember is that the <META> tag keyword list is normally used in addition to the keywords that the search engine gathers from the main text of the page. Thus, rather than simply repeating keywords that appear in the main text, you may want to concentrate on related topics or variations of the primary keywords. For example, if the keyword is *writer*, you can use variations such as *write*, *writing*, and *written*.

You can also create various combinations of keywords or phrases in the keyword list. When I say various combinations, I don't mean that you should repeat the keyword several times. Instead, create word combinations, such as business news, entertainment news, and sports news. Keep in mind that some search engines penalize you for repeating specific keywords too many times. In fact, the search engine may disregard the keyword list entirely if you repeat keywords too many times, as in the following:

```
<META NAME="keywords" CONTENT="news, news, news, news, news,
    news, news, news, news, news,
business, business, business, business, business, business,
business, entertainment, entertainment, entertainment,
entertainment, entertainment, entertainment, sports, sports,
sports, sports, sports, sports, sports">
```

The following example instead uses word combinations and variations of the topic for the keyword list:

```
<META NAME="keywords" CONTENT="news, business, entertainment,
    sports, current events, business news, entertainment news,
    sports news">
```

Just as the length of your description is important, the length of your keyword list is important as well. Generally speaking, limit the keyword list to fewer than 1,000 characters. Further, try to restrict the number of times that you repeat any word in the keyword list. A good rule of thumb is to use a keyword or a word combination that uses the keyword no more than seven times. In the previous example, the keyword news was repeated four times.

After you update your home page and top-level pages with meta-information, consider adding meta-information to the rest of your Web pages. Although this may be a mammoth undertaking, the payoff makes the time investment worthwhile. I recommend tailoring the meta-information to the individual page rather than the site as a whole.

A Last Look at Search Engine Fundamentals

As you have seen, you can do many things to improve the odds of someone finding your Web page through a search engine. The idea here is not to trick the search engine into displaying references to your pages. Instead, you are structuring your pages so that search engines can clearly identify the subjects that your pages cover and index the appropriate keywords for those subjects. You are also using techniques that make identifying the subjects your pages cover easier for your readers. Figure 3.11 shows the main design concepts to follow when you optimize your Web pages for search engines.

If you haven't done so already, create descriptive blurbs for your Web site. Start by identifying the most popular areas at your Web site, and then use the subjects that these areas cover to come up with a brief description that identifies your site's niche. Next, create separate descriptions for each popular area at your Web site. When you finish this, take a few minutes to apply the concepts discussed in the search engine fundamentals section to your home page and other top-level pages at your Web site. This will prepare you for registering with search engines of all types.

Take a Break

You've already accomplished a lot today. Stretch. Relax for a moment. Go get a cup of coffee or tea. Then take a virtual stroll over to WebTutor (**http://www.web-tutor.com/**). You'll get to see where I hang out on the Web and with any luck, I'll finally have given the site a much-needed update.

Registering with the Top Search Engines on the Planet

Now that you've optimized your Web pages for indexing, you are ready to submit your Web pages to search engines. Although hundreds of search engines are out there, trying to submit your Web site to every single one of them is not practical or worthwhile. Instead, you should start by registering your site with the major search engines. Because the search engines covered in this part index tens of millions of Web pages, they are the ones used most often to search the Web, and you can make the most of your time and resources by focusing your efforts on these search engines.

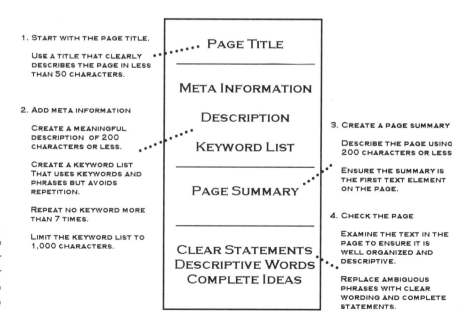

Figure 3.11

Optimizing your Web page for search engines: step by step

To find the top search engines on the planet, I visited, compared, and tested more than 500 different ones. I came up with a list of the best search engines available on the Web, and you will find them featured in this and other sessions in this book. The idea was to do the hours of legwork for you so that you could get the most out of your promotion efforts with the least amount of work.

Submitting Your Site to a Search Engine

When you register with a search engine, you let the search engine know that your Web site exists. Many search engines take a preliminary look at your site immediately after you submit your site and, in doing so, verify that the address you provided is valid. Afterward, the search engine schedules your site for indexing.

Although several days may pass before the indexing begins, the actual time that you have to wait to get into the database depends on the backlog of new sites waiting to be entered into the database and the efficiency of the indexer. Some search engines may index your Web site within hours. Other search engines may not index your Web site for weeks.

How Does Indexing Work?

Most search engines use the URL that you submit to find other pages at your Web site. Give the search engine the URL to your home page in this form:

```
http://www.your_isp.com/~you/
```

The indexer uses this page as a launching pad to all the other pages at your Web site. Generally, the indexer creates an indexed reference to the current page and then searches all the links on the page one by one. If the first link that the indexer finds is to a page called background.html, the indexer accesses the background.html page, creates an indexed reference, and then searches all the links on this page one by one. Eventually, the indexer crawls through every page at your Web site.

TIP ■■■
If an area of your Web site is not linked from a main page that the indexer can find, that area will not be indexed. The solution is to add a link on a top-level page that the indexer can find, or to register the area separately.
■■

How Can You Exclude Directories and Pages?

Although indexing your site is a good thing, sometimes you might not want the search engine to index your entire site. You can control what pages are indexed and what pages aren't by using a robot exclusion file. The exclusion file is a plain-text file placed in the top-level directory for your Web server. In the exclusion file, you specify the directories or pages that search engines are not allowed to index. The name of the exclusion file must be robots.txt.

Because you will generally want the exclusions to apply to all search engines, the first line of the file should read as follows:

```
User-agent: *
```

Here, user-agent refers to the search engine accessing the file and * is a commonly-used symbol that means all. After you specify the search engines to make the exclusions, you specify the directories or pages to exclude. You can exclude an entire directory as follows:

```
Disallow: /cgi-bin/
```

or

```
Disallow: /images/
```

You can exclude a single page as follows:

```
Disallow: /prg/webstat.html
```

You can put all these entries in an exclusion file as follows:

```
User-agent: *
Disallow: /cgi-bin/
Disallow: /images/
Disallow: /prg/webstat.html
```

TIP If you publish a large Web site or publish your Web site as part of a larger domain, you should strongly consider using an exclusion list. With so many Web pages, search engines are finding it harder and harder to index everything at a Web site. For this reason, some search engines index only 500—750 pages per domain.

How Often Is Your Site Reindexed?

Indexing your Web site is not a one-time deal. Most search engines periodically reindex your pages. By reindexing your pages, the search engine verifies that the pages still exist and can update the indexed reference to your page if necessary.

In an ideal world, search engines would rapidly remove references to pages that no longer exist and just as rapidly create references to new areas that you build. In reality, search engines do not remove pages or find new areas as quickly as we would like.

The reason search engines don't immediately remove pages that can't be found is that the dreaded 404 -File Not Found error occurs all too often. Whenever your site is busy, down, or can't respond to a request, the search engine simply marks the page and moves on. If the server can't find the page on several occasions, the page is removed from the database.

Search engines don't add new areas as fast as one would like because they often don't reindex the entire site and all its contents. Instead, the search engine may check only for changes by comparing page headers or modification dates. The result is that the search engine may need several visits to find and index a new area of your Web site.

Why Won't This Search Engine List Your Site?

Sometimes you register with a search engine only to find, days or weeks later, that you can't locate the site anywhere in the search engine's database. A search engine may not list your site for several reasons, but the main reason is usually that the URL you provided couldn't be read or

used. To avoid this problem, ensure that you type the complete URL to your Web site. Because URLs can be case-sensitive (depending on the Web server), ensure that your URL uses the proper case. For example, the URLs **http://www.tvpress.com/HOME.htm** and **http://www.tvpress.com /home.htm** refer to different documents.

You should also watch the syntax of the URL. Some search engines will not use an URL that includes reserved characters, such as:

= The equal sign

$ The dollar sign

? The question mark

Another reason for a search engine not indexing your site is that you use frames and the search engine doesn't know how to deal with them. To ensure that the search engine can find your page links, add a <NOFRAME> area to the page that contains the main text and links (see Listing 3.3). The <NOFRAME> tag allows browsers and search engines that can't understand frames to display other text so the page doesn't become a dead end.

Listing 3.3   Using a <NOFRAME> Area in a Web Page

```
<HTML>
<HEAD>
<TITLE>Las Vegas Virtual Tour Guide</TITLE>
<HEAD>

<FRAMESET ROWS="25%,*" BORDER=0>
    <FRAME SRC="side.htm" NORESIZE>
    <FRAME SRC="main.htm" NORESIZE>
</FRAMESET>

<NOFRAMES>
    <BODY>
    Add text and links here for version of Web page without
    frames.
    </BODY>
</NOFRAMES>
</HTML>
```

Scripts and graphics-only pages can also present problems to search engines. To ensure that your page has a description and keywords, use the techniques discussed previously this afternoon under "Capitalizing on Search Engine Fundamentals."

Additionally, if you don't have your own domain, a robots.txt file may be the cause of your problems. As discussed previously, the robots.txt file can be used to keep search engines out of specific directories. To check the contents of the robots.txt file for your domain, use this URL:

```
http://www.your_domain.com/robots.txt
```

in which *your_domain* is your actual domain. If the robots.txt file excludes your directory or all public directories on the server, you've found the cause of the problem. If you find that your files are excluded in the robots.txt file, definitely ask the server administrator whether this can be changed.

Search Engines: Tricks to Improve Your Standings

Earlier I talked about the proven techniques for improving your standings in the search engines. Now, I'll focus on unconventional promotion tricks for search engines. These tricks are designed to fool search engines into giving your Web site a better standing. You should only use these tricks if you want to take your Web site promotion to the extreme.

However, before you use these tricks, you have to weigh the benefits against the risks. Search engine developers consider these tricks to be a form of spam, and when you use spam, you have to expect a penalty. The penalty here is often delisting from a search engine. Thus, you'll need to experiment with these tricks to see how various search engines handle them. If you are delisted from a search engine that you consider important to your Web site's success, you'll have to remove the offending trick from your pages and resubmit your site.

Title Tricks

Page titles are a very important means of improving your standings with search engines. When you want to get more oomph out of your titles, you

can do several things. First, try a technique called keyword loading. Here, you add important keywords to the title to give them more relevance, such as:

```
<TITLE>Daily News: entertainment news, business news, current
    events</TITLE>
<TITLE>Sports Connection: baseball, football, basketball,
    hockey</TITLE>
<TITLE>Book Nook: rare book, collector book, first print
    book</TITLE>
```

While it may be tempting to use lots of keywords in the title, stick with the top 10 or so. This will give the keywords greater importance. You could also omit the page title entirely and only include keywords:

```
<TITLE>Entertainment news, business news, current
    events</TITLE>
<TITLE>Baseball, football, basketball, hockey</TITLE>
<TITLE>Rare book, collector book, first print book</TITLE>
```

Although more than one <TITLE> tag isn't proper HTML, you can repeat the page title to give your site better standings on some search engines. When you repeat a page title, you take a standard title (without keyword loading) and copy it several times. Thus rather than using:

```
<HEAD>
<TITLE>Daily News: Your news source</TITLE>
</HEAD>
```

You use:
```
<HEAD>
<TITLE>Daily News: Your news source</TITLE>
<TITLE>Daily News: Your news source</TITLE>
<TITLE>Daily News: Your news source</TITLE>
</HEAD>
```

If you use this trick, don't worry about confusing the user's browser. Browsers only display the first title in a Web page and ignore the additional titles.

Hidden Text and Fields

Earlier, I talked about adding descriptive summaries to your pages as a way of improving your standings. While this works in many cases, some-

times you don't want a summary paragraph in the midst of your polished page and may need to hide this text from readers. Other times, you want to load up the page with additional descriptions or keywords that are all hidden from readers.

One way to hide text from readers is to add descriptions or keywords that use the same color as the background for the page. For example, if the background color is black, you could add hidden text by setting the font color to black. Because you want these extras to have a small footprint on the page, you should also set the font size to 1:

```
<FONT COLOR="#000000" SIZE="1"> Writer's Gallery is a place
  for
anyone who loves the written word. You'll find links to hun-
  dreds
of writing-related resources as well as new works of fiction
published at our site.</FONT>
```

TIP

To avoid the watchful eye of search engines, you may need to use a color that is close to the background color but doesn't match it exactly because search engines look for these types of tricks and will delist you if you use the same color for both the font and background. Delisting means that none of your Web pages will be available in the search engine. Another technique to avoid a penalty is to use a background image with colors that your hidden text can blend into.

HTML comments also let you hide text from readers. With HTML comments, you place text on the page that the search engine can see but your readers can't:

```
<!— Entertainment news, business news, current events —>
<!— Rare book, collector book, first print book —>
```

Some search engines also read values associated with input fields. This allows you to use hidden input fields to boost your standings. Here, you use the input type HIDDEN and add a VALUE attribute that contains your descriptive text or keywords:

```
<INPUT TYPE="HIDDEN" VALUE="baseball, football, basketball,
  hockey">
```

Multiple Versions of Your Pages

Mirror sites have long been used to provide additional ways to access popular Net resources. What many promoters discovered is that if they mirrored individual Web pages, they could drive additional traffic to their Web site. When you mirror a page, you create copies of a page.

To give mirrored pages greater importance, keep the pages short and stick with text descriptions and keywords. You should use different descriptions and keywords to tailor the pages to specific audiences and search engines, and then save the pages with unique names. Usually, you will name the pages sequentially, such as index1.htm, index2.htm, index3.htm, and so on. When you are finished, register each individual page.

Remember the idea isn't to dazzle readers with these mirror pages, but rather to get the readers to your door. Once at your door, readers will need a way to get to the rest of your Web site. You can do this by placing a link to your main page or by using a <META> tag that automatically redirects the reader to your main page. (Redirecting readers to a new page is discussed in the Saturday Morning session titled "Redirecting Lost Readers.")

Increasing Your Web Traffic with the Top Search Engines

Registering with the major search engines is the best way to increase traffic to your Web site. If you've followed the techniques for optimizing your Web site for search engines as discussed previously under "Capitalizing on Search Engine Fundamentals," you should see marked improvements in your Web traffic simply by registering with the search engines listed in this section. Don't expect a great flood of traffic the day after you register your Web site, however; rather, you should see a steady increase in the level of traffic that your Web site receives over time. The actual level of traffic increase that you see will depend on the subject of your site, the size and quality of your Web site, and your use of search engine optimization techniques.

Although you could use the techniques that I discuss here to register with hundreds of other search engines, the reward for all your hard work usually isn't worth the effort. Millions of people use the major search engines to find what they need. Every day, these search engines collectively handle about 90 percent of the searches performed by general search engines. Obviously, this means that the hundreds of other general search engines handle only about 10 percent of the search transactions. Do you really want to spend countless hours registering with hundreds of other search engines when you can potentially reach the vast majority of users simply by registering with the most-used search engines? Probably not.

When you register with a search engine, you generally provide the URL to your top-level page. The search engine uses this single URL to find all the other resources at your site. Because of this, you should register the URLs to the top-level pages that cannot be reached from your home page as well.

The registration section is designed as a quick reference resource that you can use time and again. The idea is to provide only the information you need. With this in mind, you'll find the sections are organized alphabetically based on the name of the search engine. You'll also find the URL to the main page and the relevant registration page (if available). If you find that the URL for the registration page is no longer valid, go to the main page and follow the submission link to the appropriate page. Usually, the submission link is labeled Add URL, Add a Page, or something similar. To make the task of registering your Web site even easier, you may want to visit the search engine area at the companion Web site. Use this URL:

`http://www.tvpress.com/promote/search.htm`

NOTE Keep in mind that these are general search engines, not specialized or category-specific search engines. In upcoming sections, I show you how to increase your traffic using other types of search engines. Note also that there are many popular alternatives to search engines, such as directories and guides, which I discuss later in the book as well.

Figure 3.12

With millions of accesses every day and millions of indexed pages, AltaVista is one of the busiest and largest search engines on the Web.

AltaVista

Main Page (see Figure 3.12): http://www.altavista.digital.com/
Submission Page: http://www.altavista.digital.com/av/content/addurl.htm
Instructions: Submit your top-level URL to the submission page.

Anzwers

Main Page (see Figure 3.13): http://www.anzwers.com/
Submission Page: http://www.anzwers.com/addurl.html
Instructions: Submit your top-level URL and your e-mail address to the submission page.

Excite

Main Page (see Figure 3.14): http://www.excite.com/
Submission Page: http://www.excite.com/Info/add_url.html
Instructions: Submit top-level URL and your e-mail address to the submission page.

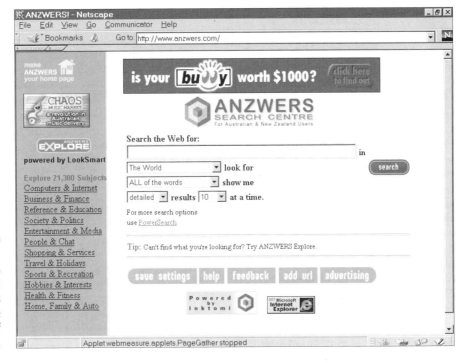

Figure 3.13

Anzwers is a search engine for users from Australia and New Zealand. This up and coming site has a lot of potential.

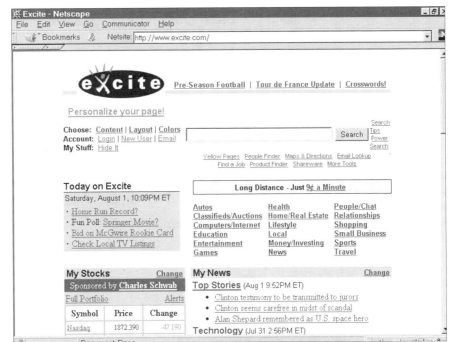

Figure 3.14

Excite maintains a huge database of well over 60 million Web pages, making this search engine one of the largest on the Web.

HotBot

Main Page (see Figure 3.15): http://www.hotbot.com/
Submission Page: http://www.hotbot.com/addurl.asp
Instructions: Submit top-level URL and your e-mail address to the submission page.

Infomak

Main Page (see Figure 3.16): http://www.infomak.com/
Submission Page: http://www.infomak.com/add_url.sh
Instructions: Submit your top-level URL to the submission page.

InfoSeek

Main Page (see Figure 3.17): http://www.infoseek.com/
Submission Page: http://www.infoseek.com/AddUrl?pg=DCaddurl.html
Instructions: Infoseek only indexes the pages that you submit directly. Enter individual URLs and submit them one at a time. If you have more than 50 pages to submit, submit them by e-mail to www-request@infoseek.com. Each page that you submit must be listed on a separate line.

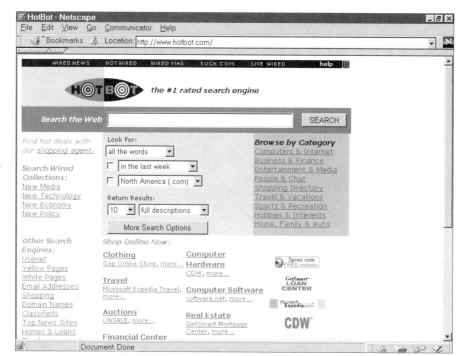

Figure 3.15

HotBot stormed onto the scene in 1996, sporting millions of pages in its database. Driven by its strong relationship with Wired magazine, HotBot quickly became one of the most popular search engines on the Web.

Figure 3.16

Infomak features a sleek design and solid search features, making this one of the up-and-coming search engines you'll want your Web site to be in.

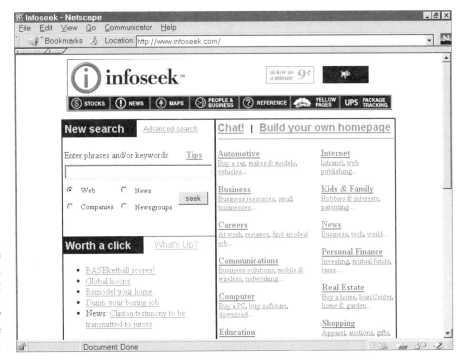

Figure 3.17

Infoseek maintains one of the largest search engines and combines this nicely with an extensive Web directory.

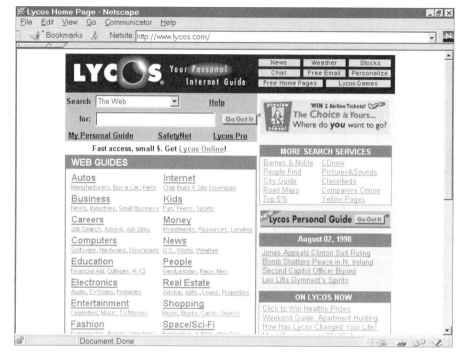

Figure 3.18

Lycos has one of the best-known search engines on the Web. Like many other search engine sites, Lycos maintains both directory listings and guides to the Web.

Lycos

Main Page (see Figure 3.18): http://www.lycos.com/
Submission Page: http://www.lycos.com/addasite.html
Instructions: Submit top-level URL and your e-mail address to the submission page.

NetFind

Main Page (see Figure 3.19): http://www.aol.com/netfind/
Submission Page: http://www.aol.com/netfind/info/addyoursite.html
Instructions: Submit top-level URL and your e-mail address to the submission page.

Northern Light

Main Page (see Figure 3.20): http://www.northernlight.com/
Submission Page: http://www.northernlight.com/docs/register.htm
Instructions: Submit top-level URL, your name, and your e-mail address to the submission page.

Figure 3.19

NetFind is a search engine from America Online. The site is powered by Excite and is definitely a search engine to keep on your radar scope because so many AOL subscribers use it.

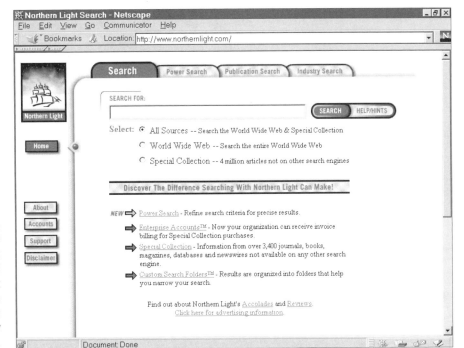

Figure 3.20

Northern Light combines Web and electronic document search in a single resource, making it a site you definitely want to be listed at.

Planet Search

Main Page (see Figure 3.21): http://www.planetsearch.com/
Submission Page: http://www.planetsearch.com/?a=19&flags=7&count=10
Instructions: Submit your top-level URL to the submission page.

PowerCrawler

Main Page (see Figure 3.22): http://www.powercrawler.com/
Submission Page: http://www.powercrawler.com/add.htm
Instructions: Submit your top-level URL to the submission page.

WebCrawler

Main Page (see Figure 3.23): http://www.webcrawler.com/
Submission Page: http://www.webcrawler.com/Help/GetListed/AddURLS.html
Instructions: WebCrawler indexes only the pages that you submit. You must submit each page separately. WebCrawler asks that you not submit more than 25 pages for a single Web site.

Figure 3.21

Planet Search is another up-and-coming search engine to keep an eye on. This search engine lets users search the Web and many other information resources.

Figure 3.22

PowerCrawler is a small but growing search engine with potential. Register here to reach a growing network of subscribers.

Figure 3.23

WebCrawler features an extensive search engine, Web site reviews, and the WebCrawler 100. Don't forget to submit individual URLs.

Figure 3.24

What-U-Seek is a
growing search
engine that you'll
want to be listed in.

What-U-Seek

Main Page (see Figure 3.24): http://www.whatuseek.com/
Submission Page: http://www.whatuseek.com/addurl.htm
Instructions: Submit top-level URL and your e-mail address to the submission page.

Submitting Your Web Site to the Top Guides, Lists, and Directories

The phenomenal popularity of resource directories such as Yahoo! ushered in a whole new era of guides, lists, and directories designed to help people find things on the Web. Whereas the focus of Web guides is usually on the top or best sites, lists and directories focus on categorizing information found on the Web.

Just as hundreds of search engines are available, you can find hundreds of guides, lists, and directories to the Web as well. Unfortunately, trying to

submit your site to every guide, list, and directory is a waste of your time and resources. Instead, you should focus on the top resources that you find in this section.

To come up with the list of Web sites featured in this and other parts of the book, I visited, compared, and tested thousands of Web sites—more than 5,000 of them, as a matter of fact. Searching, categorizing, and comparing all these Web sites to produce a list of the ones that would truly help increase your Web traffic took weeks. Fortunately, you don't have to scour the Web; you just need to work your way through this book.

Submitting Your Site to Lists and Directories

Guides, lists, and directories are all terms used to describe Web resources that provide links to Web pages. Web guides usually provide pointers to the best or top sites. Think of a guide as something that you might buy at the bookstore to help you learn about a country you are visiting. Lists are exactly what the name implies: lists of Web sites that are usually organized into several major categories. Think of a list as something that you might put together before you go grocery shopping. Beyond lists, you will find directories, which usually have rather extensive listings of Web sites divided into many categories. When you think of a directory, think of the Yellow Pages directory, that huge yellow tome that lists tons of businesses.

Although size is usually the major factor that distinguishes a list from a directory, don't get hung up on the terminology. Generally speaking, lists and directories serve the same purpose, and for this reason, I don't dwell on the difference between a list and directory. More often than not, I simply use the word directory when I am talking about both lists and directories.

Web site listings in guides and directories are very different from the results returned by a typical search engine. Guides and directories do not index your Web pages at all. They simply use the information that you provide to create a listing for your Web site.

When you submit your Web site to a list or directory, you submit the URL for your home page or other top-level page at your site. Along with

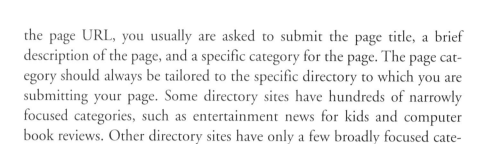

the page URL, you usually are asked to submit the page title, a brief description of the page, and a specific category for the page. The page category should always be tailored to the specific directory to which you are submitting your page. Some directory sites have hundreds of narrowly focused categories, such as entertainment news for kids and computer book reviews. Other directory sites have only a few broadly focused categories, such as entertainment and travel.

Most directory sites screen all new submissions rigorously. If the same page has been submitted previously, the site usually disregards the submission. If the page is submitted to the wrong category, the site may disregard the submission for that reason also.

Rather than place your listing in a category that you think is popular, you should place your listing in a category that strongly relates to the topic your site covers. Placing your site in a category that fits your content ensures that readers who are looking for a site like yours will be able to find it.

Trying to submit the same page to multiple categories will usually get you in trouble. Rather than submit the same page to multiple categories, examine the type of content that you publish to see whether different areas of your site fall into different categories. You could, for example, list your home page in one category, your writing area in another category, and your job center in yet another category. Whenever possible, I recommend that you list each of the major areas at your Web site separately in directories, which gives your Web site a better chance of getting noticed. And the more your Web site gets noticed, the more your Web traffic will increase.

Submitting Your Site to Web Guides

The focus on the top or best sites puts Web guides in a league of their own. When you submit your site to a guide, you are betting that the guide's reviewers will find your site useful, informative, or well presented. If the guide's reviewers count your site among the best, they will write a review of your site, and your site will show up in their database of the Web's top sites. If the guide's reviewers don't like your site for

whatever reason, they will move on to the next site in their long list of sites to review.

A typical review rates a Web site in several categories. The Lycos Top 5% Guide rates sites in presentation, content, and the overall experience of visiting the site. NetGuide rates sites in content, design, and personality. These scores are the site's rating. Contrary to what you might think, the Web sites with the fancy graphics and multimedia don't always have the best ratings. In fact, some of the most highly rated Web sites have mostly text.

You can improve your odds of getting your site reviewed by taking the time to learn what the guide looks for and what the guide's reviews look like. When you have gained a clear understanding of how the guide works, submit your site with descriptive information that will catch the eye of the reviewers. Along with the summary information, you may want to include a rating for your Web site. If this rating is realistic, you may give the reviewers a reason to visit your Web site.

Another way to improve your odds with Web guides is to focus on the top-level areas of your Web site. My primary Web site publishes two key resources: Writers Gallery and Internet Job Center. When I submit my site to a guide for review, I submit entries for both of these areas rather than the Web site as a whole. The reason for this is that these areas have very different focuses and can't be realistically rated in the same review.

As a final note, remember that reviewers are real people. With thousands of Web sites to review, several weeks or even a month could elapse before a reviewer gets a chance to look at your Web site. If reviewers don't review your site, there isn't much point in inundating them with e-mail or repeated submissions. Instead, wait a few months and then try again.

How Do People Find Your Listing in the Guide or Directory?

Most guides and directories can be searched in two ways:

- By category
- By keyword

When you search by category, you follow links from a broad category to a progressively more focused category. In a category search, the categories themselves are the main elements driving users to your listing. Yet when users finally get to the detailed page that shows your listing, it is the page title and summary description that will influence their decision to visit your Web site.

A keyword search in a guide or directory is handled in a very different manner. Rather than follow links, you use a search interface to find categories and listings within the guide. If the keywords that you enter lead to several different categories, you see category headers. If the keywords that you enter lead to a specific listing, you see either the listing itself or the page of which the listing is a part. The main elements driving a keyword search within a Web guide or directory are the category headers and page titles, which are usually the only elements that are indexed.

How Often Is Your Site's Listing Updated?

Unlike search engines that periodically schedule your site for reindexing, most guides and directories rarely update their listings. The problem with updating listings is a logistical one. To update a listing in a Web guide, a reviewer needs to take another look at the Web site. To update a listing in a directory, the directory site needs to have someone check the validity of the link and the description. Both actions require time and resources that could be directed at new listings.

Don't rely on someone from the guide or directory site to update your listing in six months or a year; take a proactive stance instead. If you move the furniture around a bit or add a new addition to your Web home, let the folks who run the guide or directory site know. Generally, you will want to send a message to the folks who maintain the directory or guide. The key things to tell them are what the old information looked like and what the new information should look like.

TIP Definitely limit the number of updates that you send to the maintainers of the guide or directory. Here, an annual or semiannual update message may be just what the doctor ordered.

Increasing Your Web Traffic with Guides and Directories

Getting your Web site listed in a popular guide or directory will definitely increase the traffic to your Web site. As with search engines, you will find that you get the most out of your time investment when you submit your site to the top guides and directories, which is why this part of this section focuses on the best guides and directories.

Although you know that a Web page or area within your Web site will be listed in the directory, there is no assurance that you will get listed in a Web guide. Still, I firmly believe that submitting your site to the guides listed in this section is worthwhile, especially when you consider that getting your site listed in any one of these guides will bring thousands of visitors to your Web site every single day. For many Web sites, an extra thousand visitors a day would effectively double or triple the site's traffic. Doubling or tripling your Web traffic from a single listing may seem like a pipe dream, but the reality is that people often seek out the best that the Web has to offer. After all, do you settle for bronze, when silver, gold, and platinum are waiting in the wings?

As you read this section, you should submit your Web site to the featured guides and directories. As discussed earlier, directories often ask for detailed information, which can include: page URL, page title, keywords, description, contact information, and categories/topics. Before you submit your listing, you should have this information plotted out. To make the task of registering your Web site easier, you may want to visit the Web guides and directories section at **www.tvpress.com/promote/guide.htm.**

Alcanseek

Main Page (see Figure 3.25): www.alcanseek.com/
Submission Page: www.alcanseek.com/add.shtml

Can Links

Main Page (see Figure 3.26): www.canlinks.net/
Submission Page: www.canlinks.net/addalink/

CANDirectory

Main Page (see Figure 3.27): www.candirectory.com/
Submission Page: www.candirectory.com/add.htm

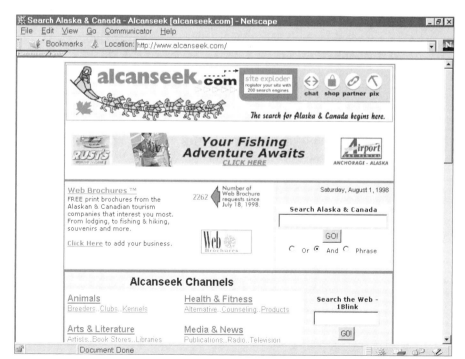

Figure 3.25

Alcanseek is a Web
directory for Alaska
and Canada.

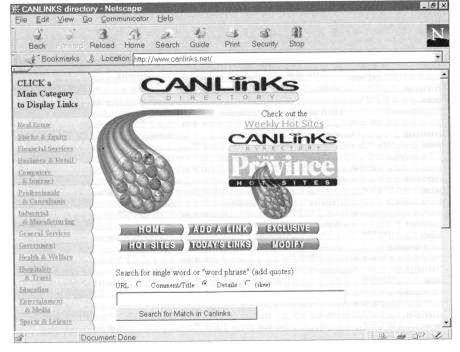

Figure 3.26

Can Links is a Web directory for Canada.

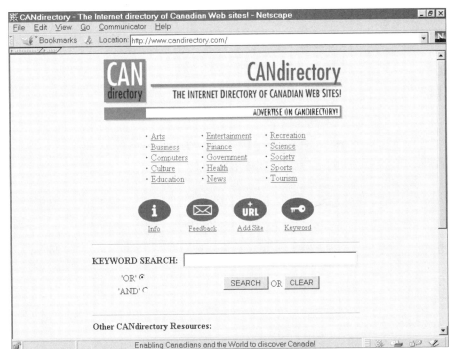

Figure 3.27

CANDirectory features Web sites from Canada.

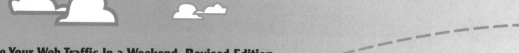

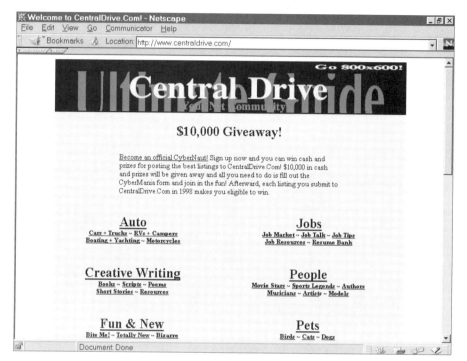

Figure 3.28

CentralDrive is a growing online community that features topic-specific Web directories.

CentralDrive

Main Page (see Figure 3.28): www.centraldrive.com/
Submission Page: Visit a specific topic area and follow the submission links.

EuroSeek

Main Page (see Figure 3.29): www.euroseek.net/
Submission Page: addsite.euroseek.net/

Galaxy

Main Page (see Figure 3.30): galaxy.einet.net/
Submission Page: galaxy.einet.net/cgi-bin/annotate?/galaxy

Figure 3.29

EuroSeek is one of the most popular Web directories in Europe.

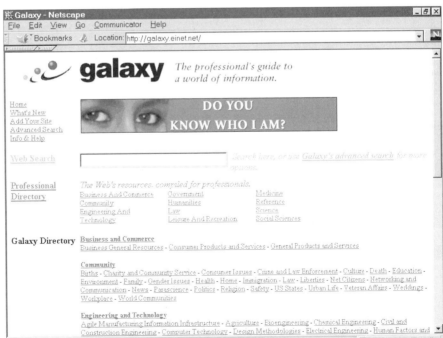

Figure 3.30

As one of the oldest Web directories, Galaxy has a lot to offer, and although it may take a while to get listed, it's worth the wait.

InfoHiway

Main Page (see Figure 3.31): www.infohiway.com/
Submission Page: www.infohiway.com/isn/addurl.shtml

InfoSpace

Main Page (see Figure 3.32): www.infospace.com/
Submission Page: www.infospace.com/submit.htm

Jayde Online Directory

Main Page (see Figure 3.33): www.jayde.com/
Submission Page: www.jayde.com/submit.html

Figure 3.31

In addition to a Web
directory, InfoHiway
provides value-
added services, such
as a shopping
agent, that can
bring in visitors,
making it an
important site to
get listed at.

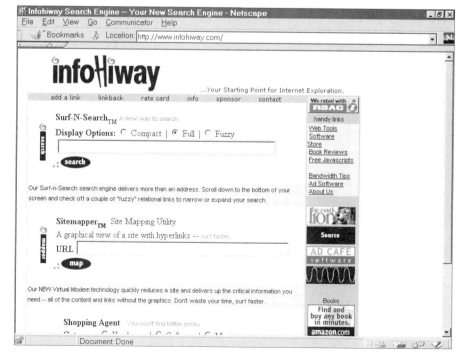

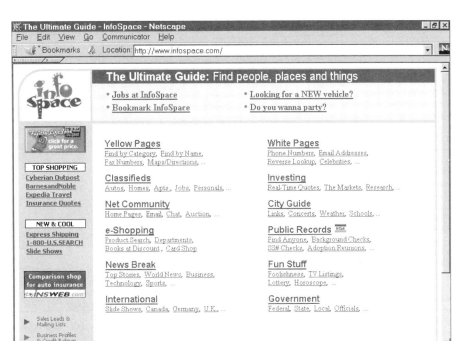

Figure 3.32

InfoSpace combines Web, White page, and Yellow page directories into a single resource.

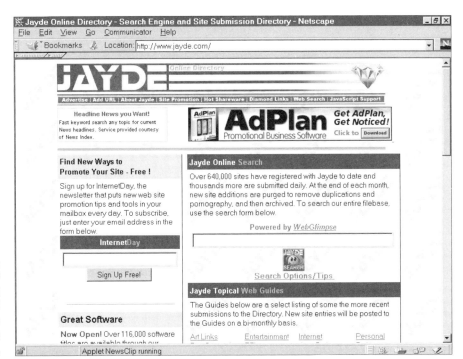

Figure 3.33

Jayde is a growing Web directory and guide that can help bring visitors to your Web site.

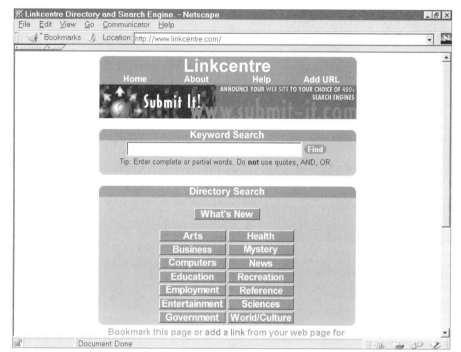

Figure 3.34

Linkcentre features
a well-organized
directory that is
easy to browse
and search.

Linkcentre

Main Page (see Figure 3.34): www.linkcentre.com/
Submission Page: Visit the category most relevant to your page, and then click on the Add URL link. You'll then be able to submit a listing.

LinkMonster

Main Page (see Figure 3.35): www.linkmonster.com/
Submission Page: www.linkmonster.com/add.html

Lycos Top 5%

Main Page (see Figure 3.36): point.lycos.com/
Submission Page: Selected based on submissions to Lycos.
www.lycos.com/addasite.html

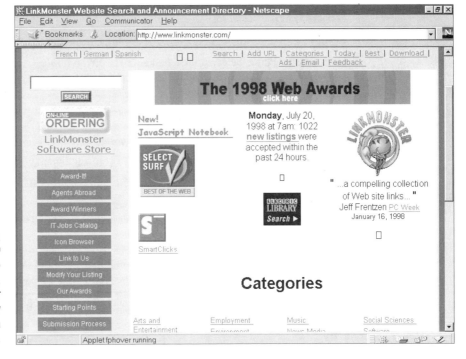

Figure 3.35

In addition to traditional listings, LinkMonster features newly submitted links in a what's new area.

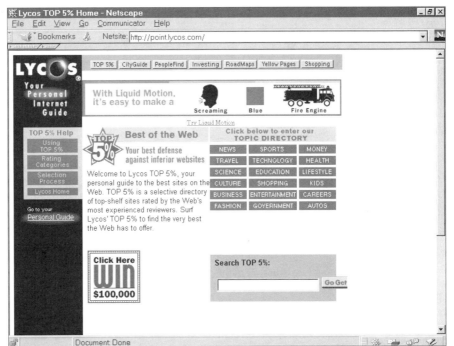

Figure 3.36

Getting listed in the Lycos Top 5% is tough to do, but the rewards are certainly worth it.

Magellan

Main Page (see Figure 3.37): www.mckinley.com/magellan/
Submission Page: Selected based on submissions to Excite.
www.mckinley.com/magellan/Info/addsite.html

NerdWorld

Main Page (see Figure 3.38): www.nerdworld.com/
Submission Page: Find the specific category your site fits into using the search form at
www.nerdworld.com/cgi-bin/nwadd.cgi, and then fill out the submission form.

NetGuide

Main Page (see Figure 3.39): www.netguide.com/
Submission Page: Searches are based on submissions to the Lycos search engine. Site
reviews are selected based on e-mail sent to appropriate editors. The necessary e-mail
addresses can be obtained at www.netguide.com/aboutus/aboutreviews.html.

Figure 3.37

Magellan is a
discerning Web
guide. You'll have to
submit your site
via the parent
organization, Excite.

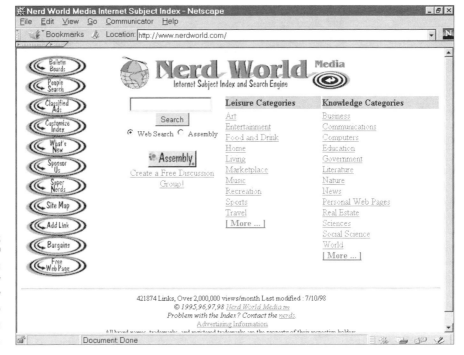

Figure 3.38

NerdWorld is a stylish Web directory that heavily promotes the top 10 listings in various categories.

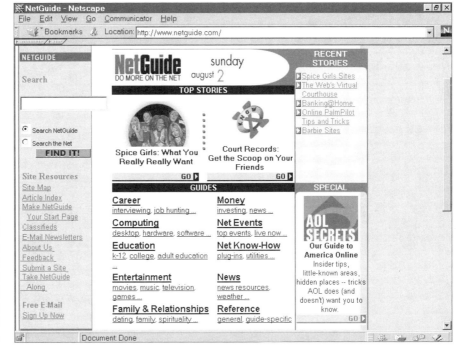

Figure 3.39

NetGuide features category-specific reviews selected by various editorial teams. Getting listed takes patience.

Figure 3.40

Online Canada is
another fine Web
directory
for Canada.

Online Canada

Main Page (see Figure 3.40): www.onlinecanada.com/
Submission Page: www.onlinecanada.com/addurl.cfm

Peekaboo

Main Page (see Figure 3.41): www.peekaboo.net/
Submission Page: www.peekaboo.net/index1.html

Yahoo!

Main Page (see Figure 3.42): www.yahoo.com/
Submission Page: Visit the category your site fits into, and then click on the Suggest a
Site link.

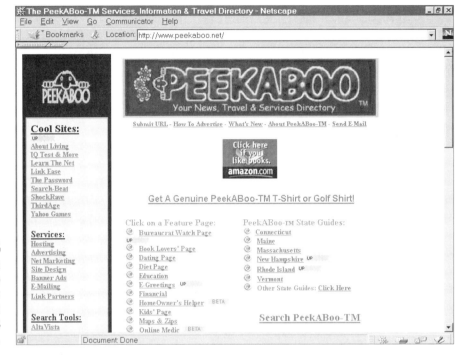

Figure 3.41

Peekaboo is a growing Web directory that can help you reach small groups of users.

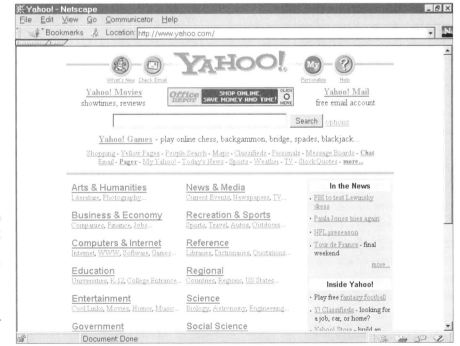

Figure 3.42

Yahoo! is the most popular Web directory on the planet; getting listed here can certainly bring visitors to your Web site.

Wrapping Up and Looking Ahead

Registering with search engines is a terrific way to build traffic to your Web site, especially when you consider that millions of people use search engines to find information every day. Guides, lists, and directories can also help get your Web site noticed. Although you aren't guaranteed a listing in a guide to the best of the Web, your time is still well spent when you consider that a single award could bring a flood of thousands of visitors to your site.

Tomorrow morning you'll examine many different types of search engines and Web directories. You'll learn about the best directories and search engines for business-oriented Web sites, industry and category-specific directories, getting more mileage from What's New directories, and a whole lot more.

So take a break this evening and spend some time with the family. I'll see you back here tomorrow.

The Coolest, the Hottest, and the Best

- The Best Business Search Engines and Yellow Pages Directories
- Directories by Industry and Category
- Getting More Mileage out of What's New? Directories
- Getting Your Site Listed As the Cool Site of the Day

Several hundred business search and directory sites are currently available, but the first part of this morning's coverage focuses on the best of these sites so that you can get the most exposure for your time investment.

I have spent many hours compiling these resources so that you don't have to. If you have time, go ahead and make use of these resources as you learn about them; that is, proceed with the registration process that I describe as you go through this section. If you don't have time to get them all in now, come back when you do. It will be worth your while, I promise.

Later this morning, you'll find out how to vie for awards that help get your site noticed by cyberspace travelers. Awards abound on the Web, and your site can sizzle as Hot Site of the Day or freeze out the competition as Cool Site of the Week. Some awards are more likely to increase your Web traffic than others, though, and this part of the book introduces you to some of the best.

The Best Business Search Engines and Yellow Pages Directories

Business search engines and Yellow Pages directories provide great resources for anyone who offers products, services, or business-related information on the Web. Most business-oriented search engines and directories provide much more detailed information than other search sites and directories. These detailed entries allow you to list your Web site and tout your products and services as well.

Submitting Your Site to Business Search and Directory Sites

Hundreds of thousands of businesses offer products and services on the Web. The sites that help Web users make sense of all these offerings are the business search engines and Yellow Pages directories. Because these search and directory sites are tailored for businesses, you can search for specific businesses by company name, location, and industry as well as the products and services that the companies offer.

Although they are similar to traditional search engines, most business search engines do not index your Web site or the pages that you submit for listing at the search site. Instead, these search engines create an indexed reference to your site based solely on the information you submit, which doesn't necessarily include the URL to your Web site. In this respect, this type of business search engine is more like a directory listing than a traditional search engine.

Because business search engines don't actually index your site, many business search sites are called Yellow Pages directories. Although some Yellow Pages directories are modeled after the Yellow Pages of your phone book, most Web-based Yellow Pages directories have features of both traditional directory sites and traditional search engine sites.

Due to their very direct focus, business search sites and directories often want a great deal of information from anyone registering with the site. For this reason, before you register with these sites, you should have all the following information planned out:

- What subject category you want to be listed under
- How you want the company contact information to read
- Who you will list as the contact name at the company
- What keywords you want to associate with your site
- What page URL you want to be listed at the site
- What e-mail address you want to use for inquiries
- What description you will use for your company, products, and services

You should also know that, by their very nature, business search sites and directories are out to make a profit. The worst of these sites exist only to push paid services at unwitting souls who want to get listed at the site. Again, I recommend that you don't sign up for anything that will cost you money. Plenty of sites are happy just to have your listing and will list you without charge. These sites get their money from advertising rather than listings.

Increasing Your Web Traffic with Yellow Pages Directories

Just as the top search engines and directories receive millions of visitors every day, so do the top Yellow Pages directories, and accordingly, registering your Web site with Yellow Pages directories will increase the traffic to your Web site. That said, Yellow Pages directories generally don't drive thousands of visitors to a particular Web site; rather, you can reasonably expect relatively modest increases in your Web traffic over time.

By *relatively modest*, I mean that the average Web site, which may have 500 visitors a day at present, may see an additional 50 visitors daily as a result of registering with a popular Yellow Pages directory. The traffic

depends, of course, on the types of products and services that you offer. Right now you may be thinking, is it really worth the effort? The answer in this case is a resounding yes if you focus your efforts on the top Yellow Pages directories listed in this section.

Although Yellow Pages directories are popular and do receive millions of visitors every day, Yellow Pages directories are business-oriented. Visitors to these directories are usually looking for very specific types of information—for example, information on a management consulting service. Furthermore, because Yellow Pages listings contain addresses, phone numbers, and other contact information, people visiting the Yellow Pages directory may not visit your Web site at all. Instead, they may visit your physical storefront or otherwise contact you by phone, fax, or e-mail.

Whether visitors to a Yellow Pages directory go to your storefront, contact you, or visit your Web site, you have managed to bring in the all-important consumers who are actively looking for a business that offers products or services like yours. With a listing in a traditional search engine or directory site, you simply cannot bring in this type of visitor on a consistent basis. Most businesses I know of would much rather have 50 people browsing the aisles, virtual or otherwise, than 500 people racing past the windows on their way to somewhere else.

As you follow along with the discussion, I recommend that you submit your Web site to the search engines and directories found in this section. If you are in a hurry and don't have time to register with all the sites I examine, simply start with the first site and register with as many sites as you can. To make the task of registering your Web site easier, you may want to visit the companion Web site for this book at **www.tvpress.com /promote/yellp.htm**.

NOTE Any Yellow Pages directories that you find at the online site and that are not listed in this part are discussed later in the book. I recommend that you not register with these other sites for now.

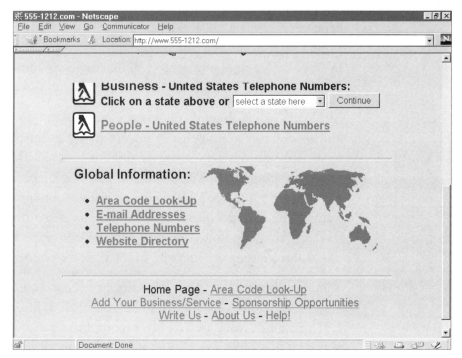

Figure 4.1

555-1212 is designed as an information resource for businesses, people, and Web sites.

555-1212

Main Page (see Figure 4.1): www.555-1212.com/
Submission Page: www.555-1212.com/addbiz.html

All Business Network

Main Page (see Figure 4.2): www.all-biz.com/
Submission Page: www.all-biz.com/directry.htm

Big Book

Main Page (see Figure 4.3): www.bigbook.com/
Submission Page: Submissions handled via GTE Super Pages.

Figure 4.2

All Business Network offers services to businesses as well as a Yellow Pages directory. On the submission page, click on the Add button to enter a new directory listing and follow the prompts.

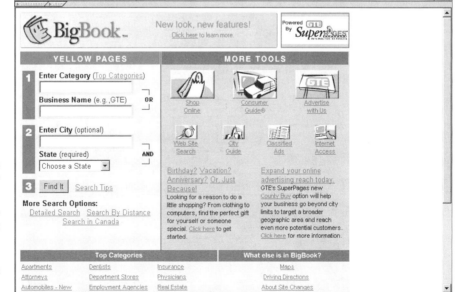

Figure 4.3

Big Book is one of the best-known Yellow Pages directories. Because Big Book is owned by GTE, all submissions are handled through GTE Super Pages.

BizWeb

Main Page (see Figure 4.4): www.bizweb.com/
Submission Page: www.bizweb.com/InfoForm/

Business Seek

Main Page (see Figure 4.5): www.businesseek.com/
Submission Page: www.businesseek.com/business/engalta.htm

ComFind

Main Page (see Figure 4.6): www.comfind.com/
Submission Page: www.comfind.com/intro.html

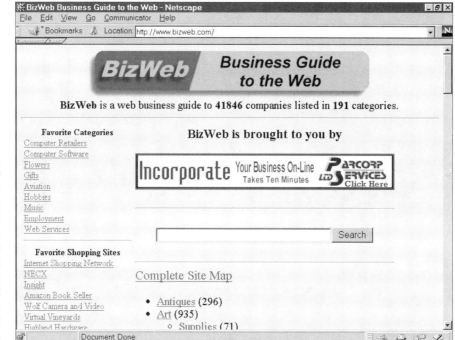

Figure 4.4

BizWeb is a growing directory to businesses that have Web sites. Read the information on the submission page and then submit your listing to submission @bizweb.com.

Figure 4.5

BusinessSeek is an international Yellow Pages directory with listings for businesses throughout the world.

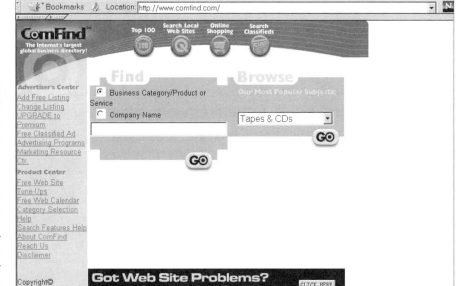

Figure 4.6

ComFind is one of the best business directories on the Web. Follow the instructions on the submission page. From the submission page, you'll need to browse or search for the appropriate category for your Web site and then click on the Go! Register button.

Figure 4.7

Gold Links provides services to businesses as well as a Yellow Pages directory.

Gold Links

Main Page (see Figure 4.7): www.goldlinks.com/
Submission Page: www.goldlinks.com/addurl.shtml

GTE SuperPages

Main Page (see Figure 4.8): www.superpages.com/
Submission Page: Click on Add or Change Your Listing on the bottom of the main page.

One World Plaza Web Directory

Main Page (see Figure 4.9): www.owplaza.com/owp/index.html
Submission Page: www.owplaza.com/Register.html

Figure 4.8

GTE SuperPages provides free basic listings. To create a listing, you'll need to enter your business phone number and then follow the submission guidelines.

Figure 4.9

One World Plaza maintains a growing directory of businesses on the Web.

Pronet Business Directory

Main Page (see Figure 4.10): www.pronett.com or www.pronet.ca
Submission Page: Click on Add URL on the main page.

USYellow.com

Main Page (see Figure 4.11): www.usyellow.com/
Submission Page: www.usyellow.com/asp/members.asp?Func=listing

WebDirect!

Main Page (see Figure 4.12): www.wdirect.com
Submission Page: www.wdirect.com/cgi-win/wdirect.exe/SUBMITIT

Figure 4.10

Pronet is an international business directory that scores big with well-organized and easy-to-read listings.

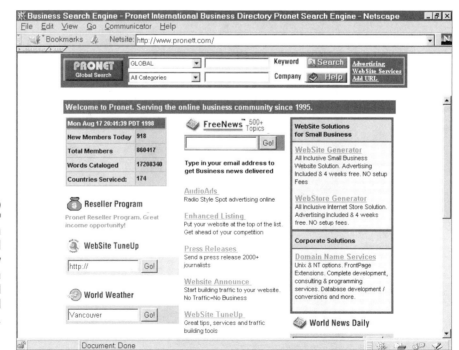

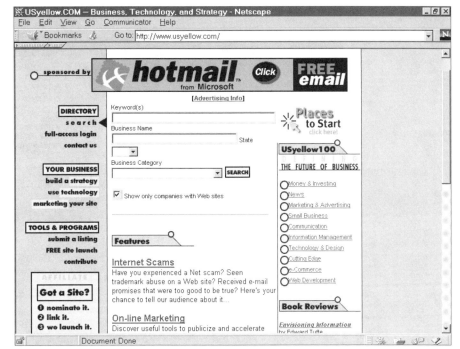

Figure 4.11

USYellow.Com is a growing Yellow Pages directory. If you have problems accessing the submission URL, visit the main page and use the Submit a Listing link.

Figure 4.12

WebDirect! provides a relatively small but useful Yellow Pages directory. If you have problems typing in the URL, visit the main page and click on the Add URL link.

Figure 4.13

YelloWWWeb is a small but growing Yellow Pages directory.

YelloWWWeb

Main Page (see Figure 4.13): www.yellowwweb.com

Submission Page: www.yellowwweb.com/freyel.htm

Figure 4.14

Yellow Web for Europe is a business directory for Europe. If your company has a business in Europe, this is a good directory to get listed in.

Yellow Web for Europe

Main Page (see Figure 4.14): www.yweb.com/
Submission Page: www.yweb.com/add-en.html

Directories by Industry and Category

The major search engines and directories are great for getting your Web site noticed by the masses, but you also want your site to be accessible to people looking for specific types of information, which is where industry and category-specific directories come into the picture. Whether your site covers fine dining in Seattle, outdoor sports activities in Australia, or one of thousands of other topics, there are directories devoted to your subject, and this portion of this morning's session shows you how to find and use them.

 NOTE Some of these directories have a fairly narrow focus. To help you better determine if a certain directory is right for you, I've organized these listings a bit differently from the previous listings. Be sure to read through the detailed descriptions before you submit a listing.

Getting the Most Out of Industry and Category Directories

Whereas industry directories focus on major industries, such as the real estate and travel industries, category directories focus on specific topics, such as resources for writers, or outdoor sports. Because of their narrow focus, industry and category directories are sought out by people who are looking for specialized or tailored information, making these directories the perfect place to get your Web site noticed.

As with most directories, industry and category directories focus on pages rather than entire Web sites. Thus, you generally submit the URL to a specific page or area that strongly relates to the topic of the directory. Along with the URL, you usually submit the page title and a summary description. Although the description of your page may not be published with your listing, the directory maintainer uses the description to determine whether the page is appropriate for the directory.

Because industry and category directories have a very specific focus, they are great for increasing the traffic to your Web site. In a way, getting listed in

these directories is like being able to conduct an advertising campaign that targets readers who are interested in the exact type of site that you publish.

Before you submit your site to industry or category directories, you should take a few minutes to plot out the industries or categories that fit your Web site. Although the first industry or category that you think up is probably the best, a typical Web site will fit into several categories or industries. Your collection of articles on Spain would probably fit in perfectly with a travel and tourism directory. But you could also look for metro or city guides that cover Spain. Additionally, your articles may cover the best restaurants in Madrid, making these pages suitable for a listing in a directory to restaurants, fine dining, or food.

City and Metro Guides

City and metro guides are becoming increasingly popular. The idea is that by focusing a directory on a specific city, state, or country, users will be able to find information directly relating to an area of the world in which they are interested. If you want to find an Italian restaurant in Denver, you access a city guide featuring Denver. If you want to find a Web design firm in the Seattle area, you access a guide to the Seattle metropolitan area.

Every single Web site in cyberspace has a place in a city or metro guide. After all, we all live somewhere. For this reason, you should register your site in a directory that covers your city or metro area.

Unfortunately, only a few metro guides actually let you submit listings. Because of this, I cover only the guides that accept submissions. Online, you will find the city and metro guide listings at **www.tvpress.com /promote/metro.htm**.

Creating a Listing in GeoCities

GeoCities (**www.geocities.com**) is a different kind of city guide. Instead of focusing on your actual location in the real world, GeoCities focuses on virtual communities of interest. The BourbonStreet community is a tribute to the Big Easy. The CapitalHill community covers politics and government. The MotorCity community is for racing fans and car enthusiasts everywhere. In all, more than 30 virtual communities exist that cover dozens of topics.

GeoCities is home to millions of Web users. To enter GeoCities or publish a page within GeoCities, you must become a member. Fortunately, membership is currently free. As you might expect, there is a catch. GeoCities displays an awful lot of advertising that you have to wade through when you visit and work with your Web page.

What Do Entries in GeoCities Look Like?

GeoCities is organized into dozens of virtual communities. Each page within a community has an address—sort of like your street address. Anytime an address has a vacancy, a new homesteader—you, for example —can create and customize a home page within the community. Figure

Figure 4.15

At GeoCities, you can create a free home page, complete with everything you need to set up an additional home on the Web.

4.15 shows the main page in Area 51, a virtual community for sci-fi and fantasy fans.

Because everyone can create a customized home page within GeoCities, no standard look to the pages exists. Your home page in GeoCities can be the doorway to your Web site. Your home page in GeoCities can also be a separate outlet for your creativity. Either way, you can use the home page in GeoCities to attract readers.

Placing a Listing at GeoCities

Before you can place a listing in GeoCities, you must become a member. When you become a member, you can create a home page. Start by visiting the virtual community of which you would like to become a part, and then follow the links that allow you to join the neighborhood. You can then choose a membership option and fill out the membership form shown in Figure 4.16. Just as with any service provider, your home page

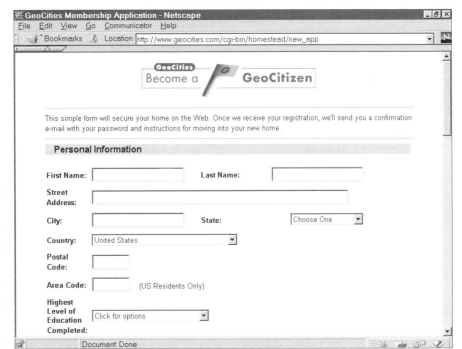

Figure 4.16

Unfortunately, there's no way to get around having to fill out this membership form. But the good news is that once you do, you can go look for your new homestead!

can be a single page or a collection of pages. Currently, your home page is limited to 2MB of disk space.

Getting Listed at Net Metro

Net Metro (**www.centraldrive.com/metro/**) is a guide to major metropolitan areas. Most major metropolitan areas within the U.S. have their own pages.

Because Net Metro is a guide to the best sites rather than a guide to all of the available sites, the directory listings within Net Metro aren't extensive. The focus on the best is what makes Net Metro a great place to give your Web site additional visibility.

Figure 4.17

Net Metro's detailed listings make it a great choice.

What Do Entries in Net Metro Look Like?

Entries in Net Metro are organized in several different ways. Entries are first organized geographically by metro area and then by category. As shown in Figure 4.17, the listings can be quite detailed, which makes this guide very effective in helping bring traffic to your Web site.

Placing a Listing at Net Metro

Net Metro has a central submission page (**www.centraldrive.com/metro /listing.htm**) for all metro areas. Figure 4.18 shows this submission page.

Before you submit a listing to Net Metro, you should examine the metro areas within the directory to determine where your site should be listed. If you live near a major metro, you should use this metro. Be sure to select the category that best fits your Web site.

Figure 4.18

Net Metro has a central submission page for all metro areas. Be sure to select a category when you fill out the listing.

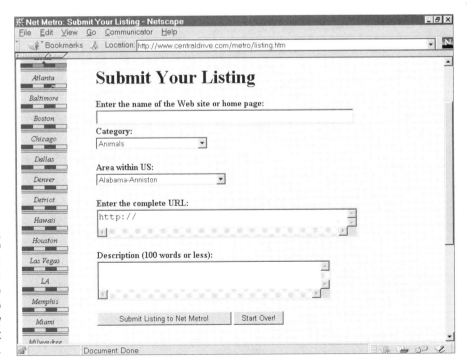

Getting Listed at USA CityLink

USA CityLink (**www.usacitylink.com**) is a city guide that focuses primarily on travel and tourism. Because of this narrow focus, most of the listings in USA CityLink focus on state- and city-specific information from government and state sources, such as visitor information published by the state. Yet you can also find information on vacation tips, tourist attractions, convention centers, airports, and many other topics that relate to travel and tourism.

What Do Entries in USA CityLink Look Like?

Although USA CityLink is a city guide, it is organized by state rather than by individual cities. Each state within the U.S. has its own area within the guide (see Figure 4.19). These areas are divided into broad categories, such as state information and city information.

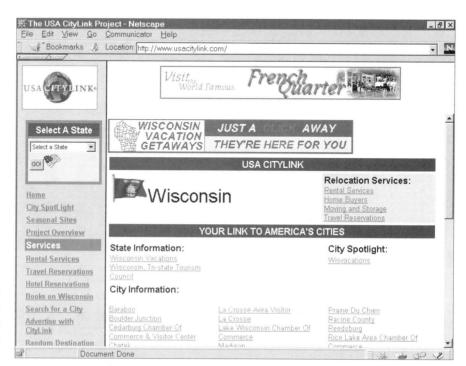

Figure 4.19

USA CityLink focuses primarily on travel and tourism.

Placing a Listing at USA CityLink

USA CityLink is another site that you should definitely browse before you submit anything. First make sure that your listing fits in with USA CityLink's strong focus on travel and tourism information. If your site does, then you should submit your site using the submission page shown in Figure 4.20 (**www.usacitylink.com/addcity.html**).

To get the most out of your listing, you should fill out the form completely, including the optional information such as the name of your organization. Because listings in USA CityLink are so terse, the name of your organization is usually the only thing that distinguishes your listing from another listing that covers a similar topic.

Other City and Metro Guides

Millions of people are lost in the endless sea of the Web. They are looking for tailored information that they can access easily and quickly, which is

Figure 4.20

Although listings in this guide are short, you should fill out the submission form completely.

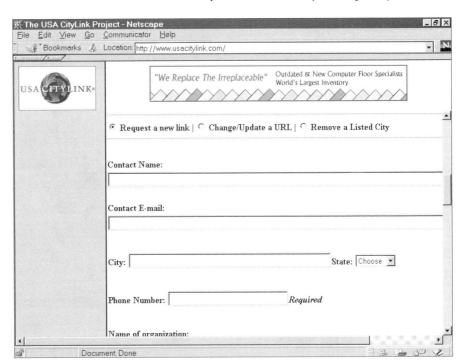

exactly what city guides provide. The growing trend to tailor information based on geographic boundaries is clearly evident when you visit the major search sites. Just about every major search site has a city or metro guide.

The Lycos City Guide (**cityguide.lycos.com**) is shown in Figure 4.21. When you visit the top-level page in the Lycos City guide, you see a map of the world. You can click on the map to visit areas within the city guide dedicated to specific countries. By following maps and links, you will eventually end up on a page with listings dedicated to a specific city or metro area. Although you cannot place listings directly in the Lycos City Guide, you can register your site with the Lycos search engine, which then places you in the Lycos database. (To learn more about Lycos, see the Saturday Afternoon session under "Registering with the Top Search Engines on the Planet.")

Not to be outdone, Excite also has a city guide called the Excite Travel Channel (**www.city.net**). Originally, the Excite Travel Channel was an

Figure 4.21

Lycos City Guide has a lot to offer. To submit listings, use the main Lycos site at **www.lycos.com**.

independent city guide called City.Net. When Excite took over City.Net, Excite changed the name. The home page for City.Net Travel is shown in Figure 4.22. Just as with the Lycos Travel Guide, you cannot submit listings directly to City.Net Travel. Instead, you must register your site in the main Excite database.

Although Excite and Lycos use their extensive databases to create city guides, Yahoo! has taken a completely different approach to creating city guides by setting up separate areas for major metros and countries throughout the world. The Web site for Yahoo! Seattle (**seattle.yahoo.com**) is shown in Figure 4.23. If you want to register your Washington-based business or Web site in the Seattle metro guide, visit Yahoo! Seattle and go through the same submission process that you do for the main Yahoo! directory. If you want to register your Web site in any other Yahoo! city guide, visit the city guide and go through the submission process as well.

Figure 4.22

Excite also has a city guide. To get your listing in this guide, you have to go through the main Excite site, **www.excite.com**.

The Seattle metro guide is only one of many other Yahoo! metro guides. Some of the other Yahoo! metro guides include:

Yahoo! Atlanta	atlanta.yahoo.com
Yahoo! Austin	austin.yahoo.com
Yahoo! Boston	boston.yahoo.com
Yahoo! Chicago	chi.yahoo.com
Yahoo! Dallas/Fort Worth	dfw.yahoo.com
Yahoo! Los Angeles	la.yahoo.com
Yahoo! Miami	miami.yahoo.com
Yahoo! New York	ny.yahoo.com
Yahoo! San Francisco	sfbay.yahoo.com
Yahoo! Twin Cities	minn.yahoo.com
Yahoo! Washington DC	dc.yahoo.com

Some of the Yahoo! national guides include:

Yahoo! Canada	www.yahoo.ca
Yahoo! France	www.yahoo.fr
Yahoo! Germany	www.yahoo.de

 NOTE To find a complete list of Yahoo! city and country guides and their URLs, visit Yahoo!'s main Web site at **www.yahoo.com**.

Real Estate Directories and Guides

When you think of real estate, you probably think of real estate agents and brokers. Although agents and brokers are the cornerstones of real estate, the real estate industry encompasses many other professions and organi-

zations. At one end of the spectrum are the construction companies, developers, engineers, planners, workers, and service organizations whose efforts create the homes in which we live and the office buildings in which we work. At the other end of the spectrum are the property managers, asset managers, trust companies, and holding companies that manage the construction and the properties. In between are the financial institutions, the appraisers, the investors, and the property owners who make the construction possible.

Because dozens of professions and organizations are a part of the real estate industry, the fact that this industry has a dominant presence in cyberspace is no surprise. In fact, real estate directories are some of the best-designed sites that you'll find online. If your Web site or business covers any of the professions or organizations related to the real estate industry, you should add a listing to the directories in this section. Further, if you publish any information that relates to the real estate

Figure 4.23

Yahoo! metros provide a lot of area-specific information.

industry, you should consider adding a listing in real estate directories as well. Online, you will find the real estate directory listings at **www.tvpress .com/promote/real.htm**.

Getting Listed at CenterNet

CenterNet (**www.centernet.com**) is a real estate directory published by Net Properties Corporation. The directory covers many different aspects of the commercial real estate industry. You'll find listings of real estate companies, retailers, products, and services. You'll find listings of trade journals, news sources, and associations that are related to the industry as well.

What Do Entries at CenterNet Look Like?

Although CenterNet primarily covers the U.S. real estate industry, it also provides fairly extensive listings for the international market. All listings in the directory are organized geographically and by topic, such as real estate companies, agencies, and related services. These sites provide separate areas for each state within the U.S. Listings within most states are further divided by county.

After the U.S., the real estate market best represented is Canada. The sites offer listings for each province.

As with most directories, CenterNet lists only the title of the company or service (see Figure 4.24). The title is linked to the home page of the company or service.

Placing a Listing at CenterNet

CenterNet accepts listings for real estate companies, agencies, and brokers. The form that you use will be similar to the one shown in Figure 4.25 (**http://199.170.0.37/comm/misc/listme/wsite.htm**).

Figure 4.24

CenterNet lists only the title of the company or service, so be sure to give the full information.

Figure 4.25

Fill out the submission form to create a listing.

Getting Listed in Estates Today

Estates Today (**www.estatestoday.co.uk**) is a terrific directory for the commercial and residential real estate industry. Although the primary countries covered in the directory are the U.K. and the U.S., Estates Today also has comprehensive listings for many other countries.

Unlike some real estate directories that focus only on companies, agencies, and brokers, Estates Today covers every aspect of the industry. In addition to the very diverse directory, Estates Today also publishes lists of the top sites by country and category.

What Do Entries in Estates Today Look Like?

The Estates Today directory has a terrific design that allows you to find information in many different ways. You can find comprehensive listings by category for various countries, or zero in on specific states and

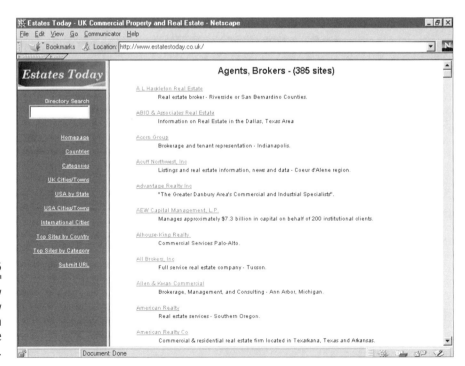

Figure 4.26

Estates Today provides summary information along with the standard links.

provinces. Estates Today also organizes listings by category for cities within the U.S. and major international cities.

As shown in Figure 4.26, listings in Estates Today appear by company name. Following the company name is a summary description of the services, products, or resources provided.

Placing a Listing at Estates Today

Estates Today accepts listings from a broad spectrum of areas that relate to the real estate industry. Because of this wide focus, you can list just about any type of Web site or company that relates to real estate, including agencies, appraisal companies, asset managers, construction services, consultants, developers, financial services, legal services, and property managers.

Before you submit a listing, you should find the category that fits your Web site or company. After you find the specific category that best fits you, submit an e-mail message to **estates@estatestoday.co.uk**. The message should provide the following information:

- Company or Web site title
- Category

Getting Listed in the International Real Estate Digest

The International Real Estate Digest (**www.ired.com**) is a comprehensive directory to the real estate industry. The goal of IRED is to be a one-stop shop for real estate information. As an actual online digest, the site features current news covering the real estate industry.

What Do Entries in the International Real Estate Digest Look Like?

The International Real Estate Digest has thousands of listings from more than 85 countries. You can browse the listings in several ways, including by world region and country. As shown in Figure 4.27, individual listings appear with titles and summary descriptions. Most listings also have graphical icons that depict the kinds of information you will find at the Web site.

Placing a Listing in the International Real Estate Digest

The International Real Estate Digest accepts listings from many different types of organizations that relate to the real estate industry. Some of these organizations include agencies, appraisal companies, brokers, builders, construction services, education, inspectors, financial services, and legal services. You can add a listing to IRED at **www.ired.com/dir/newlinks /addme.htm**.

To get the most out of your IRED listing, be sure to carefully consider the graphical icons that may pertain to your site. Each icon that you select will be displayed with your listing. In the remarks sections, you should add a brief description of your Web site; doing so should ensure that your listing is displayed with a summary description.

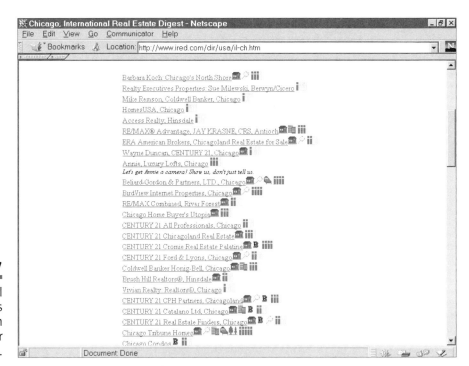

Figure 4.27

International Real Estate Digest has listings from countries all over the world.

Other Real Estate Directories

Although I've focused on the top directory sites for the real estate industry, many other real estate directories exist. Some of the other real estate directories that you may want to consider include the Real Estate Cyberspace Society and Open House America.

The Real Estate Cyberspace Society (**www.recyber.com**) provides services for real estate professionals. The home page for this site is shown in Figure 4.28. You can submit your site to the Real Estate Cyberspace Society directory at **www.recyber.com/links/links.html**.

Open House America (**www.openhouse.net**) is a site for home buyers that includes directories for realtors, financial services, and general real estate-related listings. The home page for this site is shown in Figure 4.29. You can submit a listing to Open House America at **www.openhouse.net /realtor_register.html**.

Figure 4.28

The Real Estate Cyberspace Society directory allows you to submit free links.

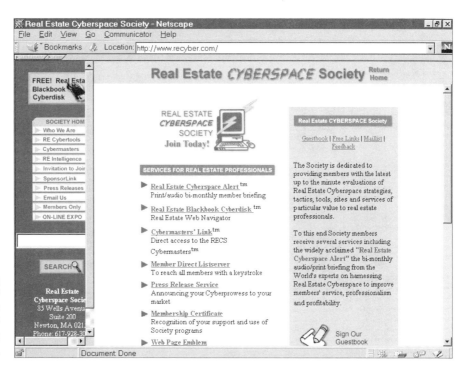

Internet Real Estate Center (**www.centraldrive.com/homes**) maintains a fairly comprehensive directory for commercial and residential real estate, real estate agencies, and real estate resources (see Figure 4.30). Real Estate agents can submit free listings by visiting the appropriate area within the directory and following the Submit Listing links.

Travel and Tourism: Guides and Directories

The travel industry covers many different professions and organizations. Travel agents book tickets; airlines, cruise lines, train companies, and bus companies provide transportation; hotels offer a place to stay; car rental agencies give you flexible mobility; recreation and amusement businesses provide entertainment.

Because travel and tourism is big business, the industry is well represented online. As with the real estate industry, many high-profile travel directories can help you build traffic to your Web site. If your Web site covers

Figure 4.29

Real Estate agents and agencies can submit listings to Open House America's real estate directory.

any of the professions or organizations related to the travel industry, you should consider adding a listing to the directories in this section. If you publish any information that relates to travel and tourism, you should consider adding a listing in travel directories as well. Online, you will find the travel and tourism directory listings at: **www.tvpress.com/promote /travel.htm**.

Getting Listed in Hotels and Travel on the Net

Hotels and Travel on the Net (**www.hotelstravel.com**) is an international directory for the travel and tourism industry. This comprehensive directory contains hundreds of thousands of listings.

You can search Hotels and Travel by keyword or by following links to specific categories of information (see Figure 4.31). Categories within the directory include hotels, airlines, airports, travel-related products, travel-

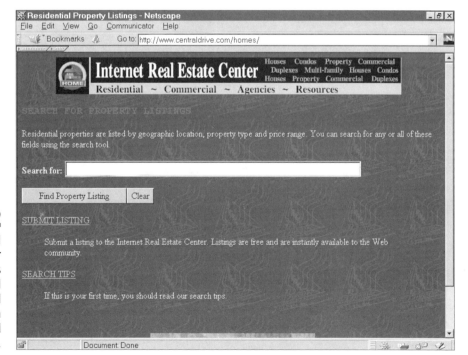

Figure 4.30

Internet Real Estate Center combines directories for commercial and residential real estate with realtor and resource listings.

related services, and travel references. Most of the major hotel chains have areas within the site as well.

What Do Entries in Hotels and Travel on the Net Look Like?

Entries in Hotels and Travel cluster around hotels, airports, and airlines. Figure 4.32 shows listings for hotels, which are organized into country/state directories, local directories, maps, and tourist information. The site indexes most of the entries according to city names.

Placing a Listing in Hotels and Travel on the Net

If your site features travel-related information, you can add a listing to Hotels and Travel. The URL for this page is **www.hotelstravel.com /addsite.html.**

Figure 4.31

Hotels and Travel is easy to browse and search. You'll find a lot of resources, which makes it a good choice for your listing.

Fill out only the information that pertains to your Web site. If you are submitting a travel-related site, be sure to specify the city, state, or country that your site serves.

Getting Listed in Ecotravel

Ecotravel (**www.ecotravel.com**) is an exceptional international directory to outdoor sports and travel. The Ecotravel directory contains much information on outdoor activities and travel destinations for the adventurous. Because of its focus on eco-tourism, the site includes listings on conservation, wildlife information, and outdoor education. It also carries listings for sites that sell outdoor equipment, sites that cover outdoor sports, and sites that describe the latest events in outdoor sports.

Figure 4.32

Listings in Hotels and Travel are organized by subject and then by geographic area.

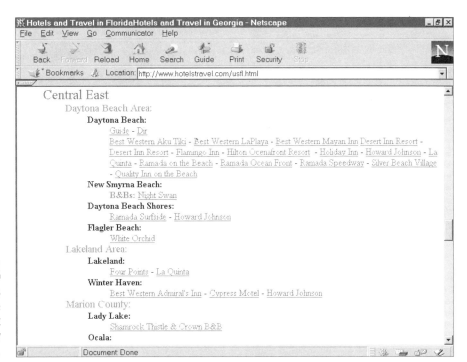

What Do Entries in Ecotravel Look Like?

Entries within the Ecotravel directory are organized by category, such as destinations and activities. Within specific categories, the directory is divided by country. Listings are displayed with a title and a summary description (see Figure 4.33).

The unique focus of the Ecotravel directory gives anyone who publishes information related to outdoor sports and travel a great opportunity to be noticed. If you publish outdoor sports information or travel information, you should be listed in this directory. If you sell sports gear or publish information related to sports gear, this directory is ideal for you as well.

Placing a Listing in Ecotravel

Before you submit your site, you should familiarize yourself with the categories within this directory. The Conservation area focuses on wildlife

Figure 4.33

ECO Travel provides a great deal of travel resources, all organized into various subject areas.

information, environmental issues, and outdoor education. The Gear area focuses on outdoor equipment manufacturers and sites that sell this equipment or publish related information. The Activities area focuses on outdoor activities, such as backpacking and kayaking. The Destinations area focuses on worldwide locations for outdoor sports and travel. The Events area focuses on upcoming events in outdoor sports. Other areas cover general travel and hotel information.

The submission page for Ecotravel is shown in Figure 4.34. The URL for this page is **www.ecotravel.com/addalink/**.

Other Travel and Tourism Directories

After you submit listings to the Hotels and Travel directory and the Ecotravel directory, you may want to try other travel directories as well. After all, you want to build traffic to your travel-related Web site, and the best

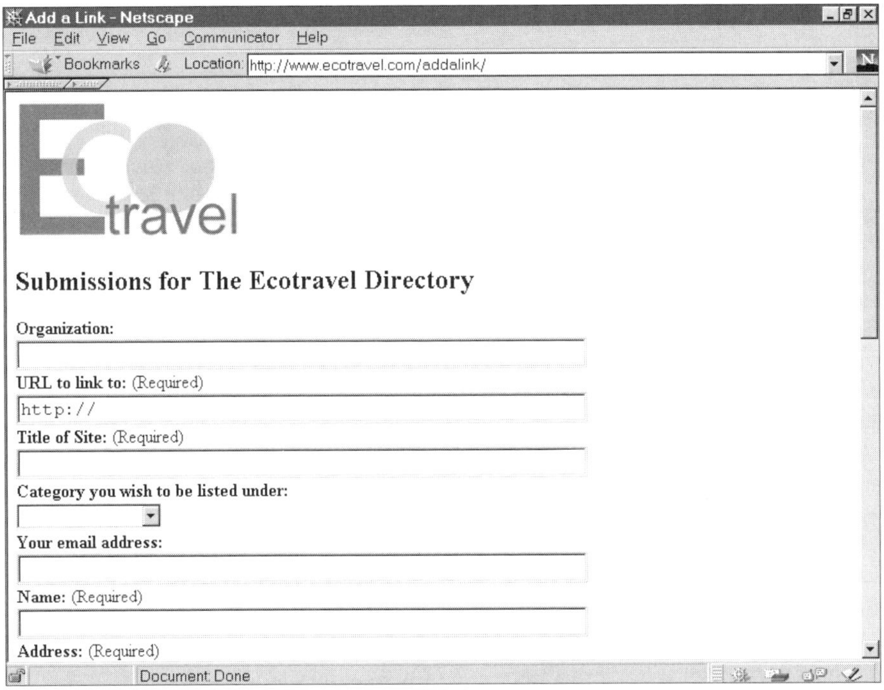

Figure 4.34

Add your link to Ecotravel using this form.

way to do this is to spread the word about your Web site through the key directories for the travel industry. Some of the other travel directories to which you may want to submit your site include SETII, TravelHub, and the Rec. Travel Library.

The Search Engine for Travel Information on the Internet (**www.setii .com**) provides a search interface to thousands of travel and tourism listings in its international travel directory. Most of the listings in the directory cover travel-related areas such as travel agencies, airlines, cruise lines, vehicle rentals, travel clubs, and resorts. To submit a listing to this site, visit the home page shown in Figure 4.35 and click on the Add button or follow the links to the free listing area.

TravelHub (**www.travelhub.com**) is a directory to travel agencies. If you are a travel agent, TravelHub provides a number of free services that can help you build traffic and boost your company's bottom line. The home

Figure 4.35

The Search Engine for Travel Information on the Internet is a growing travel directory that you should keep an eye on.

page for TravelHub is shown in Figure 4.36. To find out how you can get listed in this directory, visit **www.travelhub.com/info/.**

More Guides and Directories by Category

Category-specific guides and directories are great ways to get your site noticed. The usefulness of category guides is apparent when you want to find specific types of information without having to wade through search engine results. Because category guides are so useful, they are also extremely popular. The Web contains thousands of category-specific guides covering every imaginable topic. If you are looking for a very specific category guide, one of the best places to find it is shown in Figure 4.37 (**www.yahoo.com/Business_and_Economy/Companies/Directories/**).

Before you go on to the next part in this section, look for additional directories that relate to topics or industries discussed at your site. Rather than

Figure 4.36

Another travel directory to watch is TravelHub. TravelHub combines services with directory resources and information.

try to submit your site in dozens of categories, focus on the top three categories. After you've identified these categories, submit your site to the best directories related to these categories.

Take a Break

Now that you've raced through most of Sunday morning, it is time to take a break. Crank up the radio. Grab an ice-cold drink and something to eat. If you feel like taking a virtual stroll, launch your browser and visit Internet Daily News (**www.netdaily.com**).

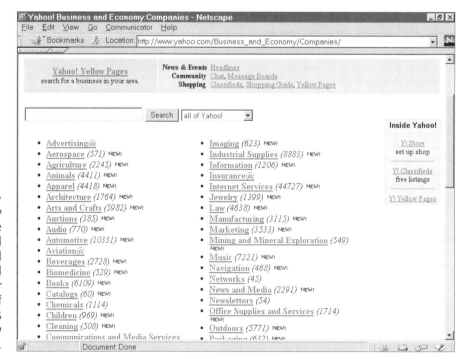

Figure 4.37

Yahoo! is the place to go to find additional directories. You'll find listings for hundreds of specialty directories organized by category.

Getting More Mileage out of What's New? Directories

Announcement sites are an effort to capture the euphoria surrounding the exponential growth rate of the Web, and simultaneously tap into the usual excitement over things that are new and fresh. One of the first What's New? directories was maintained by NCSA—the same folks who gave the world the Mosaic browser. The list at its peak received thousands of submissions for new Web sites every day. Today, the list is no longer updated, but NCSA maintains the list for its historical value. After all, by reading the list archives, you can roll back time and truly get a sense of how fast the Web grew in the early days.

Although NCSA no longer updates its What's New? list, many other sites publish extensive What's New? directories. When you visit the major What's New? lists, you will find that these well-maintained Web sites are tremendously popular. This popularity will help drive visitors to your Web site. What's New? directories are organized much like other directories, with specific broad categories such as business and entertainment. Listings within a specific category are usually arranged alphabetically by title and often chronologically as well.

What's New? lists are by nature guides to new sites. Still, if you've never submitted your site to a specific list before, your site is new to the list and you can therefore certainly submit a listing.

When you register with What's New? directories, you will generally see short-term increases in your Web traffic. The reason for this is that your site usually will be featured in the What's New? directory for only one or two days. Afterward, your listing will appear only in the site's archive files—provided that the site has archive files. If you are interested in short-term increases in Web traffic, What's New? directories are definitely for you. Considering that people often bookmark sites they like, a listing in a What's New? directory can provide modest increases in traffic over the long haul as well.

I recommend that you submit your Web site to the What's New? directories found in this part of the book. If you are in a hurry and don't have time to register with all the sites that I examine, I recommend that you submit your site to the top three What's New? directories and skip the other What's New? directories for now. At the companion Web site for this book, you will find the listings for What's New? directories at **www.tvpress.com/promote/new.htm.**

Exploring the Starting Point Directory

Starting Point (**www.stpt.com**) is a directory service that has remade itself several times over the last few years. Whereas Starting Point once strove to become a major directory à la Yahoo, the service now focuses on making a search of hundreds of Web databases easier using its central search resource, called PowerSearch. Using the PowerSearch interface, you can search individual databases all over the Web by category and keyword.

Figure 4.38

What's New at Starting Point

Despite the change of focus, Starting Point still maintains one of the best guides to new sites. The Starting Point What's New? list (Figure 4.38, **www.stpt.com/general/newsite.html**) is organized into 14 categories that range from business to weather. On the average day, Starting Point receives thousands of submissions for new sites and enhances the directory by allowing visitors to vote for new sites that should be featured as the Hot Site of the Day.

Tuning in to What's New? at Starting Point

All Web sites that are submitted to Starting Point are displayed in the What's New? directory. Within each of the 14 categories, listings are organized chronologically, with the most recent listings displayed first. Because Starting Point receives so many submissions, the directory displays only the most recent listings.

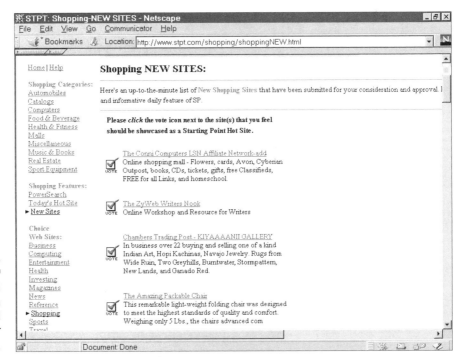

Figure 4.39

Your listing should provide a descriptive title and a clear summary for the listing.

Each listing has a page title and a summary description (see Figure 4.39). To get the most out of your listing, be sure to select a category that fits your Web site. You should also provide a descriptive title and a clear summary for the listing.

Creating a Listing in the What's New section at Starting Point

You can submit your site to Starting Point using the submission page at **www.stpt.com/general/submit.html.** When you examine the Starting Point submission form, the first thing that you may notice is that the site requests a great deal of information. Most of this information isn't used in the directory, however, which is why I recommend entering only the mandatory information. You should also note that you will be signed up for Starting Point's Web Notification Service by default. If you don't want

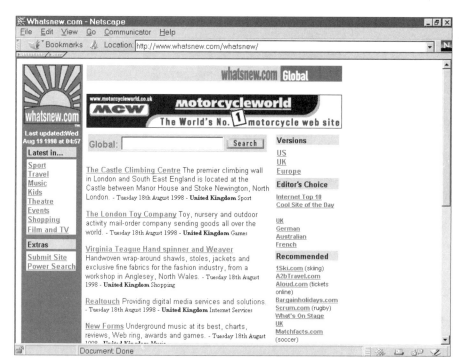

Figure 4.40

What's New on the Internet is organized geographically, so be sure to select the right region.

additional e-mail from Starting Point, deselect the check box for the notification service.

Exploring the What's New on the Internet Directory

What's New on the Internet (**www.whatsnew.com**) is a small but popular directory for new sites maintained by Emap Computing. Rather than organize the site by category, the site's developers chose to organize it geographically, allowing you to access new sites in the U.S., Europe, and the U.K., or from around the world. The home page for What's New on the Internet is shown in Figure 4.40.

Listings at What's New on the Internet

Listings in What's New on the Internet are organized chronologically, with the most recent submissions displayed first. Listings display the page title, summary, submission date, country designator, and category. Several times a day, old listings move to a current archive file. At the end of the day, the listings move to an archive of the previous day's listings.

An added bonus are the Internet Top 10 and Cool Site selections. To be eligible, all you need to do is submit your site.

Creating a Listing in What's New on the Internet

Browse the listing to get a good feel for the types of sites published in the various categories. Because the site indexes the page title and description for its search engine, your description should contain keywords that will help users find your Web site. To submit your site to What's New on the Internet, use the submission page at **www.whatsnew.com/whatsnew /submit/**.

Exploring What's New from Whatsnu.Com

What's New from WhatsNu.Com (**www.whatsnu.com**) is a comprehensive What's New? site that receives thousands of new listings every day.

Unlike other What's New? sites that are primarily directories, WhatsNu.Com provides access to listings via a search engine, allowing you to search the database by keyword and category (see Figure 4.41). When you search the database, you will find that all listings are archived, allowing you to retrieve listings for old and new announcements.

Tuning in to Listings at Whatsnu.Com

Because the site archives listings within the primary database, your submission to Whatsnu.Com will be available for quite some time. This feature is great for increasing visibility and attracting visitors to your Web site. Listings in the database appear by title, category, description, URL, and submission date (see Figure 4.42).

As with most search engines, the Whatsnu.Com search engine returns listings according to relevance. The search engine bases relevancy upon keywords used in the page title and the description.

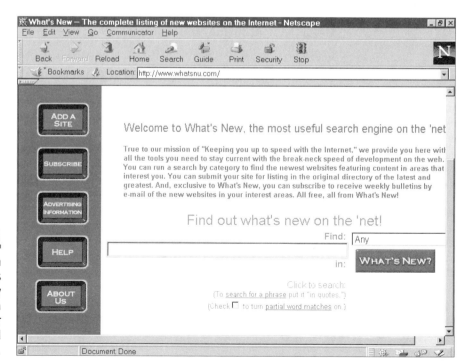

Figure 4.41

What's New from WhatsNu.Com is organized by category, which makes it easier for users to find your site.

Creating a Listing at Whatsnu.Com

To get the most out of your listing in Whatsnu.Com, you should use a title and description with keywords that strongly relate to your site's topic. This topic should also strongly relate to the category in which you submit your site. After you've plotted out the description and category that you want to use, submit your site using the page at **www.whatsnu.com /add.html.**

Other What's New Directories

Finding the new and the interesting is what announcement directories are all about. Two additional What's New directories for you to consider submitting your site to are What's New Too and Totally New for the Internet.

What's New Too (**newtoo.manifest.com**) has been around since the early days of the Web (see Figure 4.43). The name comes from the fact that the

Figure 4.42

The What's New search engine organizes listings according to their relevancy.

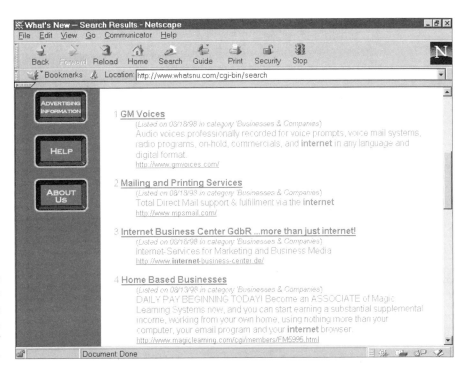

site was another choice for announcing what's new in addition to NCSA's famous What's New directory. Ironically, What's New Too continues to endure although the original What's New is no longer updated.

Because the directory is archived and searchable, you will find that What's New Too is a great choice for announcing your site. The URL for the submission page at What's New Too is **newtoo.manifest.com/submit.html.**

Totally New for the Internet (Figure 4.44, **www.centraldrive.com/splat /netnews.htm**) offers comprehensive announcements for new Web sites in over 50 categories. Listings in Totally New are instantly indexed and available for search using the online search engine. You can create a free listing at **www.centraldrive.com/splat/tnfw_post.htm.**

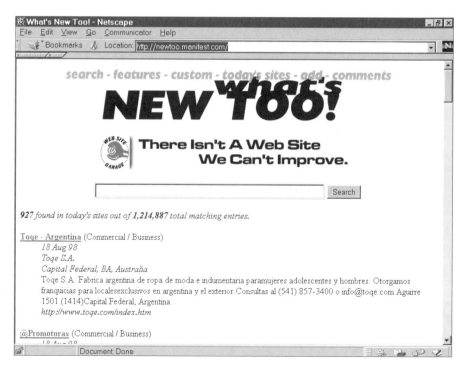

Figure 4.43

With over one million listings, What's New Too has a lot to offer.

Getting Your Site Listed As the Cool Site of the Day

One of the most famous awards on the Web is the Cool Site of the Day award. Getting named the Cool Site of the Day is an accomplishment that gets your site noticed. But the Cool Site of the Day award is only the icing on the cake as far as awards go. There are dozens of other awards that range from the fleeting to the everlasting. Making sense of all these awards and finding the awards that truly make a difference is what this part of this section is all about.

Nothing makes your site stand out from the crowd like an award. Awards are stamps of approval that tell the masses your site is worth their time. Not just any old award will do, though. The Web has more than a thousand different types of site awards. These awards range from Bubba's Cool Site of the Day to the Web 500 Best of the Web. Although Bubba's award may do wonders for your ego, the actual award itself will do very little for

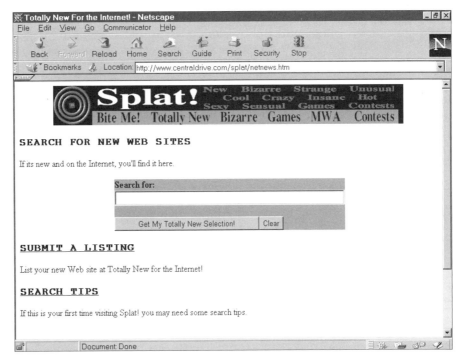

Figure 4.44

Totally New for the Internet is a fast-growing directory to What's New.

your site's traffic. On the other hand, an award like the Web 500 Best of the Web can dramatically increase traffic to your Web site.

NOTE At the time of this writing, there's no award called Bubba's Cool Site of the Day—I just made it up to make a point.

Wandering the Maze of Web Awards

Over the years, my sites have received hundreds of awards—hey, I've been around for quite some time and have created dozens of Web sites. I've discovered that awards can work miracles when it comes to building traffic to your Web site, but they can also be mere self-serving trophies that you place in a glass case to brag about your achievements. The simple truth is that displaying your awards prominently doesn't build traffic to your Web site, no matter what the sites granting the awards want you to think.

The number of awards doesn't matter, either. You could have hundreds of Bubba and Bubba-clone awards and it wouldn't make a difference as far as your site's traffic is concerned. The reality is that these days it seems everyone is offering a Web award of some type or another. There are more than a hundred Cool Site of the Day awards. There are awards for Cool Site of the Moment, Cool Site of the Hour, Cool Site of the Week, Cool Site of the Month, and Cool Site of the Year as well. Beyond the cool site awards, there are the Hot Site of the Day, Hour, Week, Month, and Year awards. Next come the Crazy Site of the Day, Hour, Week, Month, and Year awards. There are so many awards that Web neophytes have started offering backward awards such as the Mediocre Site of the Day, the Ugly Site of the Day, and the Bottom 95 percent of the Web.

If displaying your awards or the number of awards doesn't matter, you are probably wondering what does matter. Well, the true equalizers are the underlying meaning of the award and the strength of the award giver's announcement medium. When an organization such as PC Magazine rec-

ognizes your Web site as one of the Top 100 of the Year, you can expect your traffic to skyrocket. Again, the reason for this isn't so much the award itself as the significance of the award and the channels through which it is announced.

PC Magazine is well respected in the industry. The Top 100 of the Year award (**www.pcmag.com/special/web100/**) is bestowed upon sites only after thorough research and extensive review. The list of recipients of the Top 100 is published in PC Magazine, which has several million readers. After publishing the list in its print edition, PC Magazine publishes the list in its online edition, where it is available to the Web community throughout the year. The longevity of the print edition coupled with the continued traffic to PC Magazine's Web site and the Top 100 list itself are what drives traffic to the Web sites of the recipients.

Finding the Right Award

The right award can make all the difference in the world when it comes to increasing traffic to your Web site. To find the right award, you really need to visit the home of the organization or person granting the award. When you get to the Web site, spend some time reviewing the site and the techniques used to display awards.

Ideally, current awards will be showcased at the site for at least a day and then later put into an archive that can be searched. Because the popularity of the award site is also important, you should try to gauge the level of traffic at the Web site. The busier the award site, the better the chances that it will increase traffic to your Web site.

All this talk of finding the right award may seem strange. After all, these sites are giving away an award and I have the audacity to ask whether the award is meaningful and worthwhile. Unfortunately, with more than a thousand different organizations offering awards of one type or another, you really do need to make sure that the award is meaningful and worthwhile before you take the time to submit your Web site. Fortunately, I've already done the legwork for you. After searching through more than a thousand award sites, I came up with the list of sites featured in this section of this book.

Submitting Your Site

Receiving an award depends largely upon the personal tastes of the reviewer and the philosophy of the award site as a whole. Some award sites look for truly cool sites based on graphic design or coverage of zany issues. Other award sites look for great resources, with no consideration going to whether the site uses mostly text or a cutting-edge graphic design. Because personal opinion weighs heavily in the decision, truly great sites are sometimes passed by.

To improve your odds of being selected, take the time to get to know the types of sites that the reviewers prefer. If they review mostly entertainment sites and you have a business-oriented site, the odds are high that you will get passed by. So rather than submit the URL of your main business page, submit the URL for that fun area where you let customers interact with your products online, or highlight this area in the summary description that you supply with the submission.

You can also improve your odds of winning by submitting each of the key areas within your site separately. If your site has three different areas, you might submit each of these areas. Ideally, these areas would cover unrelated topics, such as sports memorabilia, music singles from the '50s, and multimedia CD-ROMs for the Mac. In this way, you are truly submitting something different.

The old adage, "If at first you don't succeed, try, try again," certainly applies to awards. Don't abuse the submission process by submitting your site every few days or weeks, though. Instead, wait a few months before submitting your site again. In the interim, you may also want to work on the design, flow, and content of your Web site.

As you read this part, I suggest that you apply the information as you go. Submit your Web site to each of the awards that I discuss. To make the task of submitting your Web site easier, you may want to visit the companion Web site for this book at **www.tvpress.com/promote /award.htm.**

Cool Site of the Day

Cool Site of the Day is one of the most popular awards. To help you make sense of the many offerings, you will find the top Cool Site of the Day awards in this section. These sites are the best of the best when it comes to the Cool Site of the Day award because they follow the guidelines for a good award discussed previously. For the most part, the awards are showcased for at least a day. Then, because they are archived, the awards can continue to generate traffic to your site over the long haul. The sites

Figure 4.45

If you're looking to get noticed, Infi.Net's Cool Site of the Day can help.

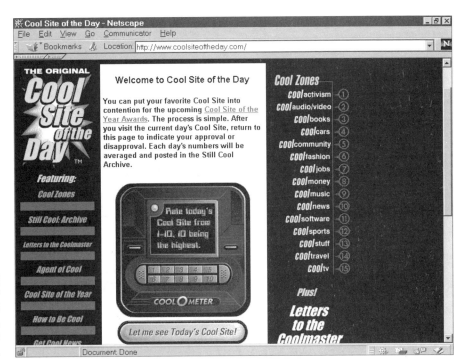

are also popular, and as I stated earlier, the busier the award site, the better the chances for increasing your Web traffic.

Infi.Net (**www.coolsiteoftheday.com/**) offers one of the original Cool Site of the Day awards. Along with the Cool Site of the Day award, this site has many other features that make the site a great destination (see Figure 4.45). All sites that receive the Cool Site of the Day are showcased on the day of the award. Afterward, they move to a page featuring sites picked that week, and then later move to an archive featuring all past awards. You'll also find a Cool Site of the Year award.

You can submit your cool home page or Web site to Infi.Net by sending e-mail to **cool@coolsiteoftheday.com**. Your message should contain the page title, the page URL, and a thorough yet concise description.

Project Cool (**www.projectcool.com**) is another hip site that recognizes the coolest sites on the Web. Project Cool features its current Cool Site of

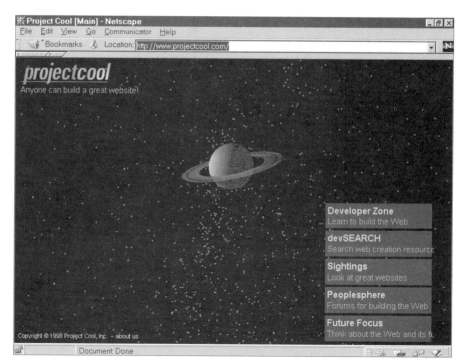

Figure 4.46

Project Cool offers daily sightings and a complete archive of past awards.

the Day in a section called Sightings (see Figure 4.46). You can access a complete archive of cool sites in the Previous Sightings section. Project Cool supplements its cool site picks with a Web site developer area and a reader discussion area. A lot of Web developers visit the developer area but end up browsing just because this site is so wonderfully designed. You can submit your site to Project cool using a submission page found at **www.projectcool.com/sightings/submit.html**.

Dr. Webster (**www.drwebster.com**) prescribes the latest cool sites every day with the Cool Web Site of the Day award. This site, produced by 123Go, has many extras that make the site a fun place to visit (see Figure 4.47). Be sure to check out the X of the Day area, where you'll find links for items such as Letterman's list of the day and the Dilbert cartoon of the day.

The current cool site is featured in Dr. Webster's zany prescription of the day style. Afterward, the cool site of the day is moved to an archive that

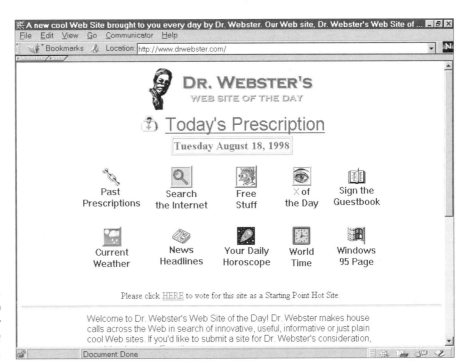

Figure 4.47

Dr. Webster prescribes new sites daily.

you can browse by month and day. To submit your Web site to Dr. Webster's Cool Web Site of the Day, send e-mail to **mmcdonald @123go.com** or visit the Dr. Webster home page and follow the Submit a Site link.

Totally Cool (**www.centraldrive.com/totally-cool/**) is an up-and-coming guide to all that's cool on the Web (see Figure 4.48). Getting Totally Cool's stamp of approval can help put your Web site on the map. Totally Cool does a great job of presenting awards and making lists of past winners available. You can submit your site to Totally Cool by visiting the site and following the Get Cool Now links.

Hot Site of the Day

The words hot site imply as much as the words cool site, so it makes sense that there are Hot Site of the Day awards. When you round up all the

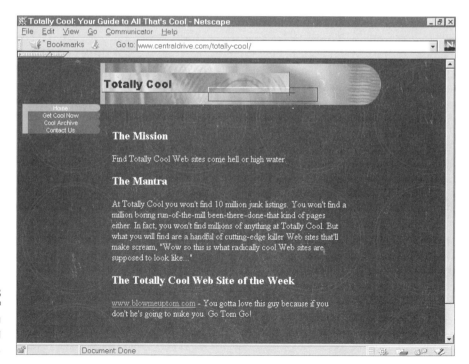

Figure 4.48

Totally Cool is an up-and-coming guide to cool.

entries in this category, you find that most aren't as polished as the sites that started the cool craze. Still, two awards sites stand out from the crowd. These sites are Cybersmith's Hot Site of the Day and HotSpots from Windows Magazine.

Cybersmith (**magneto.cybersmith.com**) is a chain of coffee houses for the wired generation. At the home page for Cybersmith's well-trafficked Web site, you will find links to lots of interesting areas within the site that promote the company and its stores. As shown in Figure 4.49, the current Hot Site of the Day is highlighted on the hot sites home page (**magneto.cybersmith.com/hotsites/**). You can access minireviews of the current week's hot sites or monthly archives of hot sites as well. You can submit your site to Cybersmith using a form found at **magneto.cybersmith.com/hotsites/suggestsite.html.**

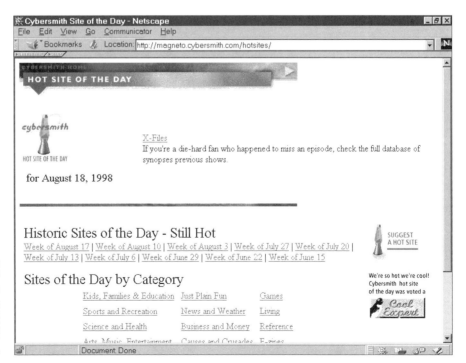

Figure 4.49

Submit your site to Cybersmith and see if you can get listed as the hot site of the day.

Windows Magazine (**www.winmag.com**) publishes a list of what it calls HotSpots, with a new one featured every day. Because of the tremendous popularity of *Windows Magazine*, the site and the HotSpots page get lots of visitors, making the HotSpot award something that will definitely increase traffic to your Web site (see Figure 4.50; **www.browsertune.com /flanga/hotspots.htm**). You can suggest your site by sending e-mail to **hotspots@langa.com**. Your message should contain the title, the URL, and a description of the page that you are submitting.

Computer Currents Interactive (**www.currents.net**) recognizes outstanding sites by designating them as hot sites or links of the week. Unlike other sites that grant only a single award, these awards usually go to several sites that cover different topics, such as entertainment, sports, and humor (see Figure 4.51). With multiple awards offered each week, you have a better chance of receiving an award. Lists of past winners are available in an archive that you can search by category.

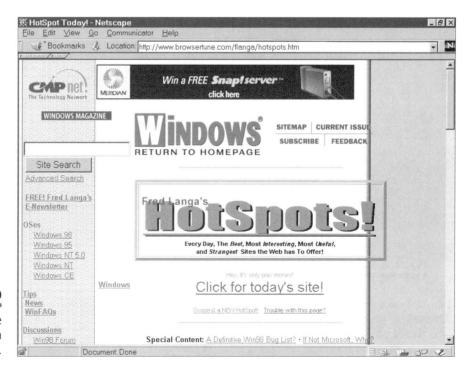

Figure 4.50

Get your Web site noticed with HotSpots.

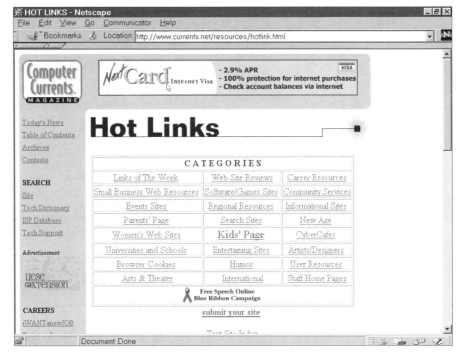

Figure 4.51

Two awards for the
price of one with
Hot Links and Links
of the Week.

You can submit your site to CCI by sending e-mail to **mmc@com-pcurr.com**. The URL for the awards pages are **www.currents.net /resources/link/linkweek.html** and **www.currents.net/resources /hotlink.html.**

Another great award site is What's New from Yahoo! (**www.yahoo.com /new/**). What's New is a daily list of cool sites. Daily picks are listed by title with a one-line summary and archived with the What's New? page.

In addition to the daily picks, Yahoo! has a weekly pick award as well (**www .yahoo.com/picks/**). Winners of the Yahoo! Weekly Pick award are show-cased in a feature article that covers about a dozen different Web sites (see Figure 4.52). All the Weekly Pick columns are archived for easy browsing.

You can submit a page to Yahoo!'s daily and weekly picks by sending e-mail to **suggest-picks@yahoo-inc.com**. Your message should contain the page title, the page URL, and a description of the page that you are submitting.

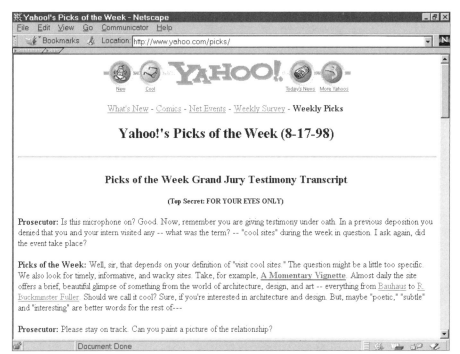

Figure 4.52

Yahoo offers daily
and weekly awards
for cool sites.

Wild, Crazy, and Zany Site Awards

Take a walk on the wild side with the wild, crazy, and zany site of the day awards. Although these types of awards are offshoots of the original Cool Site of the Day concept, this category has several terrific award sites.

When it comes to weird, Bizarre, Strange, and Unusual wins hands down (see Figure 4.53). If you have a truly weird site, you definitely want to be listed here. To submit a listing, visit the main page and follow the Submit a Listing link. You'll find the front door to Bizarre, Strange, and Unusual at **www.centraldrive.com/splat/bizarre.htm.**

Too Cool (**www.toocool.com**) offers the Too Cool award. As shown in Figure 4.54, the featured site appears directly on the home page, accompanied by a graphic and a quick review. Although the graphics are what make this site terrific, lists of all sites that have received the award are

Figure 4.53

Weird is in at Bizarre, Strange, and Unusual. If you have an unusual site, this is the place to get listed.

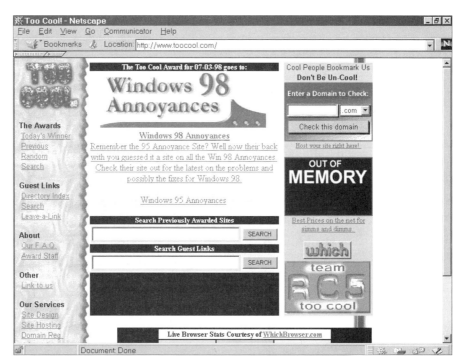

Figure 4.54

Is your site too cool? Well if it is, Too Cool is the right place for you.

archived with and without graphics. In addition to the Too Cool award, you can also use the Leave-a-Link service, which allows you to submit a link to a category-specific directory maintained at the site.

You can submit your site for consideration for the Too Cool award by sending e-mail to **webmaster@toocool.com**. To add your link to the Leave-a-Link directory, use the submission form found at **toocool.com /guest/cool_add.htm.**

Very Crazy Productions (**www.verycrazy.com**) offers an award for the craziest site of the week (see Figure 4.55). As the name implies, the award is for sites that are fun and wild. You can access the awards page directly at **www.verycrazy.com/crazysites/.** Unlike other sites that simply archive lists of previous recipients, Very Crazy Productions adds an interesting twist by allowing visitors to tour the sites of previous recipients. The actual tour is handled by a script that randomly selects the first site on the tour. Then, using an innovative browsing interface at the bottom of the featured page, you can wander through other award-winning sites.

To submit your site to Very Crazy, use the submission page found at **www .verycrazy.com/crazysites/submitsite1.html.**

Another interesting twist on the traditional cool site of the day is That's Useful, This Is Cool (**www.usefulcool.com**). As the name of the site implies, the folks at That's Useful, This Is Cool offer awards for useful sites and cool sites. In this way, if you have a great resource that isn't necessarily hip, cool, or zany, you can get a That's Useful site of the day award.

As shown in Figure 4.56, each site that receives an award is highlighted with a fairly extensive review. Snippits from the reviews are displayed in the weekly archives. You can submit a site for That's Useful by sending e-mail to **useful@usefulcool.com**. You can submit a site for This Is Cool by sending e-mail to **cool@usefulcool.com**. Although submitting the same page for both awards is tempting, the developers of That's Useful, This Is Cool ask that you submit to one category only.

Figure 4.55

Get crazy with the Craziest site of the week.

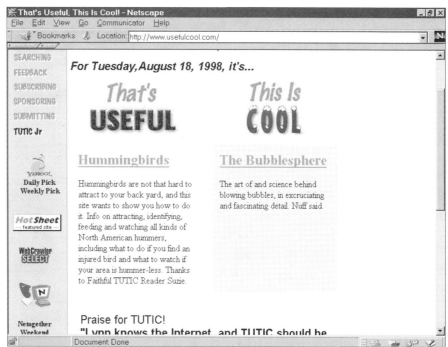

Figure 4.56

Submit useful and cool sites to That's Useful, This Is Cool.

Best of the Web

Truly great sites are designated as the best of the Web. As I've discussed previously, many Web guides offer insights into the best sites on the Web. Here, you will find additional Web guides to check out and, of course, to submit your site.

2Ask (**www.2ask.com**) maintains a comprehensive list of what it calls the best sites on the planet (see Figure 4.57). Selected sites are organized by category and feature a mini-review. You can nominate your site for possible listing at **www.2ask.com/index_nomination.html.**

Beatrice's Web Guide (**www.bguide.com**) reviews the best sites on the Web (see Figure 4.58). Although the top picks are showcased on the home page, other areas such as Getting Ahead allow you to quickly find interesting sites. You can submit your site to Beatrice's Web Guide using a submission form found at **www.bguide.com/suggest.html.**

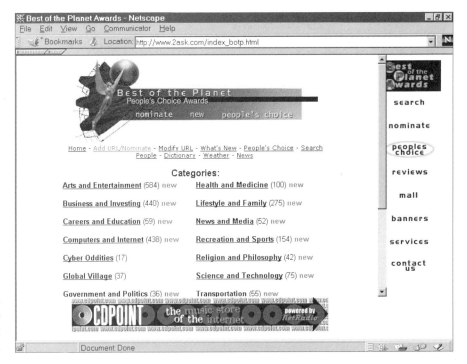

Figure 4.57

2Ask lists the best sites on the planet.

LookSmart (**www.looksmart.com/**) is one of the most well-known guides to the best of the Web (see Figure 4.59). As a tremendously popular destination, LookSmart gets millions of visitors every week. It is this overwhelming flow of traffic that makes being recognized at LookSmart's Best of the Web so wonderful. To submit your Web site, find the category within the directory that best matches your site, and then click on the Submit button found at the top of the page.

The Web 100 (**www.web100.com**) focuses on the top 100 Web sites (see Figure 4.60) Each site featured has a minireview and is searchable by position within the list as well as by keyword and category. Sites selected in the Web 100 are voted onto the list by users. Because the visitor rating is interactive, the Web 100 is constantly changing, making it a great place to get listed.

You can submit your site to the Web 100 using the submission form found at **www.web100.com/other/submit.html.**

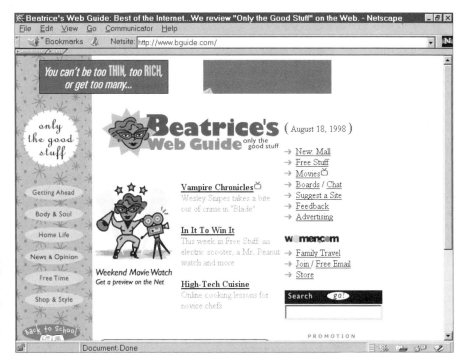

Figure 4.58

Beatrice's Web Guide mixes listings to the top sites with interesting commentary.

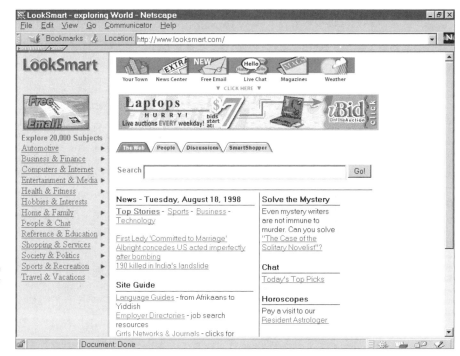

Figure 4.59

LookSmart is one of the top guides to the Web and definitely a good place to get listed.

Figure 4.60

To get listed here, you'll need to get a few friends to vote regularly for the top 100.

In an attempt to outdo the other top-of-the-Web sites, Web Side Story (**www.websidestory.com**) publishes a list called the World's Top 1000 Web pages. Unlike other top-of-the-Web lists, the World 1000 at Web Side Story is a list of the top 1,000 sites in each of more than 35 categories (see Figure 4.61). Although having a thousand sites in each category at your fingertips may seem overwhelming, Web Side Story has done a nice job of neatly organizing the listings.

The diversity of the World 1000 gives Web publishers a chance to really get noticed. You can submit a listing to the World 1000 by visiting **www .websidestory.com/wc/Addurl.index.html.**

Note that you'll have to install a hit tracker on your Web site to become eligible for this award. The hit tracker tracks visits to your Web site and lets the World 1000 rank you accordingly.

Zen Search (**www.zensearch.com/**) provides a guide to what it calls quality Web sites as well as a guide to the Top 100 Web sites in various

Figure 4.61

The Top 1000 lists sites according to their ranking. To get listed, you'll need to install a hit tracker.

categories (see Figure 4.62). The goal of the site is to give Web surfers a search engine that they can use to find only the best the Web has to offer. You can submit a listing by visiting **www.zensearch.com/AddURL.html**.

Wrapping Up and Looking Ahead

If you offer products, services, or business information at your Web site, you should definitely list your site with business search sites and directories. Business search engines and Yellow Pages offer a unique place to get your business and your business-oriented Web site noticed. After submitting your site to these search engines, you should go on to submit your site to search engines and directories that focus on specific industries. These guides can also help your Web site stand out from the crowd, especially when you consider that the major category guides attract millions

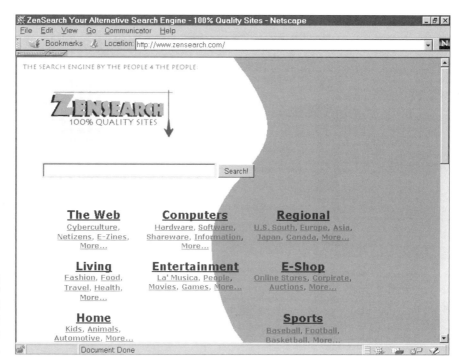

Figure 4.62

Zen Search lists the Top 100 as well as offering a guide to quality Web sites.

of visitors, yet have considerably fewer listings than mainstream directories such as Yahoo!

Finally, don't forget about awards sites. Thousands of organizations are offering Web awards. Web awards range from daily awards, such as the Cool Site of the Day award, to yearly awards, such as *PC Magazine*'s Top 100. When you work your way through the maze of Web site awards, you find that there is a tremendous difference between Bubba's Site of the Day award and an award from a well-respected, well-trafficked Web site. This afternoon you learn how to submit your site to many search engines and directories simultaneously. As always, the focus is on using resources that are low-cost or cost free.

Attracting the Masses

- ✪ Registering with Many Search Engines and Directories Simultaneously
- ✪ Selling Your Web Site through E-mail
- ✪ Attracting the Masses with Giveaways, Contests, Sweepstakes, and More
- ✪ Reviewing Your Progress and Planning More for Next Weekend

More than a dozen organizations offer services that allow you to register with multiple search engines and directories. These so-called registration services are great if you want to quickly spread the word about many different page URLs. You'll spend this afternoon learning about these and other valuable means of promoting your Web site.

Registering with Many Search Engines and Directories Simultaneously

Just as search engines and directories have different submission processes, so do registration services. This part of the Sunday Afternoon session covers registration services: how they operate, what to watch out for, and how to use these services without paying a dime.

Introducing Web Registration Services

Registration services are one of the most innovative types of Web services to come along. The idea is that instead of having to register with search engines and directories one by one, you can use the registration service to register with many different search engines and directories at once. Although one central interface for registering your Web site is wonderful, you still have to go through a rather lengthy submission process.

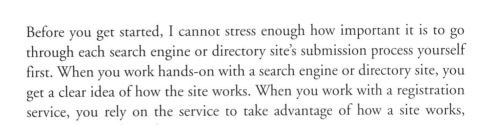

Before you get started, I cannot stress enough how important it is to go through each search engine or directory site's submission process yourself first. When you work hands-on with a search engine or directory site, you get a clear idea of how the site works. When you work with a registration service, you rely on the service to take advantage of how a site works, which doesn't always happen.

Using Registration Services

The registration process usually starts with your entering information into a form. This information includes all the elements that you would normally enter into the submission form of a search engine or directory, such as the page title, page description, and personal contact information. Next, you select the search engines and directories to which you want to submit your site. Afterward, you begin the submission process, which almost always involves having to register each site separately by clicking on individual submission buttons that will send your information to a specific search engine or directory.

Because most search engines and directories use unique categories or require you to fill out other information, you usually enter this additional information during the submission process. Before you can submit your page to the Nerd World Internet directory, for example, you need to select a category. Likewise, before you can submit your page to What's New on the Internet, you must select a category and state where the page is located. With Pronet, you have to enter state, country, and category information before you can submit your page.

All these intermediate stops along the road mean that the registration process isn't as easy as the registration services would like you to believe. Still, the process is an improvement over manual submission if you are in a rush. Generally, it takes about 30 minutes to submit your site to 20 to 25 search engines and directories using a registration service, which shaves 10 to 15 minutes off the time that submitting your site manually would take.

Working with Registration Services

Like any service-oriented business, registration services are for-profit enterprises. You can't blame these services for trying to make a buck off their hard work. The cost of registering your site can jump to hundreds of dollars, however, and most registration services base their charges on the number of URLs that you want to register and the number of places to which you submit your URLs. For example, a registration service may charge $30 to submit a single URL to 50 search engines, $60 to submit two URLs to 50 search engines, or $100 to submit one URL to 150 search engines.

Although these rates were much higher in the past, the influx of new registration services is forcing the market to be competitive, resulting in wholesale pricing and better registration engines. But before you shell out your hard-earned cash or corporate money, you should know what you are buying.

The first thing you may note when you examine the resources provided by a registration service is that you've probably never heard of most of these sites—well, when I was conducting research I had never heard of some of them either. You should note that some of the sites are invariably personal home pages with very little Web traffic at all. Worse, you may find that some of the sites listed as resources don't even function.

Additionally, you should note that resource sites are frequently for restricted types of search engines and directories. You will find Yellow Pages directories that take only business listings. You will find directories for Web sites covering specific geographic areas such as Canada, Europe, or Asia. You will also find specialty directories, such as What's New? directories, award sites, and guides to the best of the Web.

In the end, whether you can register with 50 or 500 search engines doesn't really matter. What matters is the number of search engines that you can use out of those available. With a cost of about $1 per search engine or directory registered, most Web publishers simply cannot afford to throw money away. Fortunately, the best sites are usually those included in the

first 50 or so available. Because of this, you get more bang for your buck if you stick to the basics—and the free services covered in this chapter are the ultimate in giving you your money's worth.

The most important thing to consider when you use registration services is the type of site with which you are registering. As you learned in previous chapters, there is a huge difference between a search engine and a Web directory.

Search engines use the single URL that you specify to crawl through your entire site and will usually schedule your site for periodic reindexing.

Because search engines reindex your site, you need to register with a search engine only once. Because search engines crawl through your entire site, the only URL that you need to register with a search engine is the URL to your top-level home page.

On the other hand, Web directories create a listing only for the page that you specify, and they rarely update the listing in the future. Because Web directories focus on pages rather than entire sites, you can register multiple URLs for the same site. The URLs that you submit should be for separate areas that cover different topics, however.

Because Web directories rarely update listings, you are responsible for updating your listing in the directory if you move the furniture around at your Web site, which doesn't necessarily mean that you should reregister with the directory. Instead, you should check the directory to see whether it has an update or change process. To make life easier on yourself and avoid having to submit changes for your listings, you can use the redirection techniques discussed in the Saturday Morning session under "Gaining Lost Readers from the Error Logs."

In the end, if you use a registration service, don't waste your time reregistering with search engines and directories that you've already used. Concentrate on the search engines and directories with which you haven't registered yet. Online, you will find the registration service listings at **www.tvpress.com/promote/reg.htm.**

Using Submit-It! to Register with Multiple Search Engines

Submit-It! (**www.submit-it.com**) is the original Web registration service. Although Submit-It! got its start by offering freebies, the service today is largely a commercial for-profit operation. An alternative to the Submit-It! premium service is Submit-It! Free (**siteowner.linkexchange.com /Free.cfm**), which is produced by the same folks who created the original Submit-It! site.

Using Submit-It! Free, you can submit your site to 20 different search engines and directories without spending a dime. The key difference between the paid service and the free service is simply the number of different search engines and directories sites to which you can submit your Web site. At the time of this writing, the 20 free search engines and directories included:

AAA Matilda	Northern Light
Alta Vista	PlanetSearch
AOL NetFind	Pronet
Bizwiz	Starting Point
ComFind	The Internet Archive
Infoseek	WebCrawler
InfoSpace	WebDirect!
LinkStar	What's New
Mallpark	What's New Too!
Nerd World Media	Yellow Pages Online

Preparing for the Submission Process at Submit-It! Free

Before you can submit your site using Submit-It! Free, you need to select the search engines and directories with which you want to register. By default, all of the search engines and directories are selected (see Figure 5.1). If you have a business-oriented Web site, you will probably want to

use all of these selections. If you have a personal home page or non-business Web site, you will probably want to deselect the business-only listings such as BizWiz, ComFind, and Yellow Pages Online.

As when you are registering your site directly, the most important fields are the ones that describe your Web page. Use the techniques discussed in previous chapters to select your page title, keywords, and page description. Most of the remaining fields in the submission form ask for personal and business contact information. Although you may want to skip these fields, keep in mind that some directories, especially business directories, will not place your listing without this information.

Submit-It suggests limits on the length of your descriptive information. These limits are based on the least common denominator, such as a site that allows your descriptions to have only 255 or fewer characters. Although you can get away with adding more than the suggested limit,

Figure 5.1

Submit-It Free allows you to submit your Web site to 20 search engines and directories. By default, all of the search engines and directories are selected in the submission form. Deselect the resources you want to omit.

you may have problems when you try to submit your site. You may also find that the information is simply truncated when necessary.

Registering Your Site

After you fill out and submit the form, Submit-It! Free will load a page that allows you to verify your submission and register your site with the selected search engines and directories. All the information that you entered in the form is stored in hidden fields in the registration page.

If you find a mistake when you are verifying the data, you can use your browser's Back button to return to the fill-out form. When you change the fields containing errors, resubmit the form by clicking on the submission button. When you are satisfied with the information, start the registration process.

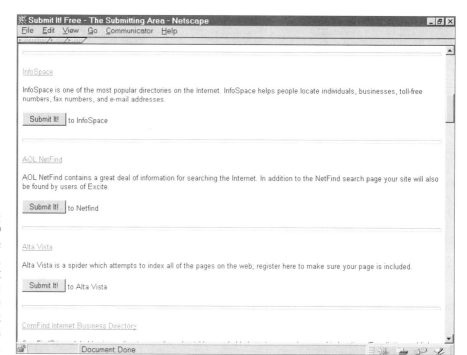

Figure 5.2

After you fill out the submission form, you need to submit entries to each resource site. Use the site-specific submission buttons to do this.

As shown in Figure 5.2, the registration page has submission buttons for each search engine and directory that you selected. If no other information is required for registration, you just click on the submission button. Doing so takes you to the search site, where you will usually see a page that confirms your registration. Some sites require you to verify the registration, which adds a few extra steps.

Each time you submit your site, you need to use your browser's Back button to return to the registration page. Doing so enables you to continue through the registration process.

After you submit your site to all the search engines and directories that you selected, you're done. If you have additional sites or pages to register, you can go back to the original submission form and start again.

Working with Addme!

Addme! (www.addme.com) offers a comprehensive registration service. Unlike with most other registration services, the developers of Addme! are hoping that advertising dollars will supplement their service and continue to allow them to provide the service without charge.

Using Addme!, you can submit your site to 34 different search engines and directories without spending a dime. At the time of this writing, these search engines and directories included:

411 Locate	New Rider's WWW Yellow Pages
Alta Vista	Northern Light
Excite	Open Text
FindLink	Peekaboo
Galaxy	Pronet
Goto.com	QuestFinder
HotBot	REX
Infohiway	Scrub The Web

InfoSeek	Snap!
InfoSpace	Starting Point
Jayde Online	USA Online
LinkMonster	WebArrivals
LinkStar	WebCrawler
Lycos	What's New
Magellan	What's New Too!
Matilda	What-U-Seek
NetFind	Yahoo

Preparing for the Submission Process at Addme!

Before you can submit your site using Addme!, you need to fill out the listing information shown in Figure 5.3. Addme! suggests that you use no more than 30 words for the descriptive field. However, keep in mind that more restrictive limits do apply in most cases. As stated previously, if you submit a field with too many characters, you may have problems when you try to submit your site. The information in the offending field may also be truncated.

Submitting Your Web Site with Addme!

After you fill out and submit the listing information, Addme! loads a page that allows you to verify your submission. If you find a mistake, you can use your browser's Back button to return to the listing information page. When you change the fields containing errors, resubmit the form by clicking on the submission button. When you are satisfied with the information, you can click on the Next button to continue with the registration process.

Rather than put all the entries on a single page, Addme! breaks the submission process down into a series of pages that allows you to register with one or more search sites. Figure 5.4 shows one of these pages.

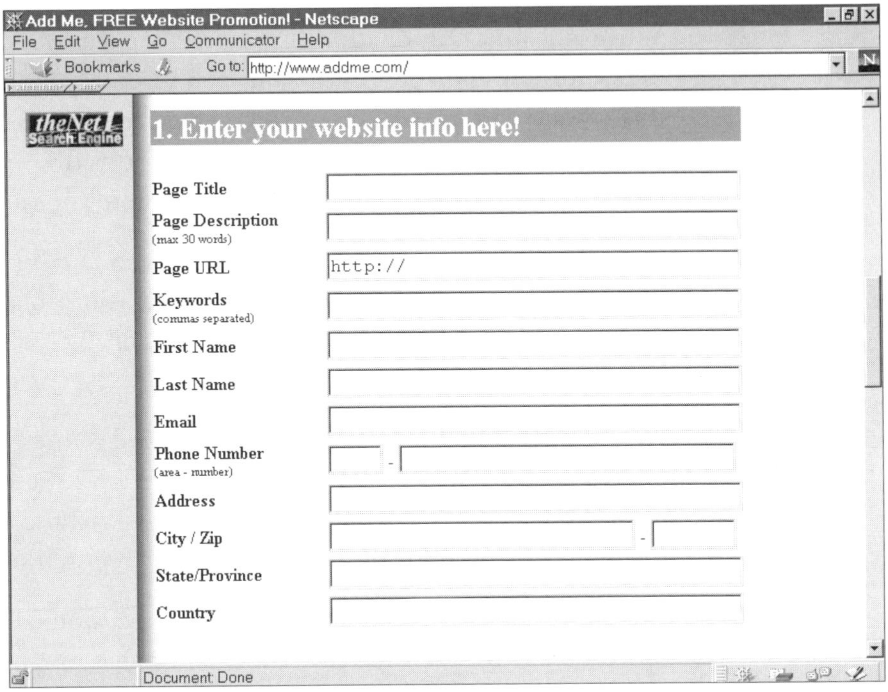

Figure 5.3

Be sure to fill out the Web site information form completely. The title, description, and keywords are the most important aspects of your entry.

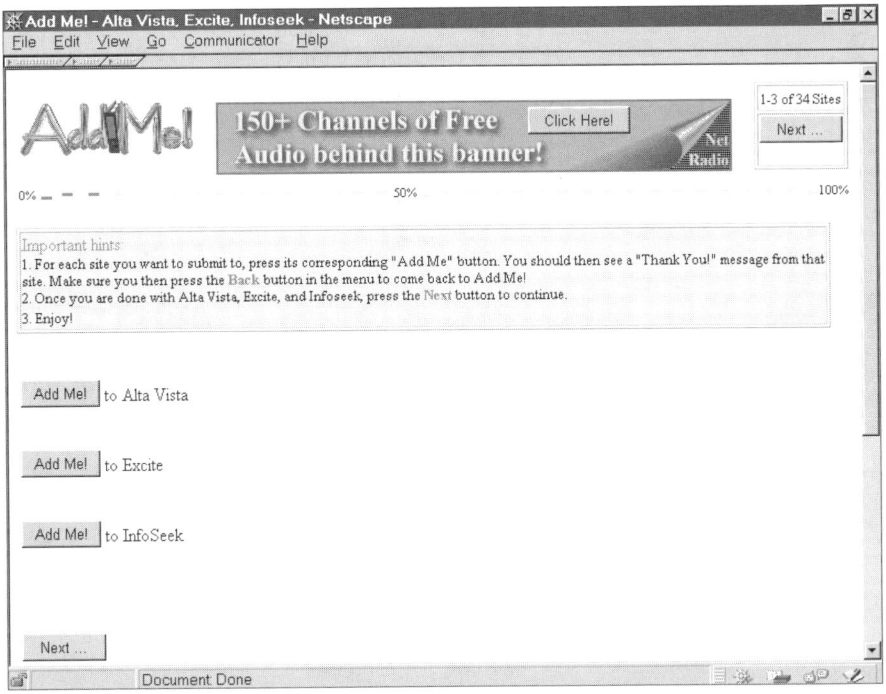

Figure 5.4

Addme! breaks the submission process down into a series of pages that allows you to register with one or more search sites. Use the navigation buttons at the top and bottom of the page to proceed through the registration process.

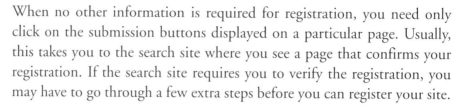

When no other information is required for registration, you need only click on the submission buttons displayed on a particular page. Usually, this takes you to the search site where you see a page that confirms your registration. If the search site requires you to verify the registration, you may have to go through a few extra steps before you can register your site.

Keep in mind that many of the search engines and directories in Addme! have a very specific focus. For this reason, you probably don't want to submit your site to every single one of the available sites. Instead, pick the sites that make sense.

Each time that you submit your site, you need to use your browser's Back button to return to the Addme! Web site. After you've submitted your site to the desired search engines on a particular page, use the Next button at the top of the page to continue through the registration process.

The individual pages within Addme! make customizing the registration process easier for each search engine, and this is one of the strong points of this service. After you've moved through all the registration pages, you will see a final page confirming that you are finished with the submission process. If you have additional sites or pages that you want to register, you may want to use your browser's history list to go back to the first entry for Addme!, which contains the submission form that you filled out at the beginning of the registration process. Alternatively, you can simply reenter the URL to the Addme! Web site in your browser's Location field.

Selling Your Web Site through E-mail

Plain old e-mail is an extraordinary means of promoting your Web site. Every day, people send more messages by e-mail than by standard mail, and why not? Messages sent by e-mail are usually free. The millions of daily e-mail messages bounce around the globe in one of three forms: messages sent from person to person, messages posted to a newsgroup, and messages submitted to a mailing list.

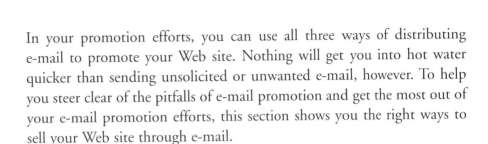

In your promotion efforts, you can use all three ways of distributing e-mail to promote your Web site. Nothing will get you into hot water quicker than sending unsolicited or unwanted e-mail, however. To help you steer clear of the pitfalls of e-mail promotion and get the most out of your e-mail promotion efforts, this section shows you the right ways to sell your Web site through e-mail.

Web Site Promotion through Direct E-mail, News-groups, and Mailing Lists

Not only has e-mail been around since the earliest days of the Internet, but also it is quickly becoming the most widely used electronic communication method. The widespread popularity of e-mail comes from the fact that it is so compulsively usable. Unlike standard mail, you can use e-mail to quickly and easily send the same message to hundreds, thousands, or even millions of recipients. Unlike the phone, you can send your message at any time of the day or night without fear of waking the recipient. Unlike the fax, you can send a message without having to worry whether the recipient has stocked the fax machine with paper or the fax line will be busy.

Just as most people don't want to receive calls from telemarketers, unsolicited faxes, or junk mail, most people don't want to receive unsolicited e-mail either. In the world of electronic mail, no four-letter word is more odious than spam. Spamming is the electronic equivalent of junk mail, and anytime you send unsolicited or unwanted messages, you are guilty of spamming. Sure, Web advertising agencies will try to sell you on the concept of bulk e-mail by telling you that the word spam applies only to unsolicited messages sent to multiple recipients, multiple discussion groups, or multiple mailing lists. In the end, however, an unsolicited message is an unsolicited message no matter whether it is sent to one or a thousand recipients.

As anyone who has ever sent unsolicited e-mail will tell you, the consequences can be severe. Your e-mail box may be bombarded with hate mail.

Your Internet service provider may pull your account. You may even run into legal difficulties. Despite these potential pitfalls, people all over the world continue to spam the electronic byways. The reason is the tremendous value of being able to send messages to anyone, anywhere, at any time.

Although you can certainly take the haphazard approach for Web site promotion through e-mail, there are ways to work within the system and current guidelines for newsgroups and mailing lists without rocking the boat. Working within the guidelines allows you to tap into the wonderful potential of e-mail, newsgroups, and mailing lists while minimizing the risk of backlash.

NOTE   I say that you can work within the system while minimizing the risk because you can't please all of the people all of the time. The simple truth is that some people like to huff and puff. When you encounter someone who cries foul for no apparent reason, you should do one of two things: simply ignore the person, or send a brief apology and then move on.

The following section offers a look at how you can effectively promote your Web site through direct communications, newsgroups, and mailing lists.

Promoting Your Web Site Directly

When you send a message to people using their e-mail address, you are using the most direct method of sending e-mail: person to person. As a rule, you should never send e-mail directly to anyone who doesn't want it. Instead, you should put together a promotional campaign that is responsive rather than proactive. This means that you ask visitors to your Web site and anyone else who contacts you whether they want to receive promotional material, rather than send the material to them unsolicited. Remember, unsolicited e-mail is spam, and some U.S. states may charge you a fine.

Sending Promotional Material

Promotional material that you send to subscribers can take many different forms. For a straightforward marketing approach, you can use advertisements and press releases pertaining to your organization as well as your products and services. You can also use an approach that focuses less on marketing and more on information. With this approach, you send subscribers information on what's new at the Web site, clips from recently published pages, or highlights of interesting places within the Web site.

The best way to invite participation is to add a subscription field to the HTML forms that are already at your Web site. In previous chapters, you saw that many forms used by search sites and directories have subscription fields. These fields ask whether you want to receive information or other promotional material by e-mail.

Subscription fields are often selected by default, which in itself isn't a bad thing, but some search sites go out of their way to ensure that most people who submit their forms join the subscription service. It is a deceptive practice to try to hide the subscription field or to blur the wording so that it isn't clear that the field is obscured.

Tips for Direct Mailings

To ensure that you receive subscriptions only from people who are truly interested in what you have to offer, place the subscription field so that it can be clearly seen, use clear wording, and deselect the field by default. Doing so makes subscribing an active process that requires a conscious effort from the reader.

If you use forms at your Web site to allow visitors to submit comments, sign a guest log, or enter any other type of data, consider adding a subscription field. The subscription field can be as simple as the Yes/No field shown in Figure 5.5. Here, the subscription field asks visitors whether they want to receive information on free promotions and contest updates. Some other subscription field descriptions that you may want to use include these:

- Can we send you press releases related to our company?
- Would you like to receive advertisements and promotional material from our sponsors?
- Do you want to receive notification when this page is updated?
- Would you like to receive weekly updates on what's new at our Web site?
- Can we send you weekly highlights of interesting areas within our Web site?

Promoting Your Web Site through Newsgroups

Newsgroups are popular gathering places for people with common interests. When you send a message to a newsgroup, you submit the message to a discussion area where everyone who follows the newsgroup may see

Figure 5.5

You can ask for subscriptions to your direct mailing list using an HTML form. When you send messages to the mailing list, be sure to add a brief statement telling the recipients they subscribed to the list and that you are not sending out unsolicited e-mail.

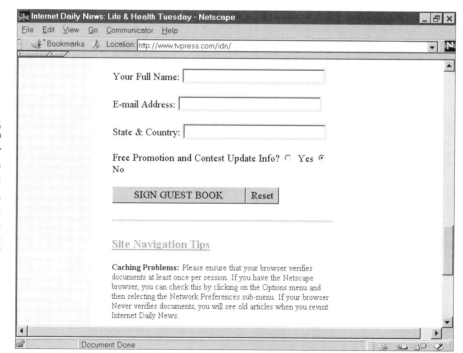

it. Newsgroups, like Web sites, cover just about every imaginable subject, and whether your Web site discusses cats or conspiracy theories, a newsgroup relating to your topic exists.

Finding Newsgroups That You Can Use to Promote Your Web Site

With thousands of newsgroups available, trying to find newsgroups without a little help is very time consuming. Rather than browse newsgroups individually, you should visit a newsgroup archive site such as Deja News (see Figure 5.6). At Deja News (**www.dejanews.com**), you can search through millions of current postings to newsgroups by keyword. Using the Interest Finder feature, you can also search by topics of interest.

If your Web site discusses cats, you would enter the keyword "cats" in the Interest Finder's search form. As shown in Figure 5.7, you would find that

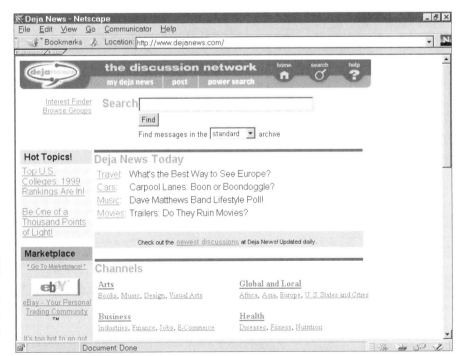

Figure 5.6

Deja News allows you to search through newsgroup postings by topics and keywords.

12 newsgroups might cover this topic. By clicking on the newsgroup names, you could access recent postings to all newsgroups that discuss the topic. Be sure to write down the newsgroups that you find.

Posting Tips for Newsgroups

After you have compiled a list of all the newsgroups that may be of interest, you should familiarize yourself with the groups by reading some of the recent postings. Nothing enrages newsgroup participants more than a promotional message that doesn't relate to the topic at hand. Going a step further, some newsgroup participants loathe all advertisements. For this reason, you should:

✪ Spend some time getting to know the newsgroup.

✪ Ensure that your promotional message strongly relates to the subject at hand.

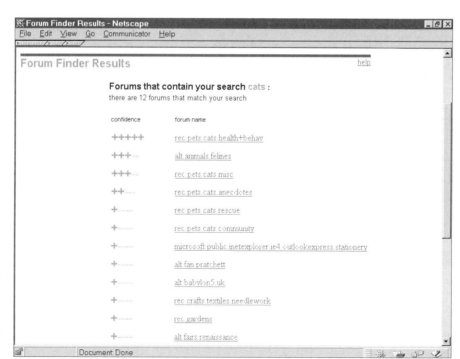

Figure 5.7

The Interest Finder lets you easily search for different kinds of newsgroups.

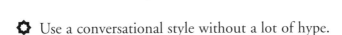

- ❂ Use a conversational style without a lot of hype.

- ❂ Keep the promotional message short, a few paragraphs at most.

- ❂ Post a message to a specific group one time and one time only; if people are interested, they'll respond.

As with direct promotion to individual users, you may want to focus less on marketing and more on information. For example, if a newsgroup participant asks about feline pneumonia and you have a terrific article on this very subject at your Web site, you may want to reply with a message like this:

> Feline pneumonia is a serious illness that affects thousands of cats every year. Because my own cat nearly died from pneumonia, I put together an article detailing the symptoms that pet owners can look for and the treatments that my veterinarian discussed with me. You can find this article at **www.centraldrive.com/pets/**.

Promoting Your Web Site through Mailing Lists

Mailing lists are similar to newsgroups but are organized in a different way. Whereas a message sent to a newsgroup goes to a central discussion area, mailing list messages get sent by e-mail directly to all the people who join the list. Because of the way mailing lists work, you must subscribe to a list before you can participate in the list. After you subscribe to a list, you can read messages posted to the list and post your own messages.

The simple act of posting a message to a mailing list doesn't ensure that it will be sent to the list members. Many mailing lists have moderators who review messages before they are actually distributed to the list members. If the moderator finds an inappropriate message, the moderator may cut out parts of the message or remove the message entirely.

Finding Mailing Lists You Can Use to Promote Your Web Site

You can find mailing lists by visiting one of the many mailing list archive or index sites. One of the best mailing list directories is Liszt (**www.liszt.com**). You can search through the directory using keywords or browse lists by subject (see Figure 5.8).

When you search or browse through the mailing list directory, you will notice that mailing lists aren't organized into hierarchies. In place of hierarchies, mailing lists use a naming system based loosely on the topic of the list or the name of the organization sponsoring the list. If you browse the philosophy category at Liszt, you will find over a dozen mailing lists that cover this topic in various ways. The mailing list maintained by the American Philosophical Association is called APACIC-L. The mailing list maintained by the Society for Women in Philosophy is SWIP-L. Other philosophy-related mailing lists are devoted to the works of specific philosophers.

When you find a mailing list in Liszt, you will see a brief summary of the list as well as the information that you need to subscribe to the list (see

Figure 5.8

Liszt is a directory for mailing lists. A fairly new feature at Liszt is the ability to see actual submissions to popular mailing lists.

Figure 5.9). Using the links provided, you can get additional subscription details and more information on the list.

Mailing lists are one of the most fluid resources on the Internet. Every day, dozens of new mailing lists are born and dozens of old mailing lists fade away into oblivion. Keeping up with this constant change is a chore made possible only with help from the list creators and moderators. Because of the constant changeover in mailing lists, I recommend that you check several different mailing list directories before making a decision about which you would like to participate in and possibly use to promote your Web site.

Another good guide to mailing lists is the Publicly Accessible Mailing Lists directory (**www.neosoft.com/internet/paml/**). You can search PAML by keyword using the search engine interface shown in Figure 5.10 (**www.neosoft.com/cgi-bin/paml_search/**).

Figure 5.9

Entries in the Liszt directory provide a brief summary of the related mailing list as well as the information that you need to subscribe to the list.

Although being able to search by keyword is useful, I found that looking for specific topics by browsing the subject index is easier. You can find the subject index at **www.neosoft.com/internet/paml/indexes.html**.

Posting Tips for Mailing Lists

As with newsgroups, you should read some of the postings to a mailing list before you submit anything. With thousands of people on the receiving end of your promotional message, you have to be very careful about the marketing approach you use. Nothing will generate hate mail faster than a blatant advertisement posted to a mailing list.

Rather than post an advertisement, you may want to focus more on information. Ideally, your posting will be helpful and useful to those who read it. For specific tips on creating your posting, refer back to the posting tips for newsgroups.

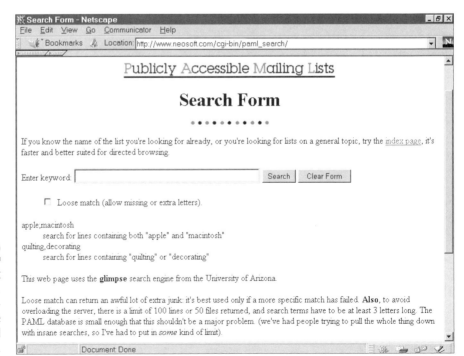

Figure 5.10

PAML is a great alternative to Liszt. Use it to double-check the information related to a mailing list.

Just about every mailing list out there has a set of rules. Usually, these rules are outlined in a FAQ (Frequently Asked Questions) for the list. Definitely try to find and read the FAQ before you participate in a mailing list. To make it easier to know and follow the rules, most mailing lists send out a confirmation message after you subscribe. In this confirmation message, you will usually find a list of the rules and lots of other good information. Save this message; you may need it later.

Announcing Your Web Site, Products, and Services by E-mail

Promoting your Web site through topical discussions is a terrific way to build traffic over the long term. Another way to build traffic is to announce your Web site, products, and services through e-mail. Although you can certainly announce your Web site in newsgroups and mailing lists that discuss topics similar to those at your Web site, you can use several additional avenues for making announcements. These avenues include:

- ✪ Using newsgroups and mailing lists specifically for announcements
- ✪ Using business-oriented newsgroups
- ✪ Using marketplace, commerce, and for-sale newsgroups and mailing lists

You can browse current postings to any of the newsgroups discussed in this section by visiting Deja News (**www.dejanews.com**). After you read some of the postings and are sure that the list is right for you, you can post your announcement. The key is to style your message in a way that is appropriate for the discussion group or mailing list.

When you make an announcement, you may want to organize your message like a press release that covers your Web site or the products and services that you discuss at your Web site. Ideally, your message will be only a few paragraphs long and fewer than 500 words. Brevity is important because most readers won't spend more than a few seconds glancing at your message.

You should work the URLs to your Web site or area within your Web site that you are promoting into the body of the message. Repeating a URL at the top and bottom of the message, or directing readers to different URLs within the Web site, is often a good idea. In this way, anyone scanning the message can zero in on the all-important URLs.

Announcement Newsgroups and Mailing Lists

Just as you can list your Web site in a What's New directory, you can list your Web site in discussion groups and mailing lists that are devoted to Web announcements. Although most announcements groups and lists focus specifically on announcements for new Web sites, some discussion groups and lists focus on products and services.

Newsgroups that you can use to announce your Web site include:

biz.infosystems.www	misc.entrepeneurs
biz.infosystems.wwwannounce	misc.news.internet.announce
comp.infosystems.www.announce	pnet.www.announce
comp.internet.net-happenings	

Mailing lists that you can use to announce your Web site include:

link-l	Web Essentials Announcement List
net-happenings	Weekly Bookmark
Net-announce	

Newsgroups that you can use to announce software products related to specific operating systems include:

comp.os.linux.announce	comp.sys.mac.announce
comp.os.ms-windows.announce	comp.sys.mac.games.announce
comp.os.netware.announce	comp.sys.newton.announce
comp.os.os2.announce	comp.sys.next.announce
comp.sys.amiga.announce	comp.sys.sgi.announce
comp.sys.atari.announce	comp.sys.sun.announce
comp.sys.ibm.pc.games.announce	

Newsgroups that cover specific Web-related products, such as browsers and servers, include:

comp.infosystems.www.authoring.html

comp.infosystems.www.authoring.images

comp.infosystems.www.authoring.misc

comp.infosystems.www.browsers.mac

comp.infosystems.www.browsers.misc

comp.infosystems.www.browsers.ms-
   windows

comp.infosystems.www.browsers.x

comp.infosystems.www.misc

comp.infosystems.www.servers.mac

comp.infosystems.www.servers.misc

comp.infosystems.www.servers.ms-
   windows

comp.infosystems.www.servers.unix

comp.os.os2.networking.www

alt.www.hotjava

alt.fan.mozilla

comp.infosystems.www.authoring.cgi

Business Newsgroups for Making Announcements

Anyone who has ever wondered whether a place exists where blatant advertising and capitalism rule the day need look no further than the biz.* newsgroup hierarchy. In the biz.* newsgroup hierarchy, you will find dozens of newsgroups devoted to announcements for products and services. Although many of the announcements in biz.* newsgroups are filled with hype, the most successful announcements are the ones that focus less on marketing and more on information.

The primary newsgroups in the biz.* hierarchy that may be of interest in your promotion efforts include:

biz.americast

biz.books.technical

biz.comp

biz.comp.accounting

biz.comp.hardware

biz.comp.jobs

biz.comp.misc

biz.comp.services

biz.comp.software

biz.entrepreneurs

biz.generalbiz.marketplace.non-computer

biz.infosystems

biz.marketplace

biz.marketplace

biz.marketplace.computers

biz.marketplace.computers.discussion

biz.marketplace.computers.mac

biz.marketplace.computers.other

biz.marketplace.computers.pc-clone

biz.marketplace.computers.workstation

biz.marketplace.discussion	biz.marketplace.services.computers
biz.marketplace.international	biz.marketplace.services.discussion
biz.marketplace.services	biz.marketplace.services.non-computer
biz.marketplace.services.computer	biz.misc

More Newsgroups and Mailing Lists for Announcements

With thousands of discussion groups available, the listings in this chapter are only the tip of the iceberg. If you know what to look for, you can find dozens of other places to post announcements. Before you get started, though, keep in mind that I searched out the best of the bunch already—you know, that old legwork stuff designed to save you time and effort.

With newsgroups, you will find that searching the hierarchy listings for keywords is usually the best way to find what you are looking for. You can do this at Deja News.

To find business-related newsgroups that may accept your announcements, the keywords you may want to use in your search include:

announce

biz

business

commerce

forsale

marketplace

www

For mailing lists, the directories at PAML or LISZT make searching by keyword easy. To find mailing lists that may accept your announcements, the keywords that you may want to use in your search include:

announce

business

commerce

marketplace

Creative Signature Files

An e-mail signature is an extra that you can add to the end of *all* your e-mail messages. This trailer can help you promote your Web site as well as your products and services anytime that you send an e-mail message. Your signature can be styled as a mini-promotion for your Web site or anything else that you want to highlight.

Although you may see e-mail signatures that run 10–20 lines, most signatures are fewer than 5 lines. As a rule of thumb, 3–5 lines are usually a good length for an e-mail signature. Because your e-mail signature will go out with all your mail unless you delete the signature, keeping the signature free of hype is a good idea.

A sample of actual e-mail signatures that I've used in the past is shown in Listing 5.1. This should give you an idea of how you can create a signature that is effective yet doesn't look like an advertisement.

Listing 5.1   Sample E-mail Signatures

```
-
William R. Stanek
Editor-in-Chief, Internet Daily News -
  http://www.netdaily.com/
Author of several tech books -
  http://www.tvpress.com/writing/
-
William R. Stanek
Executive Director, Virtual Press Global Internet Solutions
  (http://www.tvpress.com)
Providing global solutions to the Internet community since
  March, 1994
Tune in to Internet Daily News - http://www.netdaily.com/
-
William R. Stanek
Founder & Director of Virtual Press Global Internet Solutions
```

```
(http://www.tvpress.com)
Looking for something new? Why not visit: the Writer's
   Gallery
(http://www.tvpress.com/vpwg.html) or the Internet Job Center
   (http://www.tvpress.com/jobs/)
```

NOTE When you add URLs to your signature (or anywhere within an e-mail message for that matter), be sure to include the http:// as part of the URL. If you do, most e-mail programs will make this a hypertext link that users can click on.

Most e-mail applications allow you to create a signature file using an ordinary text file. After you create and save the signature file, you can use the standard features of your favorite e-mail application to add the e-mail signature to all your outgoing messages.

In Netscape Messenger, you tell Messenger about the signature file as follows:

1. Select the Preferences option of the Edit menu.

2. In the Preferences dialog box, double-click on the Mail & Groups category, and then select the Identity subcategory.

3. To the right of the Signature File field, you will see the Choose button. Click on it.

4. Use the Signature file dialog box to tell Messenger where you put the file, and then click on the Open button.

5. Click on OK and you're finished.

Outlook Express is a bit smarter when it comes to signatures. Your signature is tracked using what Outlook Express calls Stationery. Using the Stationery option, you can set up a signature without ever having to leave Outlook Express.

The steps you need to follow to create a signature are:

1. Select the Stationery option of the Tools menu.

2. In the Mail tab, click on the Signature button. Using the Signature dialog box, follow steps 2a through 2d.

   a. Make sure the Add the signature to all outgoing messages check box is selected.

   b. Click on the Text radio button.

   c. Enter your signature in the text window provided.

   d. Click on OK to close the Signature dialog.

4. Click on OK, you're finished.

Attracting the Masses with Giveaways, Contests, Sweepstakes, and More

Traditional marketers have used giveaways, contests, and sweepstakes for years to make their sponsors stand out from the crowd. The simple truth is that we all love the chance to win something for nothing, and whenever we have the opportunity to enter a contest or giveaway, we usually go for the gusto. Web advertisers have pushed traditional giveaways and contests onto the World Wide Web, where the quest for freebies can truly bring the masses to the sponsor's Web site.

Can't Get 'Em Any Other Way, Give It Away

Giving things away is a great way to build traffic to your Web site. Whether you want to pass out bumper stickers or trips to Europe, people will want to enter your giveaway. Beyond outright giveaways are contests and sweepstakes that ask the participants to answer questions or enter a creative work, such as a poem or jingle for a commercial.

Giveaways, contests, and sweepstakes promoted on the Web are often direct tie-ins to similar promotions running in print media. If your organization is already planning a giveaway or contest, advertising it on the Web can bring your message to an eager audience of millions.

Figure 5.11 shows a sweepstakes offered by Universal Studios. The sweepstakes was designed to promote Fast Times at Ridgemont High and other videos from the studio. The theme for the sweepstakes was Back to School, and all the prizes related to this theme. Universal Studios promoted the sweepstakes on- and offline.

Promotional tie-ins between your Web site and a giveaway or contest running in the print media work well if you have the clout of a major corporation behind you. But even if you are not part of a major corporation, you can benefit tremendously from running a contest or sweepstakes at your Web site.

Although many traditional promotional campaigns center around giveaways, contests, and sweepstakes, savvy marketers know that the interac-

Figure 5.11

Sweepstakes are a great way to promote your company's products and services.

tive and dynamic nature of the Web opens doors, removing the traditional boundaries and restrictions of print media. On the Web, your giveaway can become part of an interactive trivia quiz with questions that change dynamically each time the page is visited. You can even create an interactive treasure hunt with clues scattered throughout your Web site.

The Web allows you to conduct other types of promotions as well, such as online games that give something away to participants with the best scores. With an online game, contestants get to have fun while trying to win prizes. Online games can range from simple puzzles and teasers to actual video games programmed in Java or another programming language.

Figure 5.12 shows the online games available at the Headbone Zone. Kids can not only play the games at Headbone Zone (**www.headbone.com**) but also win prizes by doing so.

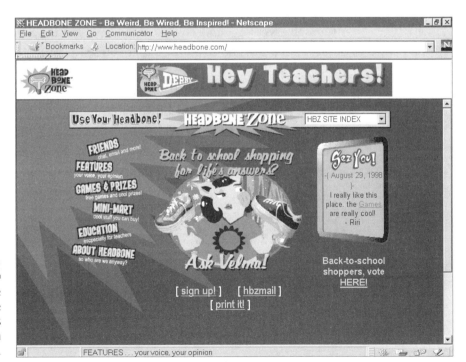

Figure 5.12

Headbone Zone provides interactive games and awards prizes based on player scores.

Using a giveaway, contest, or sweepstakes to increase traffic to your Web site is a good idea, but definitely not the only reason to give things away. You can use the giveaway, contest, or sweepstakes to accomplish these objectives:

- Build awareness for your products and services.
- Familiarize readers with other areas at your Web site.
- Build a profile of your readers based on a survey or questionnaire that is part of the submission form.

Later in this session, I examine each of the various types of giveaways and contests that you may want to use in your promotion efforts. These include:

- Free-for-all giveaways and sweepstakes
- Contests for artists, writers, and other creative people
- Trivia quizzes, games, puzzles, and teasers

Although giveaways and contests are great for increasing your traffic, the actual amount of traffic increase that you see at your Web site will depend on what you are giving away and how well you promote the giveaway. Keep in mind that the key to success isn't so much *what* you give away, but *how* you give it away. I call this your gimmick or hook. If your hook is great, your giveaway or contest will attract the masses. To help you promote your giveaway or contest, I guide you to Web sites that specialize in freebies, giveaways, and contests. After all, people need to be able to find your giveaway or contest in order to participate.

What to Watch Out For: The Legalities

Although nothing builds traffic like a good giveaway or contest, there are many things you should consider before you get started. Your primary concern should be the legal ramifications of publishing your giveaway or contest on the Web.

By putting your contest on the Web, you make it available to participants throughout the world, which may make your contest subject to certain laws. Every country has its own laws, and these laws often vary by region within the country as well. For example, each state in the U.S. has its own rules regarding giveaways and contests.

Disclaimers for Age and Residency

Because of the extreme diversity of international laws, most organizations that run contests and giveaways restrict their promotions to specific countries. When you restrict your contest to a specific country or countries, you should post a clear disclaimer along with any contest information. The purpose of the disclaimer is to protect your interests and ensure that you don't accidentally violate the laws of another country.

If you've browsed Web sites that run contests or giveaways, you have probably seen a disclaimer that says "U.S. and Canadian residents only" or "U.S. residents only." By restricting a contest to the U.S. and Canada or the U.S. only, you limit your liability—which is always a good idea.

Another thing to consider is the age of the participants. Because many U.S. states require that participants in contests be at least 18, you should place an age restriction on the contest. You can blend the age restriction right into your original disclaimer, such as "U.S. and Canadian residents 18 and older only" or "U.S. residents 18 and older only." Granted, verifying a person's age over the Internet is difficult; however, clearly marking the age restriction can only serve your best interest.

Other Disclaimers

Generally, within the U.S. and Canada, your sweepstakes or giveaway should be free, meaning that you shouldn't require entrants to purchase something in order to enter and win. In this way, your sweepstakes or giveaway is truly giving something away for nothing. You should post a clear disclaimer at the contest site that notifies readers that no purchase is

necessary to enter the contest. An exception is a creative contest, such as an art contest or writing contest that charges an entry fee.

You should also publish a statement to ensure that participants know that local laws apply to the contest and that the contest is void where prohibited. Voiding the contest where prohibited protects you from inadvertently violating the local laws.

Putting the Rules Together

Now that you have made a start on the rules for your contest or giveaway, you should put these rules together in an official form that you can publish on your Web site. In the official rules, you should spell out exactly what you will be giving away and the value of the prizes. If you will be giving away one Sony 19" TV valued at $399, specify this exactly.

After you've decided on the rules for your contest or giveaway, you should publish these for all the world to see. Ideally, you will place a summary of the rules on all the contest pages and make the detailed rules available with a hypertext link.

Listing 5.2 shows an example set of rules for a fictitious contest called the Happy Peacock Sweepstakes. As you read the listing, keep in mind that this is a made-up example that serves only to illustrate some of the points made in this section.

Listing 5.2   An Example Set of Contest Rules

```
Rules for the Happy Peacock Sweepstakes
1. No purchase necessary in order to enter.
2. To enter the sweepstakes, fill out the official entry form
   at the Happy Peacock Web site. We accept only fully com-
   pleted entry forms. Only one entry per person is allowed.
3. Sweepstakes begins January 1, 1998, and ends on December
   31, 1998. Your entry must be received no later than mid-
   night on December 31, 1998. Winners will be selected in a
   random drawing.
4. Sweepstakes is open to residents of the United States who
   are eighteen years of age or older. All submissions become
```

the property of Happy Peacock. All federal, state, and local laws and regulations apply. Any taxes due are the responsibility of the winner. Void where prohibited or restricted by law.

5. One first-place prize: Happy Peacock gift set, valued at $299. Ten second-place prizes: Happy Peacock T-shirt, valued at $25. Twenty third-place prizes: Happy Peacock coffee mug, valued at $9.

6. A list of prize winners will be published at the Happy Peacock Web site within 15 days after the end of the sweepstakes. Happy Peacock reserves the right to substitute a prize of equal or greater value.

Before you publish your contest or distribute any information related to your contest, you should check applicable federal, state, and local laws regarding contests and giveaways. The best places to research global law are the Law Library of Congress (**lcweb2.loc.gov/glin/lawhome.html**) and the Guide to Law Online (**lcweb2.loc.gov/glin/worldlaw.html**).

Boosting Traffic with Giveaways and Sweepstakes

Giveaways and sweepstakes are great for boosting traffic to your Web site. Every day, thousands of people search the Web looking for the latest giveaways and sweepstakes—and why not? They can win hats, T-shirts, books, jewelry, trips, and much more simply by filling out a form. Although there is not much difference between a giveaway and a sweepstakes, the term sweepstakes is often used when prizes are donated by sponsors or advertisers.

Creating a Giveaway or Sweepstakes

When you put together a giveaway or sweepstakes, remember that the prizes themselves are not what attract readers so much as is your execution. As a matter of fact, you could give away T-shirts and get more visitors than a site giving away trips to Europe.

Although I'm sure the organization giving away trips to Europe would argue their case heatedly, the reality is that a well-designed and well-pro-

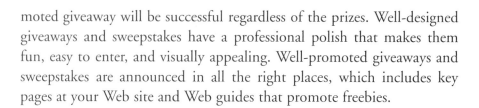

moted giveaway will be successful regardless of the prizes. Well-designed giveaways and sweepstakes have a professional polish that makes them fun, easy to enter, and visually appealing. Well-promoted giveaways and sweepstakes are announced in all the right places, which includes key pages at your Web site and Web guides that promote freebies.

NOTE You'll learn all about Web guides that promote freebies shortly, under the heading "Sites That Promote Your Freebies."

The best giveaways and sweepstakes have a theme that helps sell people on the idea of the giveaway or sweepstakes. If you are giving away trips, it is not just a "trip," but a "passport to adventure." If you are giving away cruises, it is not just a cruise, but "barefoot strolls along windswept beaches, romantic dinners for two, and quiet, moonlit evenings topside."

After you decide on the type of giveaway or sweepstakes to run, consider the prizes that you will award. As stated earlier, the prizes don't have to be extravagant, but they should be worth the time and effort that entering the contest takes. Additionally, entering the giveaway or sweepstakes should be as easy as filling out an entry form that asks for contact information, such as name, address, and phone number.

You may also want to add a questionnaire or survey to the entry form. Questionnaires can help you learn more about the type of people who visit your Web site. You can find out whether they use your products and services. You can also learn about reader preferences, such as their favorite area within your Web site, or their interests.

Looking at an Actual Sweepstakes

A good case study for a well-designed and well-promoted sweepstakes is PC Magazine's Fifteenth Anniversary Sweepstakes. On PC Magazine's Web site, the sweepstakes area shows off the prizes in a highly graphical and attention-grabbing manner (see Figure 5.13). The sweepstakes not only builds traffic to PC Magazine's Web site but also shows off the products of the sponsor.

PC Magazine enhanced the main sweepstakes page with a trivia quiz that asks you questions about technology (see Figure 5.14). After trying your hand at the trivia quiz, you could check out the answers, which were posted right on the Web site. By combining the trivia quiz with the sweepstakes, PC Magazine gave visitors an extra reason to browse the area; meanwhile, the sponsor and the magazine were getting wonderful exposure.

The official sweepstakes entry form required participants to enter key contact information, such as their name, address, and phone number, but it also featured an optional reader survey. The survey asked participants a series of questions that helped the magazine put together a fairly comprehensive reader profile.

Figure 5.13

Prizes are what bring in visitors, but you may be surprised to learn that a simple T-shirt contest can bring in as many visitors as a $50,000 giveaway. The secret is in the presentation.

Gaining Readers with Contests

Contests reward people for their talents or creativity. Because contests often require judging and extensive work on the part of the producer, some contests charge a nominal entry fee, such as $5, to enter a writing contest. Charging an entry fee for a writing contest that offers prestige, publication, and cash awards to the winners. Charging an entry fee for a contest that is meant more for fun than to be a career builder doesn't make sense.

Running a Contest

Contests can be just as much fun for you as they are for the participants. Your goal should be to use the contest to build traffic to your Web site. Ideally, your contest will tie in to and promote your business, products, and services as well. For example, developers of word processing applications may want to sponsor a write-off for the most creative or bizarre advertising gimmick for their product.

Figure 5.14

You can spice up the sweepstakes with trivia quizzes, puzzles, or brainteasers.

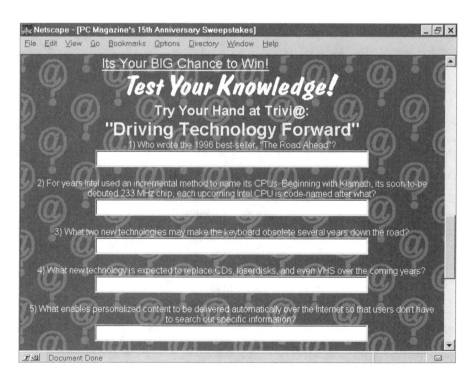

The type of contest that you run will depend largely on your interests. If you are interested in comedy, you may want to have a contest that rewards the funniest submissions. If you are interested in graphic design, you may want to have a design contest. If you love poetry, you may want to have a poetry contest.

To keep your contest as hassle-free as possible, you will want to decide on the specific formats that are acceptable for submissions. For a writing or poetry contest, you may want to specify in the rules that all submissions must be saved as standard ASCII text files with the .txt extension. Similarly, for a design or art contest, you may want to specify that all submissions must be saved in either GIF or JPEG format.

Additionally, anytime that you ask for creative submissions, you should set limits on the size or length of entries. For a writing contest, you may want to limit entries to 5,000 words. For a design contest, you may want to limit the size of the artwork to 1280 x 1024 with a file size of less than 2MB.

After you decide on the type of contest you want to run, you need to think about how you will judge the contest. Most small contests are judged exclusively by the contest developer. Creative contests, such as writing, art, or design contests, are usually voted on by a panel of judges. You can remove yourself from the judging process entirely by letting visitors to your Web site vote for the best submissions. The bottom line is that your judging process should be fair yet manageable using your current resources.

As with giveaways, you can use an entry form to accept submissions for the contest, and you may want to add a questionnaire to the entry form as well. Keep in mind that if you run a creative contest, many participants will have their entry in separate text or graphic files. Currently, the easiest way to submit files is as an attachment to an e-mail message. For this reason, you may simply want to supply an e-mail address for submissions rather than use an entry form.

With creative works, you must consider one more thing: U.S. and international copyright law. Creative works are the property of the creator unless the rights are granted or sold. Thus, if you plan to publish the winning works at your Web site, you need permission, and you should ask for this permission right in the entry form. The minimum rights that you will want to retain are one-time world electronic rights to the winning entries. Furthermore, you should state that winning entries will be published at your Web site.

Looking at an Actual Contest

An example of a contest that promotes a company's products is the Decorating Disaster Contest from Copper Canyon (see Figure 5.15). The words "decorating disaster" have a wonderful ring that describe the contest's theme. The idea behind the contest is to have participants describe their biggest decorating disaster and then to reward the best entry by allowing them to choose any item they want from the company's catalog.

The folks at Copper Canyon kept the submission form simple. As you can see from Figure 5.16, the form has fields for basic contact information and then asks participants to write an essay of 75 words or fewer, describing their decorating disaster. The entry form also has a field that lets participants subscribe to the company's mailing list.

When you consider that many people will use search engines or directories to find your contest, trying to build cross-traffic from your contest pages makes sense. As a reminder that the Copper Canyon site has more to offer, the last item on the entry page is a link to the company's home page. This link is also displayed on the page, confirming that the entry was received.

Using Games, Puzzles, and Teasers to Attract Visitors

Games, puzzles, and teasers can bring in the masses simply because they are entertaining. People of all ages love to play games that are challenging,

Figure 5.15

A great contest theme can help sell your contest. Just think about the thoughts that come into your head when you hear the words "Decorating Disaster Contest."

Figure 5.16

Submission forms can help you obtain important demographic and geographic information about your sites visitors. But if you collect this information, be sure to specify how the information will be used.

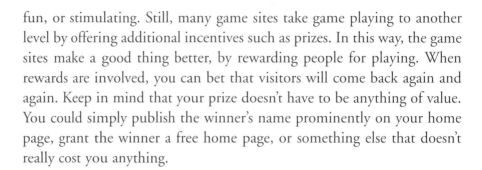

fun, or stimulating. Still, many game sites take game playing to another level by offering additional incentives such as prizes. In this way, the game sites make a good thing better, by rewarding people for playing. When rewards are involved, you can bet that visitors will come back again and again. Keep in mind that your prize doesn't have to be anything of value. You could simply publish the winner's name prominently on your home page, grant the winner a free home page, or something else that doesn't really cost you anything.

Creating a Game, Puzzle, or Teaser

When you think of games, you probably imagine the zippy video games that you see in the arcades. Although you could certainly spend months programming a truly awesome game for your Web site, some of the best games are those that are simple and compulsively playable. Most card games, such as poker or solitaire, aren't popular because of rip-roaring action; they are popular because they are easy yet challenging to play.

One game to consider is a treasure hunt. Treasure hunts are really popular during the holidays, especially at Easter. In a treasure hunt, you hide clues or treasures throughout your Web site and sometimes at participating Web sites. You can display clues or treasures directly on your Web pages using text and graphics. You can also link standardized treasure icons to secret pages at your Web site that describe an item in the treasure hunt.

With a treasure hunt, you need a submission page that lets participants submit a list of all the clues or treasures that they've collected. Usually, prizes in a treasure hunt are awarded to the participants that find all the treasures first. To ensure fair play, you may want to periodically change the clues and treasures during the hunt.

Another game that is a lot of fun and easy to produce is a trivia quiz. Although trivia quizzes can cover any topic, you may want to link the quiz to the theme or topic of your Web site. The best trivia quizzes have at least five challenging questions to which participants can get answers immediately. To keep visitors coming back, you may want to make the trivia quiz a weekly or monthly feature.

If you are giving away prizes based on a trivia quiz, you can post answers with a list of winners at a later date. Because many people may know the answer to your trivia questions, you really don't want to award prizes to everyone who submits the right answers. Instead, you may want to award prizes randomly from the list of participants who submitted the right answers.

Another type of game to consider is a puzzle. The best puzzles are word-based brainteasers, such as a crossword puzzle or a word association game. With a puzzle, you will probably want to reward participants simply for playing and submitting their answers.

A great way to build steady traffic with a puzzle is to change the puzzle often and award prizes randomly to the participants who answer a certain number of puzzles correctly in a given period of time. For example, you can publish a different puzzle every week and award prizes randomly to anyone who gets the answer to four different puzzles in a particular month.

Looking at an Actual Treasure Hunt

MacroMusic features an online scavenger hunt called Web Hunt (see Figure 5.17). The goal of the scavenger hunt is to follow a set of clues to various Web sites. Then once you find the items referenced in the clues, you can submit an entry for a chance to win a prize.

Before you can play, however, you have to join the treasure hunt by filling out a membership application. The application asks for contact information and important demographic information. Each time you want to obtain a clue or submit answers to the week's treasure hunt, you need to enter your user name and password. MacroMusic is able to use this information to track detailed statistics related to the contest participants.

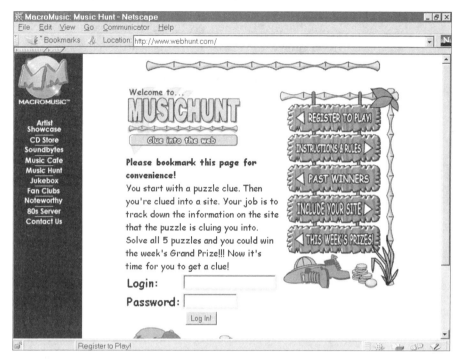

Figure 5.17

A well-designed scavenger hunt can be a terrific promotional vehicle for your Web site.

Another important aspect of the treasure hunt is the fact that participants need to find items related to five different clues. Because only one clue is given each day of the week, participants have to come back to the Web site over and over—building a long-term relationship with MacroMusic in the process.

Sites That Promote Your Freebies

You need to promote your giveaway, contest, or sweepstakes to make it successful. Although your promotion efforts should definitely begin at key areas within your Web site, you should also promote the contest through guides and directories that specialize in freebies.

In this section, you will find brief guides to some of the most popular contest directories. When you submit your freebie to a contest directory, be sure to provide the URL to the main contest page and a brief descrip-

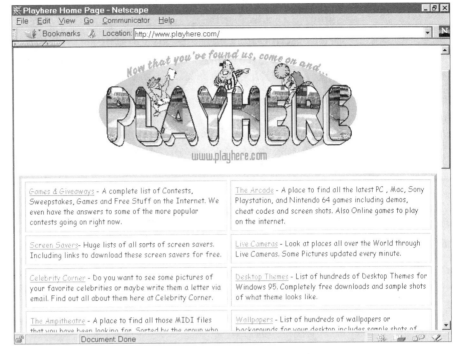

Figure 5.18

In addition to a great contest directory, Playhere provides lots of other fun resources.

tion of the contest. The contest description should specify when the contest ends as well as any age and residency requirements.

Promoting Your Freebie at Playhere

Playhere (**www.playhere.com**) is a terrific guide to fun things on the Web. The site is neatly organized into areas that cover broad, entertainment-related topics (see Figure 5.18). A section called Live Cameras is a directory to the hundreds of live cameras that you can find all over the Web. Celebrity Corner is a guide to Web sites dedicated to famous people. The Arcade covers sites that host online games as well as sites that talk about the latest video games.

One of the main attractions at the site is the games and giveaways section, which has extensive listings for contests, sweepstakes, and other freebies. Because Playhere appeals to a very diverse audience, it is a good place to

submit a contest listing. Playhere listings are displayed alphabetically, with brief descriptions and a submission date (see Figure 5.19). To show how many times a particular contest has been accessed, the listings also show clickthrough. This feature makes it easy to track the popularity of your contest at Playhere.

To submit your contest, giveaway, or sweepstakes to Playhere, visit one of the contest areas and follow the Add-A-Link URL. Be sure to provide a description of your contest.

Promoting Your Freebie in the Contest Catalogue

The Contest Catalogue (**contest.catalogue.com/contests/**) is an extensive guide to contests, sweepstakes, and giveaways on the Web. Features in the catalog include a What's New section and areas devoted to specific types of contests, such as treasure hunts and trivia quizzes (see Figure 5.20).

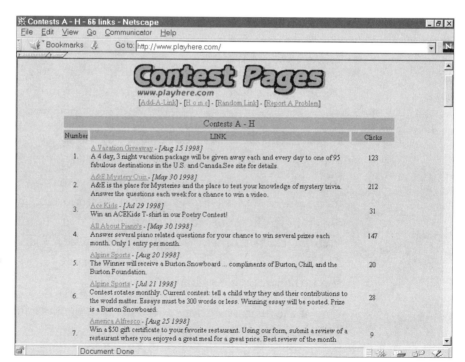

Figure 5.19

Playhere listings are displayed with descriptions, submission dates, and clickthrough information.

Before you submit a listing to the Contest Catalogue, you should wander through the site to familiarize yourself with the various listing categories. A sample of listings from the Games section is shown in Figure 5.21. As you can see, listings are displayed with a fairly detailed description that includes the cash value of prizes, the contest deadline, and the eligibility requirements.

To submit your contest, giveaway, or sweepstakes, visit the Web site and then follow the Submit A Contest links. Be sure to include the URL to the contest home page, a description for the contest, contest start and stop dates, and any other requirements.

Promoting Your Freebie at Virtual Free Stuff

Virtual Free Stuff is a guide to freebies that you can find anywhere, regardless of whether they are available on the Web (see Figure 5.22). You can

Figure 5.20

The Contest Catalog is a growing resource guide to contests, giveaways, and sweepstakes.

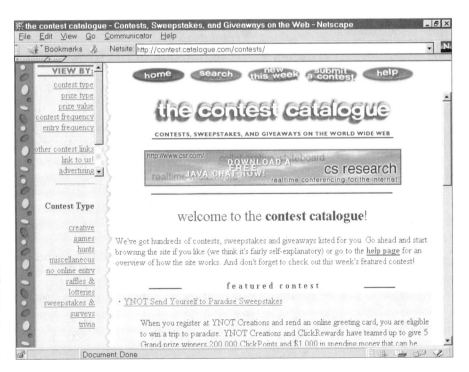

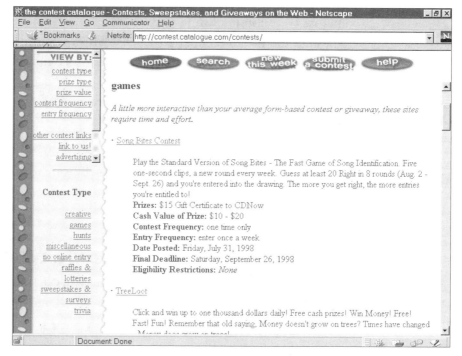

Figure 5.21

Contest Guide
listings are a bit
more detailed than
those in other
guides, so be sure
to fill out the
submission form
completely.

find the home page for this directory at **www.dreamscape.com/frankvad /free.html.**

Rather than organize the guide by contest type, the developers chose to organize the site according to the type of freebies offered, where they are offered, and how often they are given away. Because of this unique approach to showcasing freebies, the directory is divided into nearly a hundred different categories. CD-ROMs alone have a half-dozen categories. Categories exist for daily, weekly, and monthly awards. There is even a category for "almost free" stuff.

Listings at Virtual Free Stuff are fairly extensive and include requirements as well as a description (see Figure 5.23). Keep in mind that most of the listings in Virtual Free Stuff appear in more than one category. For example, your daily contest that gives away T-shirts may be listed in the free daily contest section and the T-shirts section.

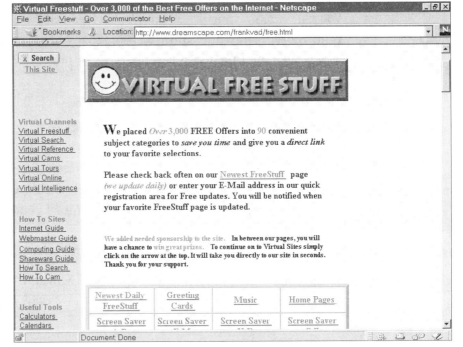

Figure 5.22

Organization by freebie type makes it easy to find what you are looking for at Virtual Free Stuff.

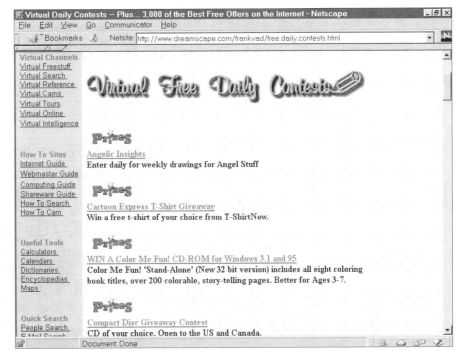

Figure 5.23

To get the most out of your listing, take the time to explain the types of prizes that you give away, as well as how often prizes are awarded.

You can submit your listing to Virtual Free Stuff by sending e-mail to **frankvad@dreamscape.com**. To ensure that you get the most out of your listing, take the time to explain the types of prizes that you give away, as well as how often prizes are awarded.

Other Places to Promote Your Freebies

With thousands of organizations giving away freebies, the existence of dozens of Web guides to free stuff is no surprise. Other freebie guides that you may want to submit a listing to include Free-n-Cool, the Contest-Guide, and the ThreadTreader's WWW Contests Guide.

Free-n-Cool (**www.free-n-cool.com**) is a guide to everything that is free and that the site's creators consider cool on the Web. The guide is divided into several key sections including: free stuff, win stuff, and cool sites (see Figure 5.24). To promote your contest or giveaway, check out the free

Figure 5.24

Free-n-Cool is a guide to what's free and cool on the Web.

stuff and win stuff sections. The distinction here is between outright give-aways and contests that award prizes to participants.

Within the free stuff and win stuff areas, you will find pages with extensive cross references based on category, type of offer, method of request, and more. You can submit your freebie to Free-n-Cool by sending e-mail to **info@free-n-cool.com**. Be sure to provide the contest rules, description, and requirements.

The ContestGuide (**www.contestguide.com**) is a fairly comprehensive guide to contests. This site has a unique focus in that it organizes listings according to how often you can enter a contest (see Figure 5.25). It has listings for contests that let you enter one time only, daily, weekly, and monthly. You can submit a listing to the ContestGuide by sending e-mail to **contests@contestguide.com** or using the submission form at **www .contestguide.com/webmasters.html**.

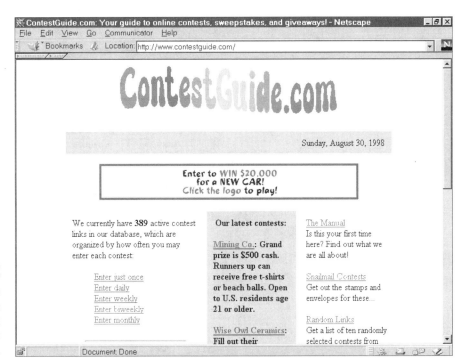

Figure 5.25

Most of the listings in the ContestGuide are organized based on how often you can enter the contest.

Another great contest guide is ThreadTreader's WWW Contests Guide, shown in Figure 5.26 (**www.4cyte.com/ThreadTreader/**).

The goal of this contest directory is to make entering and winning as easy as possible for participants. Toward this end, the site is organized alphabetically, by prize type and by theme. You can also search the directory by keyword. To submit a listing to the directory, use the submission form found at **www.4cyte.com/ThreadTreader/addform.html**.

Cost-Free Banner Advertising: No Joke

If you have browsed the Web, you have probably seen hundreds of banners. The banner is the most frequently used advertising method on the Web. A typical banner ad is placed at the top or bottom of a Web page so that it can catch the viewer's eye and possibly prompt the viewer to click on it. Most advertisers pay thousands of dollars to display a banner

Figure 5.26

ThreadTreader listings are organized alphabetically by prize type and theme.

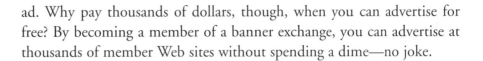

ad. Why pay thousands of dollars, though, when you can advertise for free? By becoming a member of a banner exchange, you can advertise at thousands of member Web sites without spending a dime—no joke.

What the Heck Is a Banner Exchange?

Ever since the first banner exchange sprang onto the scene in 1996, banner exchanges have spread like wildfire. Most banner exchanges have a broad focus that allows just about any type of banner advertising. There are also specialty banner exchanges that focus on specific communities of interest, such as travel Web sites.

You can think of a banner exchange as a cooperative advertising program in which participants work together to advertise each other's Web sites, products, or services using banner advertising. I use the word cooperative because the amount of cost-free advertising that you receive is directly related to the amount of advertising you give to other participants.

Although cooperative advertising isn't exactly a new concept, it is definitely a breakthrough for anyone who wants to get his or her Web site noticed. Because most banner exchanges have a network of thousands of participants, you can use the exchange to promote your Web site, products, and services to a massive and extremely diverse audience.

How Do Banner Exchanges Work?

The wonderful thing about banner exchanges is that the exchange is responsible for managing the network. To accomplish this, most exchanges have a banner management system that tracks when and where banners are displayed throughout the network. Every time you display the banner of another member, you receive a credit. Based on these credits, the management system ensures that your banner is displayed at other sites in the network.

If you had to manually edit your Web pages to change banners, the banner exchange wouldn't be of much use. Fortunately, the banner man-

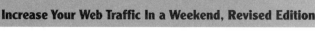

agement system is also responsible for rotating the banners as well. To enable automatic banner rotation, exchange members are given a section of HTML code that allows the management system to dynamically update banners when the page is loaded. The code snippet also includes an account number that allows the management system to track where a banner is displayed and give credits appropriately.

An added benefit of the banner exchange is the ability to track and view the performance statistics for your banner. Depending on the banner exchange, your performance statistics can range from up-to-the-minute accounting to weekly account summaries. Either way, the stats usually tell you how many times your banner was displayed as well how many times someone clicked on your banner. Generally, you will need to visit the banner exchange to view these stats.

Each time your banner is displayed is called an *impression*. The number of times that someone clicks on your banner is called the *click through*. When you divide the total click through by the total impressions, you come up with a *click through ratio*. Some banner exchanges use the click through ratio to determine the effectiveness of your banner advertising.

Exchanging Your Banner

Before you can participate in a banner exchange, you must become a member, which usually involves filling out detailed contact information on yourself, your Web site, and your business. You are also asked questions about the type of material that you publish at your Web site and the types of sites that can be promoted at your site. Although most banner exchanges unanimously prohibit promoting explicit or offensive Web sites, a rating system usually is in place that covers everything from kids-only sites to sites for mature audiences.

The purpose of the rating system is to protect the interests of the exchange members. After all, if your Web site is for kids, you don't want someone to display a banner that is directed at adults. By the same token, you may not want to display advertising for kids at your adult-oriented Web site.

After you complete the membership process, you will be given a section of HTML code that you can add to any pages at your Web site. The purpose of this code is to display the banner advertising of other exchange members. Your unique account number for the exchange is a part of the HTML code. For this reason, you should copy the code that the exchange gives you and paste it into your Web pages.

Because you receive a credit each time that someone views a banner advertising at your Web site, your first instinct may be to add the banner code to every page at your Web site. Instead, I recommend that you place the banner advertisements in well-visited areas of your Web site and primarily on top-level pages. You shouldn't inundate visitors with advertising or make them wait for banners to load on every page.

TIP

Banner exchanges have many checks and balances in place to ensure that the exchange system is fair. For example, exchanges typically prohibit the use of more than one banner from a single exchange on a single page. Nothing stops you from putting banners from other exchanges on a single page, however.

After you receive the banner code, the next step is to submit your banner to the exchange. Most exchanges have a form that you can use to submit your banner, but your browser must comply with the latest HTML standards to use this feature. If you don't have the latest and greatest version of your browser, you may have to send your banner to the exchange as an e-mail attachment.

Creating a Banner Advertisement

The banner exchange process starts with creating a banner to be displayed at other Web sites. Your banner doesn't have to be designed by a professional but should entice people to read it and click on it. Although you will see banners with high-power graphics, it is not the catchy graphics that attract the viewer's eye so much as it is the information.

Information is the key to a successful banner, especially when the file size of your banner is severely limited by the banner exchange. Most banner exchanges restrict your banner to a file size of less than 8K—a tiny amount in the world of high-power graphics. When you develop your banner, the file size limit should be one of your overriding concerns.

Banner exchanges also specify the exact dimensions of the banner. A typical banner size is 468 pixels wide by 60 pixels high. To enforce these dimensions, the HTML code from the exchange usually sets the height and width of the banner to these dimensions. Still, you should create your banner with these dimensions in mind. The reason for this is that Web browsers will use the dimensions to resize a nonstandard banner, which may distort your image and make it unreadable.

The last restriction most banner exchanges enforce is that your banner must be a noninterlaced GIF image. Further, you usually cannot use transparent or animated GIFs. If you don't know what noninterlaced, transparent, or animated GIF means, don't worry. Simply save your banner as a standard (noninterlaced) GIF. Most graphics programs will use this standard format unless you specifically change the settings. So don't change the save options.

TIP If you want to work with multiple banner exchanges, you should note the file and image size limits enforced by each of the exchanges with which you plan to work. Then, you should design the banner with these limits in mind. By resizing your banner to fit the requirements of the exchange, you can use the same banner repeatedly.

Selecting a Banner Exchange

Here I go, looking a gift horse in the mouth again—but the simple truth is that no two banner exchanges are the same. When you select a banner exchange, you need to look past the gilded doorways that say you can promote your Web site for free, and look into the heart of the exchange's management system.

Banner exchanges use what is called an exchange ratio to indicate the display-to-credit ratio offered by the exchange. The most common exchange ratio is 2 to 1. If an exchange has a 2-to-1 exchange ratio, this means that for every two times that someone views a banner on your Web site, your banner will be displayed at a member site one time.

A quick check of the math tells you that, at an exchange ratio of 2 to 1, half of the impressions are going somewhere other than to banner exchange members. Here is where sponsorship comes into the picture. To make up for the costs of running the exchange, most banner exchanges sell the additional space to sponsors. With the average banner exchange racking up millions of impressions every day, a 2-to-1 exchange ratio has a pretty hefty profit margin. I say this to help you make an informed decision, not to dissuade you from using a wonderful service that is free for members.

Beyond the exchange ratio, you should look at the features of the exchange's banner management system. Everything that you do at an exchange should be handled through a password-protected account. Standard features of the account should be to view your current statistics, modify your account profile, and submit a banner. What's more, you should be able to access any of these features directly at the exchange's Web site, and the management system should handle updates automatically.

Some exchanges offer additional features, such as targeting. With *targeting*, you can select the specific categories of Web sites that will display your banner and, often, the categories of banners displayed at your own Web site. In this way, your banner is seen only by audiences that you select, which includes audiences that are interested in products, services, or information similar to what you offer at your Web site.

Finally, you should look at the total membership of the exchange and the throughput of the exchange's Web connection. Together, the number of members and the throughput can suggest an average throughput, which in turn tells you how long visitors to your Web site will have to wait for banner ads to display. For example, a banner exchange with 25,000 member sites and a T1 connection to the Web is probably overloaded. As a result, visitors to your Web site may experience longer-than-normal delays while the banner loads.

Without getting into specific measurement criteria, one way to check the performance of a banner exchange is simply to visit pages of current members and see how long banners take to load. To get a solid assessment, you should check on several different days and at different times of the day. Keep in mind that peak usage times are typically during the week and specifically at midday.

NOTE At the Web site for this book, you will find a banner exchange page that provides summary information about all the exchanges featured in this section. You will find this page at **www.tvpress.com/promote/bann.htm**.

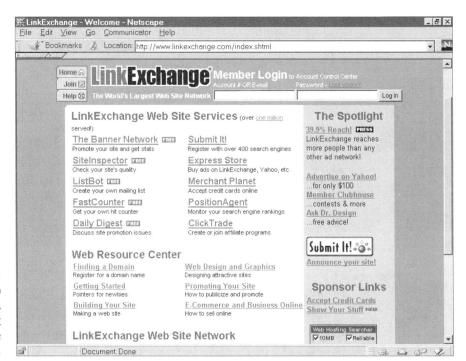

Figure 5.27

LinkExchange is one of the largest banner exchange networks.

Banner Swapping Walkthrough

LinkExchange (**www.linkexchange.com**) is one of the largest banner exchange networks, making it a good choice for your banner swapping walkthrough. At the time of this writing, LinkExchange was offering a 2-to-1 exchange ratio. During the times when other member banners are not displayed, the exchange displays its own banner as well as the banners of paid sponsors.

The LinkExchange home page is shown in Figure 5.27. LinkExchange has many extra features that make it a great choice. These features include:

- Performance stats updated hourly and daily
- Automatic profile updating
- The ability to submit and update your banner online

Creating Your Account at LinkExchange

To join the LinkExchange network, follow the appropriate links from the home page to the account creation area. The sign-up form helps LinkExchange develop a comprehensive profile of your Web site (see Figure 5.28). Keep in mind that Link Exchange uses this information to determine the appropriateness of your banner advertisement for display on other sites.

The URL that you supply is the one that users will access when they click on your banner. Before you enter anything in the URL field, you should therefore carefully consider the page or area of your Web site to which you want to direct traffic. Although your banner ad doesn't directly use the rest of the information in the Site Information area, you must fill these fields in. If you use the Surf Point search engine at LinkExchange, you will find that these fields are indexed in the database.

 TIP

If you have separate sections with separate topics that you want to promote, you may want to set up different accounts for each section.

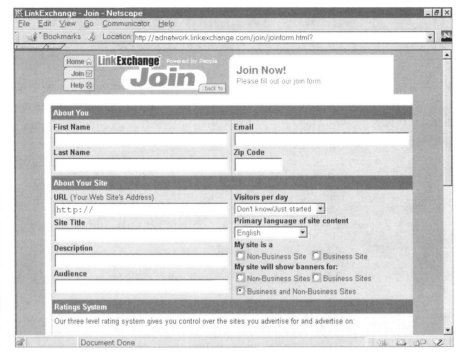

Figure 5.28

Registration forms provide the key information about you, your advertising needs, and the appropriateness of your advertisements for other Web sites.

You also need to specify whether you are running a business or nonbusiness Web site. The exchange uses this information to restrict commercial banners from sites that don't want to advertise such sites. Afterward, you need to select a content rating category for your Web site.

LinkExchange rates the content of all member sites. A level-1 site is for children. A level-2 site is for general audiences. A level-3 site is for mature audiences. To ensure that nobody posts possibly controversial banners on your Web site, you may want to specify that only level-1 and level-2 sites may advertise on your pages.

Once you complete and submit the registration form, the exchange will ask you to verify the information. After you do so, you will get your account number. Be sure to write this down; you will need it later.

Next, LinkExchange asks you to select categories that best describe your site. These categories are used for targeted advertising and ad filtering. To

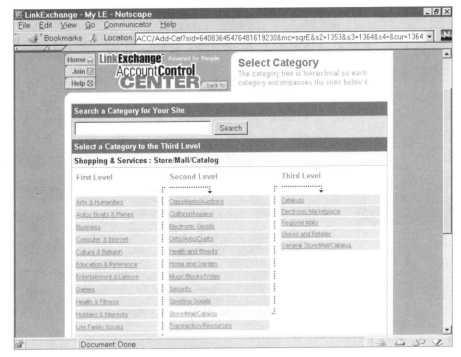

Figure 5.29

If a link exchange offers targeting or filtering features, you will usually have to specify detailed information about your Web site, which can include the category it fits into, the market it serves, and other important marketing information.

complete the registration process, you must drill down to a specific level-3 category (See Figure 5.29). When you click on the level-3 category, you will have the opportunity to select another category or complete the registration process.

Adding the Code to Your Web Site

Completing the registration process takes you to the Account Control Center, where you can obtain the code that you need to add banners to your Web site. Rather than type this code, use your mouse and browser's copy feature to highlight and select the code. If for some reason you have problems obtaining this code, don't worry; you can view it at any time by going to the member services area and selecting the Get HTML option.

LinkExchange also has a utility that lets you automatically insert the code in your Web pages. To use this tool, you will need to know how to access your Web site using FTP.

The HTML code for the LinkExchange looks like this:

```
<!-- BEGIN LINKEXCHANGE CODE -->
<center><iframe
  src="http://leader.linkexchange.com/1/X764816/showiframe?"
  width=468 height=60 marginwidth=0 marginheight=0 hspace=0
  vspace=0 frameborder=0 scrolling=no>
<a href="http://leader.linkexchange.com/1/X764816/clickle"
  target="_top"><img width=468 height=60 border=0 ismap
  alt=""
  src="http://leader.linkexchange.com/1/X764816/showle?"></a><
  /iframe><br><a
  href="http://leader.linkexchange.com/1/X764816/clicklogo"
  target="_top"><img
  src="http://leader.linkexchange.com/1/X764816/showlogo?"
  width=468 height=16 border=0 ismap alt=""></a><br></center>
<!-- END LINKEXCHANGE CODE -->
```

The code displays a banner that is linked to the banner advertiser's Web site, and a text link that is linked to the LinkExchange. At the time of this writing, the LinkExchange FAQ states that you can remove the text link to LinkExchange.

In this example, the account number is X764816. When someone views a page containing this code, the account X764816 gets a credit. Because of how LinkExchange is set up, the same banner will be displayed on each page that a user visits within your Web site. Although this behavior is intended to reduce the amount of frustration on the part of the visitor, you don't get any credits for page views beyond the first page view for this individual visit. You can override this feature by assigning a unique designator to each page containing the LinkExchange code.

The unique designator is a number that you insert before the account number. Because the account number is specified several times in the code, you must insert the unique designator on each line that contains the account number. Rather than updating the code manually, you can tell LinkExchange to generate the page-specific code for you. On the main Get HTML page, tell Link Exchange the number of Web pages that will have the LinkExchange code. Now when you generate the code, you'll see

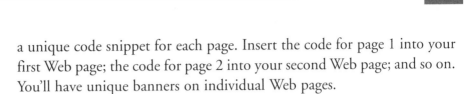

a unique code snippet for each page. Insert the code for page 1 into your first Web page; the code for page 2 into your second Web page; and so on. You'll have unique banners on individual Web pages.

Submitting Your Banner to LinkExchange

Submitting your banner to LinkExchange requires logging in with your account number and password. If you publish your banner on your Web site, you can submit your banner using its URL path. Otherwise, retrieve the banner from your file system using the option provided.

The banner that you submit to LinkExchange must be 468 pixels wide and 40 pixels high. When your banner is displayed, LinkExchange will add its logo to the banner, making the effective size of the banner 468 x 76. The file size of your banner must be 10K or less. The only format that you can use is GIF. Additionally, if you use animated GIFs, you must follow the guidelines posted at the Web site.

NOTE The banner requirements are subject to change. Please check the current requirements before you create and submit your banner ad.

Banner Exchanges for the Masses

Now that you know the ins and outs of banner swapping, you are ready to take the next step and join the exchanges of your choice. To help you on your way, this section lists some of the most popular banner exchanges.

Exchanging Banners with SmartClicks

SmartClicks (**www.smartclicks.com**) is one of the few banner exchanges that allows everyone to conduct targeted advertising for free. Although targeted advertising is one of the key reasons for the success of SmartClicks, the exchange has many other features that make it a winner. The SmartClicks home page is shown in Figure 5.30.

SmartClicks offers a 2-to-1 exchange ratio to its members. When other member banners are not displayed, the exchange displays its own banner as well as the banners of paid sponsors.

The banner that you submit to SmartClicks must be 468 pixels wide and 60 pixels high. SmartClicks adds a logo to the banner, making the effective size of the banner 468 x 76. Although SmartClicks allows you to use animated GIFs, the file size of your banner must be 10K or less. Additionally, your banner must be in noninterlaced GIF format.

Exchanging Banners with BannerSwap

BannerSwap (**www.bannerswap.com**) provides an effective banner exchange service with a to 2-to-1 exchange ratio. Unlike other exchanges that may restrict adult material, BannerSwap allows the advertising of adult-only Web sites. Figure 5.31 shows the BannerSwap home page.

Figure 5.30

SmartClicks allow you to target your ads to specific audiences.

BannerSwap's rating system is divided into three levels: G, PG, and NC-17. Here, a G-rated site is suitable for kids, and a PG-rated site is suitable for general audiences. The NC-17 rating is for sites with material suitable only for adults over the age of 17. To keep adults-only material that may be offensive to mainstream viewers off your Web site, set the maximum site rating for advertising on your site to PG or G.

All banners submitted to BannerSwap must be 400 pixels wide and 50 pixels high. As with most other banner exchanges, BannerSwap adds a logo to your banner, making the effective size of the banner 450 x 50. Additionally, your banner must be in GIF format only and have a file size of 8K or less.

Using the LinkTrader Exchange

LinkTrader (**www.linktrader.com**) set out to give the best exchange ratio out of all the banner exchanges on the Web. The idea was that by limiting

Figure 5.31

BannerSwap is one of the few banner exchanges to allow the advertising of adult-only Web sites. If you don't want adult-only ads to be displayed on your Web site, set the maximum site rating for advertising on your site to PG or G.

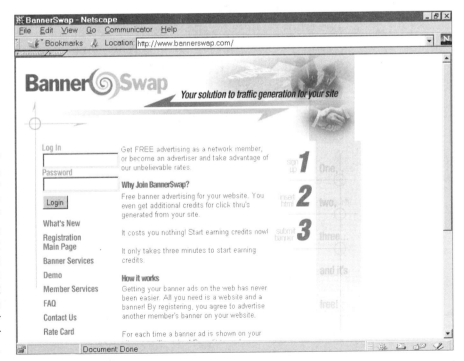

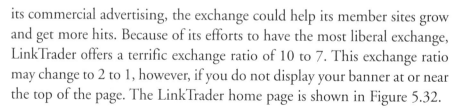

its commercial advertising, the exchange could help its member sites grow and get more hits. Because of its efforts to have the most liberal exchange, LinkTrader offers a terrific exchange ratio of 10 to 7. This exchange ratio may change to 2 to 1, however, if you do not display your banner at or near the top of the page. The LinkTrader home page is shown in Figure 5.32.

Your banner for LinkTrader should be a 400 x 50 pixel GIF image. Because LinkTrader adds a logo to your banner, the effective size of the banner is 450 x 50. LinkTrader restricts the file size of banners to 7K or less. Although this is a relatively small file size, the reduced bandwidth requirements increase the efficiency of the network across the board. LinkTrader also accepts animated GIFs.

Using the Net-On Banner Exchange

Net-On Banner Exchange (**www.net-on.com/banner/**) is one of the few exchanges to break most of the rules set by other exchange networks. Net-On offers a variable exchange ratio that ranges from 2 to 1 up to 5 to 4. The ratio you obtain depends on the popularity of your Web site and the position of your banner ads. The more popular your Web site, the better the exchange ratio. The higher on the page you place the banner ad, the better the exchange ratio.

Figure 5.33 shows the home page for Net-On. Banners submitted to Net-On must be noninterlaced GIF images with a screen size of 468 x 60. When the Net-On logo is added to the banner, the effective banner size is 468 x 76.

Net-On sets the maximum file size to 20KB, which allows you to create more detailed ads. Net-On also allows you to use animated GIFs.

Using Cyberlink Exchange 2000

Another exchange to consider is the Cyberlink Exchange 2000 (**cyberlinkexchange.usww.com**). Although this exchange doesn't have the polished appearance of most other exchanges, it offers many extras, including a fairly advanced system for targeting specific audiences

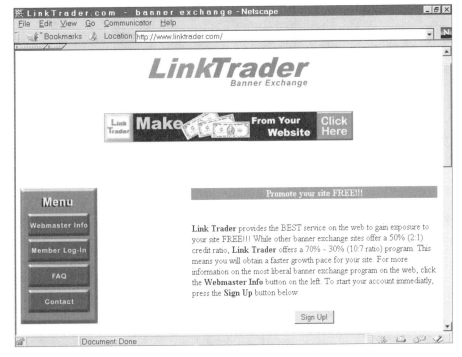

Figure 5.32

LinkTrader offers a better exchange ratio than most other banner exchanges, but only if you display your ads at the top of the page.

Figure 5.33

Net-On allows you to use ads that are up to 20KB in size, which is great if you want to create more detailed ads.

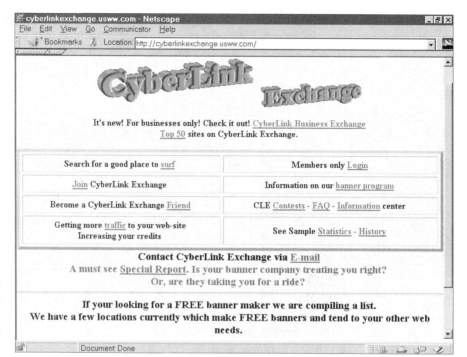

Figure 5.34

Cyberlink Exchange
2000 is a small
banner service with
a lot of attitude.

The Cyberlink Exchange 2000 home page is shown in Figure 5.34. Cyberlink offers a variable exchange ratio that ranges from 2-1 to 3-2. To submit your banner to the Cyberlink Exchange 2000, you must make the banner a noninterlaced GIF image. Further, the banner should have a screen size of 400 x 40 and a file size of 7K or less.

Reviewing Your Progress and Planning More for Next Weekend

Wow, the weekend is over already! I hope that after reading the sessions and following along, you have a great start on the long-term improvement of your Web site's traffic.

What Have You Done This Weekend?

As you learned on the first morning, you really need to understand what is happening at your Web site before you tackle a full-blown promotion campaign. Tracking stats gives you insight into the big picture for your Web site. You can use the big picture to help you improve your Web site and to promote your Web site as well.

One of the biggest reasons not only to promote your Web site but to work to improve your Web site is to get visitors to stay and to come back. After people have found the doorway into your slice of cyberspace, you want to give them every reason to stay. Nothing stops visitors dead in their tracks like an error. Errors are often the result of bad links in your Web pages or bad references to your pages from other Web sites. Using the access log and the error log as your guides, you can fix errors regardless of their source.

After you gather stats for your Web site and know who is visiting your site and why, the next step is to put the stats to work. Not only can you use the stats to make your Web site a better place to visit, you can also use the stats to find your niche in the wonderful world of cyberspace. Enhancing your Web site based on what the stats tell you and using your Web site's niche to your advantage are key ingredients that will help you attract the masses.

Putting the stats to work is only the first step of putting the motion in promotion. The next major step is registering your Web site in all the right places. Because search engines are the primary means of getting your site noticed, I offered you an extensive look at how search engines work and how you can optimize your Web pages for indexing. Although there are hundreds of search engines, it is not practical or worthwhile to submit

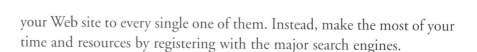

your Web site to every single one of them. Instead, make the most of your time and resources by registering with the major search engines.

Yet, registering with the major search engines is only the beginning of the promotion process. Next you need to look at Web directories. Just as there are hundreds of search engines, there are hundreds of Web directories as well. As with search engines, you should focus your efforts on the major Web directories. Afterward, you should look to business search engines and Yellow Pages directories. These business-oriented search and directory sites are great places to tout your products, your services, and your commercial Web site.

Because you also want your site to be accessible to people looking for specific types of information, the next step is to register with industry- and category-specific directories. Beyond these directories, you'll find specialty directories. Whether your site covers home decorating or famous poets, there are specialty directories that will want your listing.

Awards can make all the difference in the world when it comes to increasing traffic to your Web site. Not just any old award will do, though. The best awards are those that are long-lasting and meaningful. Still, when all is said and done, the popularity of the award site is the most important factor in determining whether the award will help increase the level of traffic at your Web site. The busier the award site, the better the chances that the site's award will increase traffic to your Web site.

One way to spread the word quickly about your Web site is through a registration service that allows you to register with multiple search engines and directories. Although registration services are useful for registering multiple URLs with directories, you get the most out of your site's listing by registering your site with individual search engines and directories.

In the final parts of the book, you saw many additional ways to increase your Web traffic, such as e-mail and freebies. Believe it or not, e-mail is a terrific way to promote your Web site. When you promote your Web site through e-mail, you can use the direct person-to-person method as well as newsgroups and mailing lists. Beyond e-mail, you can steal the thunder of traditional marketers using giveaways, contests, and sweepstakes. Because everyone loves the chance to win something for nothing, freebies can truly bring the masses to your Web site.

To wrap things up, I showed you ways to compete in the big leagues with banner advertising. The banner is the most heavily used advertising method on the Web. Although most advertisers pay thousands of dollars to display a banner ad, you can advertise through a banner exchange network without spending a dime.

Planning More for Next Weekend

Just because you've reached the end of this book doesn't mean that your promotion efforts should end. Next weekend, if you have some time, go back to the sessions or topics that you may not have explored as much as you'd like.

After you take another look at the sessions, use the main topics in this book to outline a long-term promotion plan. Your plan should focus on the items that you will need to periodically address, such as:

- Tracking Web site stats—weekly or monthly
- Looking for problem areas at your Web site—weekly or monthly
- Updating your listings in directories if you move the furniture around—only as necessary
- Resubmitting your site for awards—waiting two or three months between submissions
- Participating in mailing lists and newsgroups—daily or weekly
- Updating your banner—monthly

A Final Note

That's it! Have some fun this evening. On the other hand, if you're enjoying this creative brainstorming so much, with all the resources at hand to apply them, you might want to keep at it for a while.

Thanks again for purchasing this book. I truly hope that the discussion has helped you increase traffic to your Web site. By the way, if you see dramatic increases in your traffic, I'd love to hear about it! You can send me an e-mail message at **web_promote@tvpress.com**. And be sure to check out more resources on this book's Web site at **www.tvpress.com /promote/**.

GLOSSARY

access log. A server log that records file accesses. When a resource at a Web site is requested by a browser, the server retrieves the file or logs the error and then writes an entry in the access log for the request.

agent log. A log that records the user agent (browser) used to access files on the server.

address book. Stores e-mail addresses and personal information for your contacts.

alias. An easy-to-remember name that points to another address or a group of addresses.

animated GIF. An animated image that uses the GIF89a format.

anonymous FTP. A way to access certain FTP servers without an account. When you log into the server, you use the user name "anonymous" and set the password to your e-mail address.

ANSI. The American National Standards Institute; an organization that approves standards for computer technologies.

applet. A small program written in the wildly popular Java programming language. Applets can be added to Web pages.

archive. A compressed file that contains backup or old files for storage.

article. A message sent to a newsgroup.

ASCII. The American Standard Code for Information Interchange; a standard encoding system for text.

ASCII file. A standard text file.

attachment. A file added to an e-mail message.

authentication. A method for verifying a transaction.

backbone. A high-speed connection designed to link together multiple computers and networks.

bandwidth. The amount of data that can be sent through a given communications circuit.

banner. See banner advertisement.

banner advertisement. An image used for advertising on the Web; the typical banner ad is a GIF image at 468 x 60 pixels.

banner exchange. A cooperative advertising service in which participants work together to advertise each other's Web sites, products, or services using banner advertising; banner exchange services earn money through paid advertising displayed on member Web sites. *See* banner advertisement.

banner exchange ratio. The display-to-credit ratio offered by the exchange. The most common exchange ratio is 2 to 1. If an exchange has a 2-to-1 exchange ratio, this means that for every two times that someone views a banner on your Web site, your banner will be displayed at a member site one time.

baud rate. Tells you how much data your modem can send and receive in a given amount of time. A higher baud rate is usually better. *See* bps, Kbps, Mbps.

binary files. An application file in a machine-readable format.

BinHex. A popular way to encode files on a Macintosh computer. Most other computers cannot read files in this format without a special program or reader.

bit. The smallest piece of computer-based information, represented as a 0 or a 1.

bps. Bits per second; a transfer rate used to specify the speed of a modem or data transfer in bits.

browse. To window-shop on the Internet, wandering from place to place. *See also* surfing.

browser. A program that allows you to access the World Wide Web.

bug. An error in a computer program.

byte. A group of eight bits. Because individual characters in text are often represented with eight bits, the number of bytes can sometimes specify the number of characters transferred. *See also* bit.

cache. A temporary storage area that programs can use to store information. *See also* memory cache *and* disk cache.

case insensitive. Said of software that treats upper- and lowercase letters as equivalent.

case sensitive. Said of software that treats upper- and lowercase letters as distinct.

CERN. The European Center for Particle Physics (stands for Centre European Researche Nucleare).

CGI. Common Gateway Interface; defines how scripts communicate with Web servers.

CGI scripts. Programs that connect a Web server and other applications. Also known as gateway scripts. *See* CGI.

checksum. A computed value that can be used to check the accuracy of data sent across the network.

clickable image. An image that can be clicked on to access a resource.

client. A computer that requests the services of another computer or server.

combined log file/format. A server log file with fields that would normally be recorded separately; a log that combines the entries from the access, referrer, and agent log files.

commercial online service. A commercial service that connects people to the Internet. Most commercial services provide additional content and features for their users; these features generally distinguish a commercial service from an Internet service provider.

Common Log File Format. The most basic format for recording entries in server access logs. Access log entries in this format have seven fields: Host, Identification, User Authentication, Time Stamp, HTTP Request Type, Status Code, Transfer Volume.

communications program. A program that lets your computer communicate with other computers. *See also* terminal program.

compression. A process for making a computer file smaller. Before you can use a compressed file, you must decompress it. *See also* ZIP.

connection. A link between two computers for the purposes of communication.

cookie. A bit of information that is stored on your disk drive. This bit of information usually identifies you by a customer number and may also track how many times you've visited a particular Web page.

counter. A program used to track hits or page views.

crawler. *See* indexer.

daemon. A special program that processes requests.

delurk. To stop watching a discussion group and start participating.

digest. In mailing lists, it is a group of messages sent as a single message.

directory. On the Web, a service that lists pages and sites. Generally, you can browse a directory by category or search by keyword.

disk cache. Temporary storage of files on your computer's disk drive.

DNS. Domain Name Service; an Internet service used to look up the addresses of a particular computer.

domain. The part of an address that identifies a computer name, such as tvpress.com.

download. To retrieve a file from a remote computer to your computer.

editor. A program used to edit a file.

e-mail. Electronic mail; a service that lets users exchange messages on a network.

e-mail address. Used to identify the senders and recipients of an e-mail message. Created by combining a user name with a computer name, such as william@tvpress.com.

e-mail signature. Text that you can add to the end of your e-mail messages automatically.

encryption. The process of encoding data to prevent unauthorized persons from reading it.

error log. A server log used to record errors that occur when a file is accessed.

Ethernet. A network access method using Carrier Sense Multiple Access with Collision Detection (CSMA/CD) that was developed initially by Xerox.

exchange ratio. Generally pertains to the exchange ratio for banner ads; *see also* banner exchange ratio.

extended log file. A server log that contains custom fields for recording file access.

FAQ. Frequently Asked Questions; a list of frequently asked questions and their answers. Newsgroups, mailing lists, and other fun things on the Net often have a FAQ you can read.

finger. A program that provides information about users who are accessing a particular server.

flame. An angry message.

FTP. File Transfer Protocol; a protocol for transferring files over a network.

FTP server. The computer that stores files and allows you to access them using FTP.

gateway scripts. Programs that connect a Web server and other applications. Also known as CGI scripts. *See* CGI scripts.

GIF. Graphics Interchange Format; a compressed file format for images. The most widely used graphics format in Web pages.

.gif. A file extension used for GIF images.

gigabyte. Abbreviated GB, about one billion bytes of data.

guest book. A program used to get feedback from visitors.

guide. *See* Web guide.

GZIP. A compression format commonly used on UNIX systems.

.gzip. A file extension for files compressed in GZIP format

header. In e-mail, it is the part of a message that contains the address fields, subject line, date, and other information used by e-mail programs.

helper application. A program used to preview a data format that a browser does not directly support.

hexadecimal. A computer data format where all values are expressed in Base 16 or as a sequence of digits (0–9, A–F).

hierarchy. With newsgroups, the naming structure that helps computers track the various discussion groups.

history list. A browser-maintained list of pages or Web sites you've visited. You can use the history list to quickly revisit these pages or Web sites.

hit. The number of file accesses at a Web site. Every file that is accessed to display a Web page, including each graphic, in a browser is considered a hit.

home page. The main page for a person's or an organization's Web site. Your personal home page is the page you see when you start your browser.

host. A computer that handles requests from clients. For access logs, this field logs the host computer requesting a file from your Web server.

hostname. The name of a host computer, such as tvpress.com.

.htm. A file extension used for Web pages.

.html. A file extension used for Web pages.

HTML. Hypertext Markup Language; a text-based computer language used to create Web pages.

HTTP. Hypertext Transfer Protocol; the protocol used to distribute information on the World Wide Web.

HTTPD. HTTP daemon; the process on the Web server that handles requests from Web clients.

HTTPS. A secure protocol for transferring data on the Web.

IETF. Internet Engineering Task Force; the primary organization that develops Internet standards.

IIS. *See* Internet Information Server.

image map. An image with multiple hot spots that link to different resources on the Internet; acts as a graphical menu of sorts.

IMAP. Internet Mail Access Protocol; a protocol for retrieving e-mail. With IMAP, messages generally are accessed remotely, meaning they are maintained on the mail server.

indexer. For search engines, a utility that creates an index for all the pages at a Web site.

interface. Describes the mechanisms you can use to work with computer programs or the method by which programs communicate with each other.

Internet. A massive networked computing community or the system by which computers around the world communicate with each other.

Internet Information Server. A robust Web server from Microsoft.

Internet Protocol address. A unique numeric identifier for a networked computer.

intranet. An internal network that uses Internet technologies.

IP. Internet Protocol; a standard convention for passing information over the Internet; defines how data is packaged and sent over a network.

IP address. *See* Internet Protocol address.

IRC. Internet Relay Chat; a system for carrying on live conversations on the Net.

ISDN. Integrated Services Digital Network; a digital phone service that allows for fast communication over a standard phone line.

ISO. International Standards Organization; an organization that develops standards for networked computing in general, among other things.

ISP. Internet service provider; a company that provides access to the Internet.

JPEG. A standard for still-image compression that was developed by the Joint Photographic Experts Group.

.jpeg. A file extension used for JPEG images.

.jpg. A file extension used for JPEG images.

Kbps. Kilobits per second; a transfer rate used to specify the speed of a modem or data transfer in groups of one thousand bits.

keyword list. A list of words or phrases that help identify the topic of a Web site.

kilobyte. Abbreviated KB, about one thousand bytes of data, or sometimes (for instance, in serial communications) one thousand bytes of data.

LAN. Local area network; a computer network intended to serve a small area.

link. An element that points to a resource on the Internet and provides the method for accessing that resource.

Listproc. A program that manages mailing lists and distributes e-mail messages.

LISTSERV. A program that manages mailing lists and distributes e-mail messages.

lurking. Observing the activities in a discussion group. When you lurk, you monitor the discussion but do not participate.

mailing list. A discussion group handled through a standard mail program, or a special type of e-mail address for distributing messages to a group of subscribers. *See also* Listproc, LISTSERV, *and* Majordomo.

mail server. A computer on the Internet that distributes electronic messages.

Majordomo. A program that manages mailing lists and distributes e-mail messages.

markup. Formatting instructions for Web pages.

Mbps. Megabits per second; a transfer rate used to specify the speed of a modem or data transfer in groups of one million bits.

megabyte. Abbreviated MB, about one million bytes of data.

megahertz. Abbreviated MHz, a common term that refers to the clock speed of a computer's microprocessor (CPU). When you are comparing the same type of microprocessor, a faster clock speed is usually better.

memory cache. Temporary storage of files in your computer's random access memory (RAM).

Meta information. Data that is included in a Web page header but is hidden from the reader; generally contains instructions or special notes for Web clients.

metro guide. A Web guide to a metropolitan area. *See also* Web guide.

MIME. Multipurpose Internet Mail Extensions; used to transfer files through e-mail.

mirror. A server that provides a copy of a document or resources. Busy Web servers and FTP servers are often mirrored to provide additional ways to get a document or resource.

moderated discussion. A discussion that has a moderator. Usually, all messages submitted to a moderated discussion are checked by the moderator before they are distributed or posted. *See also* moderator.

moderated mailing list. A mailing list that has a moderator.

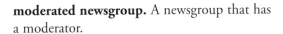

moderated newsgroup. A newsgroup that has a moderator.

moderator. A person who manages a discussion and ensures it stays on track.

Mozilla. The code name for Netscape Navigator.

MPEG. A standard for compressing video that was developed by the Motion Picture Experts Group.

.mpeg. A common file extension for MPEG video.

.mpg. A common file extension for MPEG video.

NCSA. National Center for Supercomputing Applications; part of the University of Illinois and the place where the original graphics-capable browser, called Mosaic, was developed.

netiquette. A term used to refer to the acceptable social and business practices on the Internet. Also known as network etiquette.

network. A group of computers that are all connected together.

news. Shorthand for newsgroups. *See also* newsgroup.

newsgroup. An electronic discussion group through which you can post and read messages.

newsreader. A program for reading and posting messages to newsgroups.

news server. A computer that stores discussion groups.

nickname. In IRC, the made-up name you use to identify yourself.

NNTP. Network News Transfer Protocol; the protocol used to transfer postings to and from a news server.

node. A computer on a network. Also called a host.

Octal. A computer data format where all values are expressed in Base 8 or as a sequence of digits (0–7).

packet. A group of data sent over a network.

page. A document on a Web server.

page view. A request for a Web page, which is normally in HTML format.

password. A security keyword used to protect your Internet accounts.

PDF. Portable Document Format; Adobe Acrobat's file format for documents.

.pdf. A file extension used for PDF documents.

Perl. A popular programming language for CGI scripts.

ping. A program that checks to see if a computer is available.

PKZIP/PKUNZIP. One of the most popular programs for compressing/uncompressing files using the ZIP format.

Plugin. An extension module for a browser that adds functionality to it. Plugins are used primarily in Netscape or Netscape-compatible browsers, which include Netscape Navigator and Internet Explorer.

POP. Post Office Protocol; a protocol for retrieving e-mail. With POP, messages generally are downloaded and then accessed locally, meaning they are maintained on your disk drive.

port. The line on which a computer listens for requests. Most Web servers listen on port 80 for requests.

port number. The specific numeric address of a port.

PPP. Point-to-Point Protocol; a method for transmitting information to the Internet over a phone line.

protocol. A set of rules for communicating on the network.

redirection. *See* server redirection.

registration service. An organization that registers your Web site with multiple search engines and directories.

referrer log. A log with entries that indicate the site from which the user came.

relevancy. For search engines, a term that is used to identify how strongly a Web site relates to the entered keyword query string.

resource. A general term for a file on the Internet.

robots.txt. A file on your Web server that tells search engines the files that should not be indexed.

RTF. Rich Text Format; a common format for text files.

.rtf. A file extension used for RichText Format.

search engine. A computer program that searches a database.

server. A computer that handles requests and provides resources.

server redirection. A technique used to point users at a new location.

SGML. Standard Generalized Markup Language; defines a way to share documents using a generalized markup language; was the basis for HTML.

signature. *See* e-mail signature.

SLIP. Serial Line IP; a protocol used to transmit information over serial lines, such as a telephone line.

SMTP. Simple Mail Transfer Protocol; the basic protocol for transferring e-mail messages from a client to a remote server.

spam. An unsolicited message that tries to sell you a product or service.

spammer. Someone who distributes unsolicited commercial messages.

specification. A document that describes the requirements and capabilities of a protocol or service.

spider. *See* indexer.

SSL. Secure Sockets Layer; a secure protocol for transferring information that uses encryption and authentication.

standard. The widely accepted way to handle a process or technology; usually set by standards organizations such as the ISO.

statistics. Information compiled from a variety of resources, such as server logs.

stats. *See* statistics.

status code. A three-digit number that indicates the status of an HTTP request. The code 404 indicates that a file was not found.

Stuffit/UnStuffit. A popular Macintosh program for compressing and uncompressing files.

Surfing. To browse pages on the Web.

T1. A type of digital communications line or the standard for distributing data at 1.44 million bits per second.

TCP. Transmission Control Protocol; a protocol for controlling the way data is transferred over a network.

TCP/IP. Transmission Control Protocol/Internet Protocol; the group of protocols upon which the Internet runs.

Telnet. The standard protocol for accessing remote computers.

Terminal. A basic computer with a keyboard and screen often connected to a central computer (mainframe).

Terminal program. A communications program that emulates a terminal; used to provide generic access to a remote computer.

thread. A unique subject or topic in a discussion group.

tracking software. Programs that track Web site statistics.

.txt. A file extension for ASCII text files.

unarchive. To extract files from an archive.

UNIX. A popular operating system for servers.

upload. To transfer data from your computer to another computer.

URL. Uniform Resource Locator; provides a uniform way of identifying resources on a server. Also referred to as a Web address or location. A typical URL looks like this: http://www.tvpress.com/

Usenet. The network through which newsgroups are distributed; can also be used to refer to all newsgroups collectively.

user agent. a browser; a field that records the browser used to access files on a server.

uudecode. A method for decoding e-mail attachments.

uuencode. A method for encoding e-mail attachments.

viewer. A program (helper application) for viewing files.

visit. The set of requests made by a single user in a single session; a collection of hits and page views that pertain to a specific person who requested files from your Web site during a specified time frame.

visitor. A person browsing a Web site.

VRML. Virtual Reality Modeling Language; a modeling language for rendering complex models and multidimensional documents.

WAIS. Wide Area Information Server; a distributed information service for searching indexed databases.

WAN. Wide area network; a network that covers a large geographic area.

Web address. The URL or location of a resource on the Web.

Web client. An application used to access Web-based technologies, such as a Web browser.

Web guide. A guide to the Web; tries to help you find the best Web sites.

Web page. A document on a Web server.

Web server. A computer on the Internet that stores Web pages and allows browsers to access them.

Web site. A collection of Web pages on a Web server.

Web master. The person responsible for administrating a Web site or Web server.

White Pages. A directory for finding e-mail addresses, phone numbers, and street addresses.

WHOIS. A protocol to find information on Internet users and domains.

World Wide Web. A hypertext-based system for distributing information and resources. Also known as the Web, WWW, or W3.

.wrl. A file extension for VRML files.

Yellow Pages. A directory for finding businesses on the Web and in the real world.

.Z. A file extension for UNIX compressed files.

ZIP. A popular compression format. To use the file, you will need to unzip it.

.zip. A file extension used for files compressed in ZIP format.

INDEX

A